T0309266

The Human Side of Digital Business Transformation

The Human Side of Digital Business Transformation

Kamales Lardi

WILEY

Registered Offices
John Wiley & Sons, Inc., 111 River Street, Hoboken, NJ 07030, USA
John Wiley & Sons Ltd, The Atrium, Southern Gate, Chichester, West Sussex, PO19 8SQ, UK

Editorial Office
The Atrium, Southern Gate, Chichester, West Sussex, PO19 8SQ, UK

For details of our global editorial offices, customer services, and more information about Wiley products visit us at www.wiley.com.

Library of Congress Cataloging-in-Publication Data is Available:

ISBN 9781119871019 (Hardback)
ISBN 9781119871026 (ePDF)
ISBN 9781119871033 (ePub)

Cover Design: Wiley
Cover Image: © DELstudio/Shutterstock

SKY10035997_090922

Contents

Introduction: The End of Business as Usual

Business as usual is no longer valid. For over a decade, digital disruption has impacted almost every industry. As a result, the traditional rules and assumptions of business are becoming less valid for sustainable success in the global business landscape. The time-tested rules that were developed to identify customers and engage with them, develop and market products and services, as well as manage an organization, its people and resources are no longer valid.

These rules have been upended by emerging technologies, and new business models that leverage technology to displace dominant business models. In any industry, a dominant business model emerges over time, the model that has the most efficient way to allocate and organize resources. New businesses tend to fail due to difficulty in competing with the scale and reach of these dominant business models. However, the emergence of digital technologies have upended this old business rule. New business models are able to leverage technology to create exponential scale and growth within a short time and far fewer resources, effectively displacing dominant business models.

A new business playbook has emerged, rendering the traditional rules and assumptions of business invalid. For example, the traditional rules of growth and scale are no longer valid. Incumbent organizations like Nike or Starbucks took about 24 years to achieve $1 billion dollar market valuation, while luxury brand Prada took 98 years to achieve the same financial milestone. New digitally enabled companies are not able to relate to this extended business timeline (Montini 2014). For example, companies such as YouTube, Twitter, and Instagram achieved the $1 billion valuation in three years or less by leveraging digital technologies and platforms that offered access to a global marketplace of consumers on day one of their business.

In addition, traditional industry boundaries are also becoming less relevant. Incumbent organizations are used to playing within a specific industry and competing with other players within the industry. These boundaries have developed over time, as competing companies focus on building specific expertise and capabilities within their industry. However, digitally enabled companies take an alternative approach to the market, focusing on opportunities created by technology and value created in the global market. This means forgoing traditional industry boundaries to apply technology solutions where possible and needed. For example, Amazon would be hard pressed to define an industry focus, having developed product and service offerings across multiple industries including e-commerce, consumer business and retail, health care, financial services, as well as video and content streaming. In 2021, Amazon opened a hair salon in London to trial the latest industry technologies including an augmented reality hair consultation that allows customers to visualize different hair styles and colors on themselves before deciding on a change (Vincent 2021).

A Global Paradigm Shift

A key trigger for this disruption is the rapid development of technology. In the past, one type of technology or another would be developing at a certain rate. What we're seeing over recent years is that each phase of technology development is leveraging on its previous phase to further accelerate progress. For example, research and development in artificial intelligence has actually existed since the 1950s. But it's only in the past decade or so that we've truly seen its acceleration and applications within industries explode. This is because we now have the right foundational elements not only to support rapid development of technology but also to accelerate it further, including unparalleled processing power, unlimited storage capacity, the low cost of technology production, cloud computing, as well as global connectivity and accessibility online. Soon, we will see 5G capabilities, quantum computing, and smart devices contributing further to this exponential acceleration. With these elements in place, each phase of technology development is leveraging the previous phase, resulting in breakthrough solutions constantly emerging. Technology has extended the boundaries of business reach to virtually anywhere, anytime, achieving incredible scalability and growth beyond customer demographics, physical assets, locations, or market segments.

More importantly, technology has triggered a shift in people globally. We have quickly adopted technology, almost as quickly as it is being discovered and developed. We have adapted our behaviors to suit the new digital world we live in. We have become accustomed to digitally enabled businesses that offer hyper-personalized services seamlessly across multiple channels and touchpoints, predicting our needs and wants, sometimes even before we know what they are. We are now demanding this same level of interaction from any and all companies that we interact with in our daily lives.

Scarcity versus Abundance

The foundational dynamic here is truly having a democratized emerging technology landscape. This can be illustrated by the analog camera example. As we moved away from analog cameras and the development and adoption of digital cameras increased, we shifted from a scarcity model in the industry towards an abundance model. This means shifting away from an industry that was heavily dependent on physical assets—analog camera, film, studios, lighting—where there was a limitation on the number of pictures taken, how and where they could be taken, and a cost associated with taking pictures. As the digital camera emerged in the market, we gradually shifted to an abundance industry environment, where the number of pictures that could be taken by each person increased exponentially. Digitization of the industry enabled anyone to take as many pictures as they liked and share them on digital platforms for an instant global audience. Traditional business models trapped within the scarcity environment, such as Kodak, quickly declined despite being dominant industry leaders. New digitally enabled businesses leveraging technology in the abundance environment, such as Instagram and Pinterest, grew and thrived.

'Over the past decade, technology has undermined the economics of almost every industry, enabling digitization of products and services, and democratized access for a global market of consumers. This shift of scarcity, limited access, and high cost, towards abundance, unlimited access, and low cost, has disrupted almost every industry. Digitally enabled companies thrive in the abundance offered by emerging technologies and new ways of working, while traditional businesses are trapped in the scarcity of physical assets, touchpoints, and interactions.

The Covid Impact

The coronavirus pandemic has further accelerated the shift in behavior, forcing a majority of the world's consumers into the digital ecosphere as we faced the unprecedented global physical lockdown. Unsurprisingly, traditional businesses struggled to adapt to this shift, and many were thrown into shock and standstill, while digitally enabled companies survived and thrived.

Before Covid, mindset was a significant barrier to digital business transformation in organizations. In pre-Covid times, I remember having frequent discussions with various top-level management teams about the relevance of digital disruption, and trying to convince them that the time for transformation had arrived. These conversations were even more challenging with companies that had strong performance in the market, albeit stuck in tradition operational environments. The coronavirus pandemic shifted mindsets almost overnight. Suddenly we were facing an unprecedented situation where physical interactions came to a grinding halt and organizations that thrived in the traditional business landscape were stripped of foundational elements such as physical assets, sales channels, and global supply chains.

Digital Business Transformation

Covid-19 is accelerating digital transformation at many companies, knocking through long-standing resistance and silos as illustrated in Figure I.1. It literally took a global crisis to turn people's mindsets around. On the flipside, the crisis is also setting the agenda and the priorities of where to focus digital business transformation efforts, such as facilitating the needs of a mass remote workforce.

Many companies skipped over gaining a shared understanding for what digital transformation truly means and how it aligns with the long-term business strategy, to implementing technology-based solutions in the name of business continuity. As we move into this next normal environment, this post-Covid business world, companies have a unique choice to make: they can reestablish what has existed so far, or create something new, and take this opportunity to transform and create a better, more sustainable business for the increasingly digital economy.

Digital business transformation is truly a journey—a marathon not a sprint. At the core of this journey are people, the essential element that can make or break the course of any transformation. The concept of digital business transformation goes beyond process or technology implementation. It includes the organization-wide change that is profoundly rooted in the human elements of the business. This goes beyond mindset and behavior shifts, involving the complexities of creating an environment where people thrive through the adoption of new technologies, solutions, and working models, as well as deeper interactions, engagement, shared purpose, and psychological safety. The organizations that have been proven successful in developing and implementing their digital business transformation strategies started with people rather than processes and technologies, tailoring their journey to enable the human side of transformation.

This book deep dives into the human side of digital business transformation by laying out a new playbook for business. Chapter 1 covers the impact of technologies in our lives, exploring the depth of technology application in our daily routines. We also examine the trends that have shaped the global business landscape, mapping out key elements that business leaders and transformation leaders should closely monitor as they develop. The chapter also covers the impacts of the coronavirus pandemic on the business environment, driving new trends, opportunities, and requirements.

Chapter 2 aims to create a foundational understanding for digital transformation by exploring the development of this space in the business world, as well as the critical success factors that have delivered sustainable outcomes for organizations across industries. Here, we initiate the discussion on the human factors that contribute to making or breaking digital business transformation journeys and how organizations can best prepare for it. In this discussion, it is essential to address the major shifts in human behavior that offer a deeper understanding for what to expect in the transformation process.

Chapter 3 delves into organizational cultures and their impact on the transformation journey. By comparing several examples of best in class and poor organization cultures, we explore approaches that leadership teams can take to drive sustainable change. Additionally, the chapter leverages Maslow's Hierarchy of Needs, still relevant today, to understand how best to motivate people and build a successful digital culture in the company. At the core of Chapter 3 is the symbiotic relationship between internal and external stakeholders that create a holistic business ecosystem. Every stakeholder plays a critical role in developing the transformation strategy and driving success in the long term. The chapter also explores the leadership traits that are required in the business landscape to lead an organization through the transformation journey.

Organizations often implement change management initiatives to manage the people side of transformation. Chapter 4 discusses the limitations of a change management approach, compared to the needs of the digital business transformation journey in an organization. Additionally, the chapter describes the advantages of clearly defining and communicating the purpose of the business in driving the overall transformation direction. People fall behind shared purpose and values, allowing leadership teams to manage the uncertainties and complexities of the transformation journey. The chapter also presents guiding principles for leadership teams to influence people during the digital business transformation process.

The next few chapters provide a detailed description of the Digital Business Transformation Strategy© framework, a proven approach that guides organizations through the transformation journey. Chapter 5 describes the terminology around digital transformation, setting the scene for transformation on the basis of a standard and common language. As a starting point for the transformation journey, organizations need to assess their capabilities against four levels of maturity and readiness. Digital business transformation can mean a broad set of things and can encompass quite a lot within an organization's business structure. In order to help companies truly understand where they should focus resources, investments, and efforts, I have developed a building block model. The chapter describes the building blocks and their application in detail—customer experience, products and services, people, processes and operations, as well as business models.

Chapter 6 provides a structured and detailed overview of the Digital Business Transformation© framework, a proven method that I have applied for multiple organizations across industries to drive transformation. The framework guides organizations through four phases of the end-to-end transformation journey: Situational Analysis, Disruptive Visioning, Strategic Roadmapping, and Building & Implementing. The framework helps companies move away from knee-jerk reactions of implementing technology or digital touchpoints, to really focusing on the sustainable business goals, strategies, and value propositions. Chapter 7 describes best practices and key learnings that I have personally gained from implementation of digital business transformation strategies and related initiatives.

Although digital business transformation goes far beyond technology, having a deep understanding of the capabilities of emerging technologies is important to drive innovative and agile thinking. In Chapter 8, we explore a deeper understanding of five top disruptive technologies, including artificial intelligence, blockchain and decentralized technologies, extended reality and the metaverse, 3D printing and additive manufacturing, as well as robotics and automation. I have personally seen the impacts of these emerging technologies in the business world, as well as the transformative impact in our daily lives. More importantly, I also cover the convergence of these technologies that create further exponential transformations.

In developing the content for this book, I had the opportunity to engage with global thought leaders and experts leading the charge for digital business transformation. Additionally, Chapter 9 includes case examples from global organizations, packed with insights, experiences and advice to accelerate digital business transformation in your organization.

Chapter 1

Trends Shaping the Global Business Landscape

O ver the past decade, the pace of change in the technology sector has been incredibly rapid. In the next decade, we will see more technological progress than in the whole of the previous 100 years combined, as technology reshapes industries and almost every aspect of our lives. These developments have also had a knock-on effect on various aspects of our lives, becoming a catalyst for further rapid changes. As a result, most organizations have been hit by disruption and forced to redefine their value propositions in the market. The main challenge lies in determining which trends are the most significant to the business. Understanding the impact that these trends will have on organizations, industries, and people could be critical in staying ahead of disruption.

The most successful organizations are the ones able to accurately predict the future of their industry and develop a vision of their place in that future. This is especially true in an era when increasingly affordable technology innovations are making it possible for businesses to compete on a nearly level playing field with large corporations. It can be difficult to gain a clear understanding not only of the trends affecting the business but also the most effective ways to address them, however, because both technology and business are evolving at an unprecedented rate. Recognizing that these trends exist is only the first step in tackling them. Business owners must then carefully consider how these trends will affect their company and how they can get ahead of the curve in order to take advantage of the opportunities that these trends present. A company's ability to withstand the inevitable onslaught of competition and disruption will be determined by its ability to project into the future and think strategically about change. A company's ability to identify and pursue the most promising opportunities is also essential to positioning the company for long-term growth success.

Emerging Technologies and Breakthrough Solutions

The rapid development of technology has paved the way for the constant development of new breakthrough solutions. In the current business landscape, technology-based solutions are enabling significant optimization of processes and operations, while reducing the reliance on manual activities and people costs. Organizations are able to meet the needs of their customers, anywhere, at any time, scaling meaningful and hyper-personalized interactions at a fraction of the cost. Beyond the impacts of value creation and delivery in business, emerging technologies are triggering the development of solutions that are transcending the traditional boundaries of human–machine interactions.

For example, researchers at the University of Plymouth in the United Kingdom are exploring the development of brain–computer interfaces using quantum programming. By utilizing electroencephalogram (EEG) readers, which detect electrical activity passing through the human scalp, researchers are able to track the changing brain patterns, which are then used to manipulate simulated qubits—the fundamental unit of quantum computing that reflects the mathematics of quantum physics—with nothing more than the power of thought. This marks the beginning of the construction of what the team refers to as the Quantum Brain Network (abbreviated to QBraiN). A brain–computer interface (BCI) refers to a method of controlling a computer by using brain signals. When it comes to manual input devices, the brain is technically in charge of controlling them—albeit through an intermediary such as the fingers or the voice—but a BCI makes it possible to send commands to the outside world without having to go through the process of sending commands from the brain to peripheral nerves or muscles first.

Breakthrough technologies such as QBraiN could completely change the way people engage and interact with one another, and with products or devices in the physical environment. Considering that the global voice recognition market size was forecast to grow from $10.7 billion in 2020 to $27.16 billion by 2026 (Vailshery 2022), there is already a shift in how consumers interact with brands online. Products, services, devices, and machines developed in the future will need to consider not only screenless and voice-activated capabilities, but also perhaps BCI interactivity.

Emerging technologies will continue to have a significant impact on the way we live, work, and interact with one another in a world dominated by digital solutions and innovations. Many of these technological advancements are beneficial to us—they increase our productivity, make the services we require more accessible, and generally improve the quality of our lives. Breakthrough solutions are being discovered so frequently that it can be challenging for companies to keep up. Success in staying on top of technology trends is measured in terms of fewer missed opportunities for businesses of any size. In Chapter 8 we will explore several top disruptive technologies and their impact for the business world.

Evolving Consumer Behavior

During the global pandemic lockdown in 2020, my daughter, a young Gen Zer, discovered TikTok, a video-focused social networking platform. Like most children born in her generation, she is a digital native and quickly learned the nuances of using the platform—recording creative videos on my phone, editing, posting, and even promoting videos for views. Over the next few months, she built her expertise on the site and grew her following to over 10,000 people worldwide. Soon she discovered the art of making slime, a non-toxic viscous toy product that is serious business online. For example, YouTube slime creators have gained celebrity status, with some acquiring hundreds of thousands of online followers. Building on this discovery, my daughter took her passion for slime to the next level by creating a recipe for the product through YouTube instructional videos, trial and error, and crowdsourced tips from her online followers. After perfecting the product recipe, she set up a simple e-commerce site to sell the products and has to date received requests from people all over the world.

In addition, my 10-year-old (at the time) uses online and digital technologies to engage and interact in the most natural way. She chats with friends over Snapchat, a multimedia instant messaging app, or meets them for a game on Roblox, a multiplayer online gaming platform. She is developing her passion for acting and drama by attending online classes at a professional academy located in Toronto, Canada, with a group of other talented kids.

Suffice to say, my daughter and her generation of children are growing up in a very different world from the one that many of us have known as children. Immersed in the digital world, this new generation of technology-savvy consumers will communicate, interact, engage, and consume in a very different way from past generations of people. In less than a decade, my daughter will be an adult and, I have to wonder, how will organizations built in my generation and the generations before me expect to serve this new digital-first generation of consumers?

Digitally enabled businesses have triggered a shift in consumer behaviors and expectations. Companies such as Amazon, Uber, Meta (formerly Facebook), Netflix, and many others have leveraged technology to create a new level of interaction and engagement with the global customer base. As digital natives, these companies are able to create superior customer experiences that are hyper-personalized, frictionless, flexible, and predictive.

Online and digital platforms offer personalized experiences for each individual customer. By leveraging digital technologies, these platforms not only cater to preferences and interests of individuals, but also gather insights based on their interactions and activities on the platform to further customize the experience. Leveraging technology also allows these hyper-personalized experiences to be offered at global scale but at a fraction of the cost.

Digitally enabled businesses have also transformed the customer journey. In the past, acquisition at the point of sale was a critical part of the customer journey. Here, dominant players in financial services dictated the type and speed of services that could be made available to consumers, merchants, and retailers, who were at their mercy. Today, the acquisition step has been moved to the background, while the digital customer journey focuses on creating impactful experiences. For example, when requesting services from ride-sharing app Uber, a majority of the customer journey focuses on the ease of use of the app, speed of arrival, interaction with the driver, as well as the experience in the car itself. The actual payment step takes place in the background, and goes almost unnoticed by the users. The same applies to Amazon's One Click Buy, or Netflix's subscription payments charged automatically each month. With artificial intelligence, machine learning, and predictive analytics, as well as access to extensive user data, digital businesses such as Amazon and Netflix are able to offer predictive capabilities that recommend the right product, service, and content at the right time to the individual customers.

Over the past decade, technology has triggered a change in consumer behavior. We've adopted technology almost as quickly as it's being developed. And we've become accustomed to interacting with digitally enabled businesses in a new way that has given us meaningful experiences.

Today, we have become accustomed to this hyper-personalized environment where we can get predictive interactions with companies that accurately tell us what they think we should have, as well as frictionless interactions across channels and flexibility across the entire customer journey. This has made us accustomed to these meaningful interactions, or interactions that we deem meaningful, and we're demanding the same level of interaction from all types of business, including traditional incumbent companies.

The coronavirus pandemic accelerated the adoption of digital channels across a wide range of industries and countries. In the midst of physical lockdowns, new adopters had little choice but to embrace digital channels. The number of global internet users reached 4.95 billion in early 2022, with internet penetration now standing at 62.5% of the world's total population. More than two-thirds (67.1%) of the world's population now use a mobile phone, with unique users reaching 5.31 billion by the start of 2022, and there are 4.62 billion social media users around the world as of January 2022. On average, we spent about 42% of our waking hours online, and this amounts to about two days of our week. So we are demanding more meaningful experiences because we are spending more time in these digital environments.

In this crowded digital environment, companies have really struggled to stand out. The future of consumer engagement truly lies in creating experiences that have meaning for the consumer themselves. Progressive companies should focus on moving these repetitive actions and interactions on these digital channels to the background through automation, and focus on leveraging emerging technologies to create experiences that consumers find valuable and meaningful.

Shifting Competitive Landscape

About 10 to 15 years ago, it was relatively easy for organizations and brands to determine their competitors in the global business landscape. In general, competition was direct in the business world, as key players mostly knew each other and the competitive landscape remained within industry boundaries. The current competitive landscape is far more complex and diluted. Competition can come from anywhere, crossing industry and regional boundaries with ease. The size of an organization and the length of time it has been in business no longer carry significance. Companies that have mastered digital technologies and online channels move rapidly and with purpose. In today's digital and global world, indirect and substitute competition are more significant.

Initially, these new players did not concern incumbent organizations. However, digital businesses have become hard to ignore as they rapidly reach their size, scale, and enviable commercial success. Not too long ago, it took years—in some cases nearly a century—for companies to achieve the coveted $1 billion valuation. Start-ups of today may find it hard to relate to this, gaining access to a global consumer marketplace on day one of business by leveraging digital technologies and online channels. As mentioned, YouTube reached the $1 billion valuation mark a year after its founding, while Instagram and Twitter needed less than three years. In comparison, well-known brands such as Starbucks and Nike achieved this mark in 24 years, and luxury brand Prada reached this milestone 98 years after the company was founded in 1913.

Digitally enabled companies are also demonstrating resilience, further proving that the global competitive landscape has shifted. In the midst of unprecedented global disruption, companies built for the digital age have actually grown by an incredible 42% and increased in value by $2.1 trillion with a growth rate that is 4.5 times the average growth rate for the Global Top 100 over the past 15 years (Kantar BrandZ 2021). This accelerated growth was a testament to the relationship between brands and technology. The global pandemic impacted brands regardless of size or geography, but companies leveraging technology to engage and create a point of difference in the market have proven their resilience. The digital global business landscape is also driving increased collaboration between competitors. "Coopetition"—joint ventures, outsourcing agreements, product licensing, cooperative research—is creating mutual strength for collaborators. In the current competitive landscape, companies need more than investments to penetrate and capture new markets.

Rise of the Low-Touch Economy

The coronavirus pandemic served as a shock to the global society. For example, we saw consumption patterns transform and shift as people moved away from purchasing non-essential goods towards essential goods. And consumers also abandoned brand loyalty as they started to purchase more products that were simply available to them, at low cost, during the height of the pandemic. Consumers were also forced to adopt digital channels as physical channels went into lockdown. This new environment triggered the rise of the low-touch economy—a business landscape characterized by no or minimum physical contact.

This scale of change and the speed at which it happened created a once-in-a-generation shift for most organizations. Companies accelerated digitization of customer interactions, such as e-commerce, online acquisition, and touchpoints, by up to three to four years (McKinsey 2020). The share of digitally enabled products in business portfolios has also accelerated up to seven years, offering existing products and services on digital channels, as well as creating new ones specifically designed for the digital economy. These initiatives were meant to address the surge in demand that came in through the digital channels. While it was a blessing for business continuity, organizations still struggled to deliver on the surge in digital demands through physical back-end operations and capabilities.

In the next wave of uncertainty, the low-touch economy will continue to grow and shift, demonstrating that innovation and creativity are the foundation of resilience: humans and the world will always find a way to shine through. In Chapter 2, we will delve into the development of digital business transformation over time and critical elements that influence their success in companies.

Chapter 2
A Brief History of Digital Transformation

D igital transformation is a topic that has gained focus in the business world over the last two decades. Since 2010s SMAC technologies (social, mobile, analytics, and cloud) have accelerated digital operations of businesses globally, as well as helping organizations to achieve maximum reach and closeness to consumers at minimal overhead costs. The explosion of structured and unstructured data created through global adoption and use of online channels, mobile devices, sensors and wearable technologies, connected devices, and social media, has created new business opportunities built on the basis of customer-generated data. While each of the SMAC technologies brings value and impact to businesses individually, the convergence of these technologies has created a disruptive force that has transformed the global business landscape.

As the influence of digital has increased, organizations have initiated digital transformation initiatives in an effort to leverage technology solutions to generate business returns and satisfy evolving consumer demands. With the exception of several digital leaders, most organizations across industries initiated digital transformation efforts that focused on implementing technology solutions within limited functional or market-facing areas of the business. Before 2020, digital business transformation existed for organizations as "nice to have" or "on the radar of" strategic initiatives. Although most businesses recognized the sizeable shifts that were occurring in response to digital, technological, cultural, and social factors, there was still a lack of urgency and prioritization for organization-wide transformation. Before the coronavirus pandemic, digital implementations were in reaction to specific events or needs, experienced within isolated parts of the organization.

The pandemic brought digital business transformation to the forefront of corporate strategy and the global business landscape due to the rapid acceleration in digital channel adoption for communication and acquisition. As physical lockdowns became the new normal, companies and consumers increasingly adopted digital solutions, providing and purchasing more goods and services online than ever before in the history of modern commerce. Organizations across the world rapidly shifted towards interacting with customers through digital channels, creating digital or digitally enhanced offerings, as well as overall digitization of the core internal operations (McKinsey 2020). Many organizations implemented these changes 20 to 25 times faster than expected, driven by business continuity requirements. In some cases, companies were able to implement digital solutions 40 times faster, for example in switching to remote working environments. The pandemic triggered existential challenges for most organizations, forcing business leaders to reconsider digital transformation as a top priority.

Although it may seem like a new buzz word, digital transformation has had a few waves of impact in the past. In 1948, MIT Professor Emeritus Claude E. Shannon wrote the landmark *A Mathematical Theory of Communication* (Shannon 1948). Shannon paved the way for modern digital communications with a revolutionary idea that the information content of a message consists simply of the number of 1s and 0s it takes to transmit it. This idea was gradually adopted by communications engineers, leading to the information age of today. A decade later, two critical technologies, viewed in the context of Shannon's publication, propelled the Internet into existence: the microchip and semiconductor transistor, technologies that are still commonly used today. What followed was a revolution—the ARPANET (abbreviation for Advanced Research Projects Agency Network, an experimental computer network that was the forerunner of the Internet), personal computers, and the World Wide Web propelled the enablement of analog computing to go digital.

These developments laid the foundation for digital transformation of the business world in the late 1990s, and then again in the mid-2000s when the SMAC technologies arrived. The internet boom hit in the 1990s with a bang, accelerating business ideas based on the new technology of that time. The technology developments conceived in the 1980s took flight in the e-business wave of the 90s with the rise of the Internet. I remember the sudden surge of interest that led to the hype phase in the late 1990s, when people came out of the woodwork to be part of the internet gold rush.

Hundreds of "dot-com" companies were started, and everyone wanted to invest in them. This caused valuations to shoot up and crazy ideas that crazy ideas that lacked concrete business models or a realistic chance of success were viewed as the next big thing. As millions of people decided to go online virtually overnight, companies like AOL expanded rapidly. The growth rate of technology investments averaged 24% each year from 1995 to 2000, largely in tech-to-automate solutions to create in-house efficiencies that led to better bottom line results.

Much of the current technology era of digital transformation feels similar to the late 1990s. A major drawback of digital transformation in the 1990s and 2000s was the focus on the needs of the company and was driven by operational efficiencies. The needs of the customer, or rather customer value proposition for technology implementation, were secondary. These initiatives were mainly led by IT project teams and handled through one-way dialogue by change management and training teams.

Just like in the 1990s, we are seeing many Fortune 500 companies devote significant resources, time, and investments to digitalization of business. However, a major difference to the earlier waves of digital transformation is that customers have now entered the equation in a significant way.

As described in a recent study of over 12,000 consumers worldwide (Salesforce 2020), it has become apparent that customers today have more access to information and less incentive to be loyal, and are firmly in control of their relationships with companies and brands. As the generations of digital natives grow, consumers are demanding more personalized products and services, as well as smooth interactions across multiple channels and touchpoints. Positive experiences are embraced while negative experiences spread like wildfire across online and social media channels. The same study found that 57% of customers stopped buying from a company because a competitor offered a better experience. The rise of the "cancel culture," a modern form of snubbing, and lower switching costs have made business leaders sit up and take notice of the digital power of consumers, forcing them to embrace the digital transformation.

Global spending on the digital business transformation has accelerated and is forecast to reach $2.8 trillion in 2025, more than double the amount allocated in 2020 (IDC 2021), as companies prioritize organization-wide change for people, processes, technology, data, and governance.

Many companies are still tackling digital business transformation of today in a similar way to the dot-com era of the 1990s, with a company-centric and tech-first approach. However, sustainable success in digital business transformation requires organization-wide change and a new mindset that is ready to embrace it. Digitally enabled businesses create superior customer experiences that seamlessly close the gaps between digital and physical touchpoints. Both companies and individuals need to be able to accept and thrive in the new reality to fully benefit from the possibilities of the digital world.

This point was further emphasized during my conversation with Didier Bonnet, globally recognized thought leader on digital transformation and a Professor of Strategy & Innovation at IMD

Business School. Didier pioneered the concept of digital transformation over a decade ago and is an author of the best-selling book *Leading Digital*, described as the "source code" for understanding the DNA of successful digital transformation. During our conversation, Didier indicated that organizations tended to spend 80% of the focus on digital and 20% on the transformation in their digital business transformation efforts. It should be the opposite, where a higher focus is placed on organization and people transformation enabled by digital technologies. As the global coronavirus pandemic hit, companies quickly deployed and adopted collaboration and productivity tools to enable business continuity. In the past, Didier had observed companies spending months in their attempts to train and engage employees in the use of productivity tools. I shared a similar experience several years ago when I led the charge to implement Yammer for employee communications at one of the Big Four consulting firms.

In addition, Didier highlights that the role of middle managers in particular has shifted in the business environment, where team structures are flattening and agile approaches are increasingly being utilized. The role of middle managers has shifted from leading and directing teams to enabling and shaping capabilities from the background. Managers with content knowledge are thriving in the workplace, where there is a shift of value contribution to people with high content knowledge or those with high sensitivity to the people side of business. He advises companies to use the pandemic as an opportunity to really re-think work and the business landscape. For example, as we move into the post-Covid norm, many organizations are still taking a command and control approach to discussing working models, i.e., number of days in the office or adoption of productivity platforms. This output mentality reveals short-term thinking, and few companies are truly diving deeper into the real value of work, how it is done, and whether there are better ways to structure the company and working models to create greater value in business.

This is an opportunity to innovate and shift a structure that we have set up since the start of modern business times. According to

Didier, more companies, when considering the future, think about the next generation of technologies such as AI, blockchain, and robotics. But the focus should be on innovating organizations and working models to create a new basis for tapping into the people elements and generating productivity at work. People need to start re-thinking organizational innovation, taking the pandemic as an incredible global experiment, drawing lessons from the way people have responded to the pandemic and the change in mindset that it has triggered.

In the pre-Covid landscape, companies were concerned about robots and AI taking over and people losing jobs. Didier counters this, believing that existing jobs will change and phase out, while new jobs and related tasks will be created. Organizations need to address this shift, to ensure their workforce is sufficiently prepared and upskilled to thrive in this new digital environment. For example, over the past decade, there has been a significant acceleration in automation of factories and manufacturing facilities. This has not eliminated the need for human skills, but rather resulted in increasing automation of tasks within job functions although not automating the role in full. We need to focus on getting people comfortable working with technologies and understanding algorithms, enabling more intelligent working environments.

Critical Success Factors for Sustainable Digital Business Transformation

Digital business transformation is a fundamental change of an organization's culture, operations, and ecosystem by leveraging technology to create value. A common misconception is that digital transformation is rooted in technology or disruption. On the contrary, it is about transforming value creation, capture, and delivery of the business through the intelligent use of people, process, and technology solutions. Over the past two decades, I have led numerous business and digital transformation initiatives. As part of this work, I have experienced critical challenges and opportunities created by the change efforts, as well as how to successfully navigate the complexities of uncertainty, internal politics, skepticism, and fear.

In order for organizations to jumpstart their digital business transformation efforts, several critical success factors are required to help make the case for change, earn support, and initiate the steps that lead to successful transformation.

Purpose   The starting point is an integrated strategy with clear digital business transformation goals, where the why, what, and how of the strategy are clearly described and linked to quantifiable business outcomes. The transformation should describe meaningful change that aligns with the purpose of the organization and the values embedded in the culture and people. The purpose plays a critical role in bringing stakeholders together, collectively moving towards a common direction. Chapter 4 explores the purpose-driven organization and related approach in more detail.

Customer   The customer is at the core of any organization. In today's environment, the behaviors and preferences of customers are evolving rapidly. In the last decade, mobile devices, global connectivity, and online platforms have given rise to connected consumers, who are demanding new levels of interaction with all brands. They seek hyper-personalized interactions, instantaneous responses, predictive products and services, as well as frictionless engagement across all channels. Digitally enabled businesses have been able to tap into these new requirements, further accelerating the shifts in consumers.

In this crowded digital environment, companies truly struggle to stand out. Consumers are shifting away from product-based interactions, demanding more meaningful experience-focused interactions across channels and touchpoints. Digital business transformation initiatives help organizations expand reach, engage on deeper levels, as well as scale personalized interactions at minimum cost. In reality, this involves proactively shifting repetitive actions and interactions in the customer journey to the background with automation, and prioritizing creating impactful experiences.

These experiences—moments of truth—require a laser focus on the wants and needs of current and future customers, ensuring technology adoption delivers valuable business outcomes. "Moments of truth" are defined as moments when a customer or user interacts with your brand, product, or service to form or change an impression about your company. Focus on finding micro-moments where the organization can engage with customers to further solidify the relationship and create lasting impressions.

Digital and online channels provide a great way to engage with customers. Today, other great digital solutions are easy to implement. For example, there are numerous AI-based virtual assistants and chatbots in the market today that are cost-effective and have never been so easy to implement but which create a big impact when implemented well. These enable companies to supplement customer engagement and fill the breaks in the customer journey with value-added interactions.

Process   Any transformation in the organization is supported and driven by changes to the business process landscape and operational infrastructure. New elements in the organization, whether they involve a technology solution implementation, shift in digital products and services, or even digital revenue stream, will involve process changes to scale and deliver sufficient business outcomes. This will include related policy changes, as well as effective monitoring of progress around processes and outcomes, with sufficient data availability and quality.

Digital business transformation requires organizations to go beyond improvement exercises to redesigning the process landscape through optimization, digitization, and automation.

Reengineering focuses on completely changing the process for an overall different result, as opposed to incremental improvement that tweaks an existing process to optimize it.

Technology   Identifying and implementing fit-for-purpose technology solutions that create a modern architecture driven by business needs is another critical success factor for transformation. Sustainable digital business transformation will depend on creating this environment—one that is secure, scalable, deploys and adopts changes rapidly, and is able to seamlessly interact with a range of solutions. Technology is an enabler for digital business transformation, and in many cases the trigger for change as new solutions and capabilities allow organizations to create and deliver value faster and at lower cost.

Organizations will need to reevaluate their technology architecture, including tools, applications, and platforms, to determine the effectiveness of the existing digital strategy. Additionally, it is critical to explore and make the best use of new and emerging technology solutions that are impacting the business and industry. The aim is to understand how these impact the current business operations and performance while exploring potential new opportunities.

Business leaders will face the challenge of where to focus efforts, investments, and resources—transforming the existing landscape or implementing new solutions. This situation, referred to as dual transformation, requires consideration and tough decision-making. Chapter 7 provides guidance on how to manage this environment of dual transformation.

Data & Insights   Transformation in an organization is guided by the data and often involves analyzing structured and unstructured data from a variety of sources to gain rapid insights. Organizations will be able to use these insights to determine key focus areas and strategic priorities, as well as opportunities that will guide the development and implementation of the digital business transformation efforts. In the current digital market, there is an abundance of data from various sources, including users, platforms, and devices. The combination of data and technology can help organizations review and streamline experiences across customer journeys, as well as optimize internal operations.

Emerging technology solutions also offer a new range of data sources that can add greater value to the business. For example, the explosion of Internet of Things (IoT) applications across industries is generating a plethora of real-time data from humans and machines alike. These provide an unprecedented level of granularity and detail that, when utilized appropriately, allow organizations to respond to customer needs rapidly and even anticipate new needs. As implementation of automation and digitization initiatives start to generate additional data and information about operations, processes, customers, and market offerings, these should be utilized for continuous improvement within the transformation journey.

People   At the core of digital business transformation are people. Leadership alignment, accountability and ownership, execution team capabilities and skills, as well as employees' buy-in and commitment all play a critical role in the transformation journey. The type of leadership and culture required can be described as agile and adaptable, one that is purpose-driven and gives people the space to explore, fail fast, and learn quickly. In addition, high-caliber teams involved in the transformation process should have a clear understanding of the business ecosystem, consumer needs, and technology capabilities. Leaders need to set a vision and work cross-functionally to enable the transformation team to cut across preexisting organizational boundaries to deploy better solutions.

The Human Factor: Making or Breaking Digital Transformation

In the early 2000s, while working as a consultant for one of the Big Four firms, I was assigned to one of the largest projects in the company—SAP implementation for a telecommunications client. The management consulting industry was in its prime and it was a prestigious position to hold. I was proud to be part of this large project team and passionate about delivering good work to the client. The project team spent long hours and late nights preparing for the implementation of the finance and controlling modules of the SAP Enterprise Resource Planning (SAP ERP) system.

The project began successfully enough, as we mapped the existing process landscape and scoped the transition to the new system. The existing environment at the time consisted of mostly manual, human-led processes and a patchwork of rudimentary systems, including Microsoft Excel, that enabled the flow of complex work for the company. The IT transformation project was complex in itself and the project team was divided into process, technology, and data workstreams, as we focused on understanding the process landscape, technology infrastructure, and business requirements. Once the existing processes were mapped and new processes defined, we initiated the data migration and pilot implementation phases.

To the surprise of the project team, as well as the client company management team, the project resulted in longer hours and more intensive work. A core element of the business case for the SAP ERP system investment focused on increasing efficiency and productivity. A major pain point for the company was the heterogeneous data due to disparate system landscapes that make period closing a very labor-intensive and costly process requiring manual reconciliation efforts to integrate general ledgers to sub-ledgers, causing unnecessary process delays.

The new SAP ERP system promised a single integrated solution that provided a streamlined workflow and unified view of financial data and management reporting, as well as removing the need for reconciliation of multiple manual ledgers. The system had delivered on this. However, the number of hours required to execute the process in the company increased dramatically.

The project team resorted to conducting a step-through investigation of the system to identify potential bottlenecks, errors in the workflow, or migration issues. After an effort-intensive investigation period, the issue was finally uncovered—people! The client teams working with the SAP ERP system were not sold on the new solution and did not trust that it would deliver to their requirements. In essence, they did not want to change the way they were working and felt that their original workflows and systems they had put together delivered the business requirements. As a result, they continued with the existing environment, including large Microsoft Excel sheets and manual processes in the background, while reserving time at the end of the day to enter required data into the new system. This created a shadow organization that resulted in the increase of time and effort reported.

The project team had planned for success across every part of the project, but neglected to consider the most important element that could make or break the final implementation—the human factor. Digital business transformation essentially involves change, and an essential success factor is to be able to convince users to adopt, embrace, and advocate for the change that is being implemented.

As a conclusion, I am happy to share that the consulting project initiated a communication and change management workstream that prioritized gaining buy-in from the wider client organization teams. In addition to a communication plan, we conducted project roadshows across all functional units in the organization and in-depth training sessions for users of the new system. We also identified project champions from various business units to help advocate for the new solution and respond to questions, queries, and uncertainties that the employees might have regarding the new implementation.

The result: by the time the final module implementation was complete, we had developed a community of users and supporters throughout the organization that helped drive the successful implementation of the system.

This experience is not unique as I am convinced that many technology and transformation leaders have had similar experiences in their journey to implement change in an organization. Even to this day, with my focus squarely on digital business transformation and emerging technology implementation, I often encounter the "amygdala response."

The "Amygdala Response"

The amygdala is an almond-shaped structure in the brain. It is involved in processing emotions. Early humans developed a fight-or-flight response to deal with threats and dangers. This is an automatic response to danger, and it allows people to react quickly, without the need to think. The amygdala is the part of the brain responsible for this reaction. When a person feels stressed or afraid, the amygdala releases stress hormones that prepare the body to fight the threat or flee from the danger. Common emotions that trigger this response include fear, anger, anxiety, and a feeling of loss of control.

The term "amygdala response" has been propagated in the business context in the book *Exponential Organizations* (Ismail 2014) to describe how organizations reject change. An organization can be likened to a living organism that functions to survive within its environment. As with the human body, organizations have an immune system as well, which organically develops out of systems, procedures, and mindsets that work together to remain in the comfort zone of past successes and keeps the system alive and running smoothly in the status quo. Just like the human body, an organization's immune system can also become hyperactive. The organization's immune system will go into overdrive to attack and disarm any new element or change that threatens the status quo, irrespective of whether this is a threat, disruption, or innovative opportunity. When this happens, there is a high chance of missing out on new market opportunities transforming the industry.

In the book, Ismail references the amygdala response as a major barrier to successful implementation of transformation and a critical need to address it early. For example, Walmart attempted to introduce e-commerce four times in order to compete with Amazon, but each time the immune system played a key role in preventing progress. The time and resources spent by Walmart during those four attempts were significant, by which point Amazon had grown beyond the point where Walmart would ever be able to catch up. Ismail indicates that it takes around three years for a C-suite to come around to a new idea—but in today's environment, companies do not have the luxury to wait around for this long before moving forward with transformation.

At the core of the amygdala challenge are people—board members and management teams that drive change; employees that adopt, embrace, and advocate for change; customers that trigger the change; as well as external stakeholders such as partners and suppliers that support the implementation of change. Understanding stakeholder motivations is a critical way to manage the amygdala response and drive sustainable digital business transformation. The next section explores the shifts in human behavior, their motivations, the role they play in transformation, and how to engage with them for success.

Shifts in Human Behavior

In the early 1900s, the Industrial Revolution started to spread across the world and transformed economic, health, and transportation industries, which led to numerous inventions and firsts in history. This was a major turning point in the history of the world because the Industrial Revolution impacted almost every aspect of humanity. It marked the transition to new manufacturing processes as local economies shifted from an agricultural and handiwork economy to an industrial and machine-based economy.

The most significant shift that occurred during the Industrial Revolution was the impact on society and human behavior. Traditional ideas of Western civilization began to be replaced by radical new philosophical and economic ideas. The increasing reliance on science and technology of the time, the questioning of traditional agriculture methods, and the onset of profit-oriented market economies had triggered the Industrial Revolution and gave rise to new societal structures. This marked the origins of travel to work, where, for the first time since the Neolithic era, people started to work outside of their local environment, namely in factories or industrial sites.

Additionally, the Industrial Revolution marked a major change in the skills and capabilities required. In the agricultural era, physical and manual labor was dominant. A massive shift occurred as farm workers were reskilled to work with machines that needed to be fabricated or repaired. There were some short-term job losses, but different jobs were created that did not previously exist and new working models needed to be constructed to suit these new demands.

In many ways, these working models—rules of work and time schedules for common workers—set during the Industrial Revolution have been sustained for over 200 years into modern times. At first, factories needed to be tended to all the time, forcing employees to work between 10 and 16 hours a day. However, in 1926, the Ford Motor Company (founded by Henry Ford) made a ground-breaking change by being one of the first significant companies to change their work policy to 40-hour weeks with five working days, with no change in wages. This historic change marked the first step that soon inspired companies across the world to adopt the Monday–Friday workweek.

The working models of the Industrial Revolution have been largely maintained through the Second and Third Industrial Revolutions, although developments in skillsets, physical location of work, and enhancements in technology have rapidly shifted.

The Second Industrial Revolution, which occurred between 1870 and 1914, was a period of growth for existing industries and expansion of new ones, including steel, oil, and electricity. During this time, electric power was used to create mass production and major technological advances took place, including the telephone, light bulb, phonograph, and the internal combustion engine. With the transition from steam power to electricity, there were once again short-term job losses, but as steam mechanics reskilled to become electricians, more new jobs were created.

The Third Industrial Revolution, also known as the Digital Revolution, references the advancement of technology from analog electronic and mechanical devices to the digital technology available today. The Digital Revolution started in the 1980s, with technology advances including the personal computer, the Internet, and information and communications technology (ICT). Many jobs were then replaced by computers and robots, and computer literacy and related skillsets, for example software and hardware engineers, were in high demand. Once again, new jobs were created that previously did not exist.

Today, we are in the Fourth Industrial Revolution (see Figure 2.1), built on the foundation of the Digital Revolution, representing new ways in which technology becomes embedded within society, business, and our daily lives. The Fourth Industrial Revolution is marked by emerging technology breakthroughs in a number of fields, including robotics, artificial intelligence, nanotechnology,

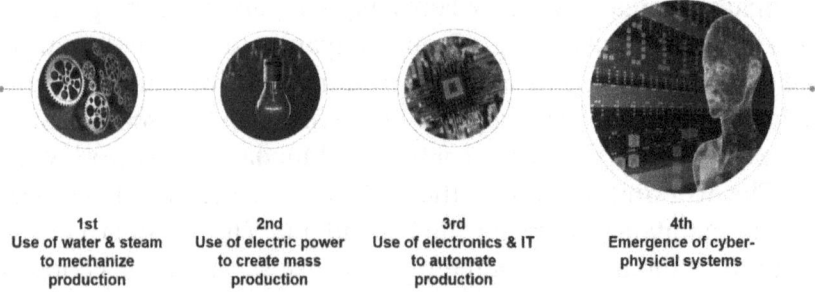

1st	2nd	3rd	4th
Use of water & steam to mechanize production	Use of electric power to create mass production	Use of electronics & IT to automate production	Emergence of cyber-physical systems

Figure 2.1   The Industrial Revolutions.
SOURCE: World Economic Forum

quantum computing, biotechnology, the IoT, decentralized consensus, 3D printing, and autonomous vehicles. The greatest aspiration of the Fourth Industrial Revolution is to improve the quality of life, reduce inequality of the world's population, and raise income levels. We will explore the human side of the top five disruptive technologies and their convergence, as well as the impact and applications for business in Chapter 8.

The impact of the Fourth Industrial Revolution is increasingly evident in the shift in skill requirements and working models across industries and companies. New digitally enabled companies are also implementing new working models that question the validity of Henry Ford's original 40-hour workweek, demonstrating that increasing autonomy could result in increased creativity and effectiveness in work output. In addition, the new generation of the workforce are wired differently from the workers of the previous industrial revolutions—they are motivated by a higher purpose, value, and quality of life, unlike previous generations that looked for security, stability, and consistency from employment. There are several key factors that have triggered the shifts in human behavior and motivations, now impacting the next industrial revolution.

Generational Shift: The Rise of Gen Y, Z, and Alpha

Today, the global workforce consists of a unique blend of four different generations of people—Baby boomers, X, Y (also commonly referred to as Millennials), and Z. Each group brings a different dynamic to the business world, and companies need to truly understand their generational characteristics to be able to harness their potential during the digital business transformation journey.

Baby boomers (born between 1946 and 1964) are the oldest generation currently still in the workforce. This was the generation that thrived before and during the Third Industrial Revolution, learning to compete for resources and success. The Boomers are known as "Traditionalist"—the generation that brought the strong work ethic of their parents into the factories of industrialized soci- ety. Having grown up following the Great Depression and World War II, Baby boomers considered work a privilege and believed that one must earn one's way through hard work.

Motivated by position, perks, and prestige, Baby boomers define themselves by their professional accomplishments and equate work and position with self-worth. This makes the Boomer generation competitive in the workplace and respectful of hierarchical struc- ture and rankism that have been traditionally established in com- panies. Baby boomers aspire to have job security and think that careers are defined by the employers.

As **Generation X** entered the workplace, we saw some shifts take place, as this generation aspired to achieve better work–life balance. Generation X (born between 1965 and 1980) make up the second-largest group in the current workforce. Known for a willing- ness to take on new challenges, these employees have the tenure, people skills, and experience to add value as leaders at work.

The Gen Xers, as they are commonly known, were the last gen- eration to grow up in the physical world, without digital tools. As such, they favor collaboration, efficiency in getting things done, and are comfortable with face-to-face engagement, and in-person conflict resolution. However, Gen Xers are also currently the most connected generation, spending the most time on digital and technology-related activities. Although Gen Xers aspire to achieve work–life balance, they are loyal to their professions and the workaholics of the group, recognized for high work ethics and commitment.

A major shift occurred when Generation Y, more commonly known as **Millennials,** (born between 1981 and 1996) entered the workforce. This generation was born into a world of technology and has grown up surrounded by gadgets such as smart phones, laptops, and tablets. Technology is a major aspect of life for Millennials, who are constantly plugged into mobile devices and online platforms. Of all the generations currently in the workforce, Millennials are considered to be the most independent. Having grown up sourcing information, they prefer to create their own way of doing things rather than being provided with instructions and being told exactly what to do.

Based on a study by Upwork, a global freelancing platform, one in three Millennials recommend working in a startup (Upwork 2013). They have a strong desire to follow independent career paths due to the freedom and flexibility that this offers—the ability to work when and where they choose (versus working in a corporate 9–5 job). Admittedly, Millennials are the brains behind some of the most innovating digitally enabled businesses that exist in the global market today. As digital natives, this generation is in tune with the true capabilities of digital and online technologies, and how to leverage these to meet the demands of the growing population of digital consumers.

In the digital world of today, anyone can launch a business online for next to nothing and start selling online in next to no time. Millennials were born with the "entrepreneurial" mindset of being self-starters and big dreamers. Additionally, they are seeking jobs that are meaningful and prioritize fulfilling that need as an integral part of their identity.

Generation Z (between 1997 and 2010) will soon surpass the Millennials as the most populous generation on earth. This generation, fundamentally different from Millennials, have an entirely unique perspective on professions and what constitutes success in life and at the workplace (Gomez 2018). The Gen Zers have come of age in a world where content and information are free and shared, where products and services are one click away, customer journeys are seamless across channels and hyper-personalized for their needs.

In the evolution of work, we are at an inflection point and Gen Z are entering the workforce at an opportune moment. Historically, a first job was always seen as a rite of passage where newcomers pay their dues, learn the necessary skills required in the business world, and work their way up. This situation is now shifting, as technology and automation are reducing or even eliminating the mundane, manual, repetitive tasks traditionally done by the newcomers.

Organizations are having to rethink and redesign the current jobs landscape, in order to attract and engage Gen Zers and continue the pipeline of future talents.

The **Alpha Generation** (born from the 2010s onwards) will shape the future of work in ways that are unimaginable for generations of the past. Although the oldest of the Alpha generation are now barely 12 years old, their behaviors, attitudes, and preferences are already being affected by both the proliferation of technology and the uncertain times we live in. The term "Alpha" is used because this is the first generation born entirely in the twenty-first century.

The Alpha workforce will be the most diverse and educated, prioritizing equal opportunity, real-world simulations, as well as highly personalized and engaging on-the-job training. With early access to new technologies such as AI-based systems, augmented and virtual learning-based systems, the Alpha generation will learn at a faster pace and be able to apply these learnings in new, innovative ways, quickly collecting skills at a whirlwind speed as they move forward. To this generation, technology is not just considered as a means to serve their needs to collaborate with peers, but also as a channel to transform the work around them.

The Millennials, Gen Y, and Alphas will demand more from companies and their employers than the generations before them. They are looking for companies that closely align with their values and beliefs and directly contribute to the betterment of society. These generations will seek to continuously improve and innovate, motivated deeply by their sense of fulfillment in life, and they will want recognition for their successes.

Additionally, across the generations, success and happiness mean very different things. The newer generations seek flexibility, in terms of working models, type of work, and the environment that they work in. Apart from flexible working hours and normalizing the digital-nomad work culture (i.e., working from anywhere both virtually and remotely), these generations will not be confined by physical boundaries, organizational hierarchies, and traditional job descriptions. Additionally, Gen Y and Alphas already think diversity is the norm and will see no barriers to ascending the professional ladder, demanding to see this generational composition reflected in the organizations they work with.

The Millennials, Gen Y, and Alphas also expect companies to support their emotional, physical, and mental well-being as part of this new social contract. During the coronavirus pandemic, we saw a rise in companies prioritizing mental health discussions—this was previously almost a taboo topic at the workplace. The newer generations will further normalize this topic, prioritizing it as a basic requirement for any work environment. These generations want companies to treat them as humans first and workers second, yearning for teams to act as a support structure.

These generations also deeply understand the impact of societal, political, and climate changes in which they are growing up, and the need to take responsibility for the world around them to establish critical systemic changes.

Rapid Adoption of Digital Technologies

For decades, the rate of technology development, production, and adoption in the global market has been accelerating rapidly. A common illustration of this is the adoption rate comparison of the telephone, which took decades to reach 50% of households, and the cellphone, that took up to five years (see Figure 2.2). Technology innovations that were introduced more recently are being adopted more quickly. More than 50 years after the formulation of Moore's law—which holds that computing power doubles in capability every 18 to 24 months—mobile devices, sensors, AI, and robotics affect our lives more quickly and more pervasively than ever before.

The technology adoption life cycle is a description of customer behavior related to the acceptance of a new product or feature, which is often broken into innovators, early adopters, early majority, late majority, and laggards. Classical theory would suggest that the majority of customers could be the early majority and the late majority adopters.

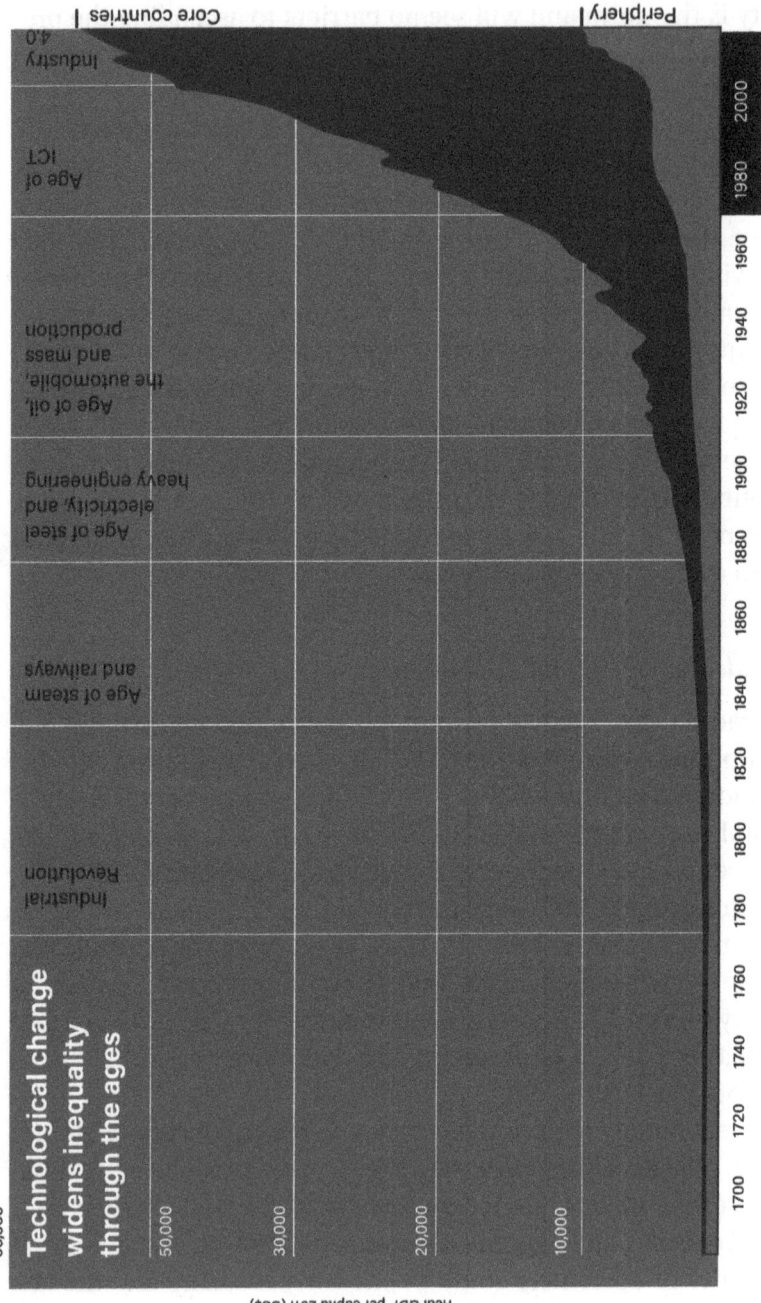

Figure 2.2 Technology adoption curve.
SOURCE: Adapted from UNCTAD, 2021

40

While this rings true for Boomers and Gen Xers, the generations after these are characterized by increased levels of technical acumen, demonstrable by the ever-shortening times that pass between the introduction and full-scale adoption of new technologies. As such, the customer majority has shifted to early adopters and the difference between the late majority and laggards becomes insignificant.

In the current digital age, it is more than possible to achieve higher levels of market penetration for new technologies and innovations in shorter amounts of time. The speed of adoption also means that these technologies will lose their novelty and achieve mass adoption quicker, forcing innovators and companies to continuously improve and update to stay competitive, further driving the rate of technology development.

A 2017 study (Deloitte University Press 2017) highlights that business productivity has not kept pace with technological progress.

According to the study, the problem is rooted in the increasing gap between technological sophistication and rate of productivity in organizations. Essentially, organizations with low productivity quickly lose to competitors, and this comes down to how businesses organize, manage, develop, and align their people at work.

In the current digital world, people are fairly quick in adopting new digital technologies and innovative solutions. However, organizations are moving into the digital space and adopting technology solutions at a relatively slower pace, despite the fact that consumers and employees alike are demanding greater digital integration. The traditional functional areas of corporate planning, organizational structure, job design, performance measures, and management have not truly changed since the first industrial age. As illustrated in Figure 2.3, the curves demonstrate the need for organizations to adapt to technology and societal changes. Additionally, public policy relating to income, unemployment, immigration, taxes, and legislation, is developing at an even slower pace, resulting in further imbalances and challenges for businesses.

What appears to be happening

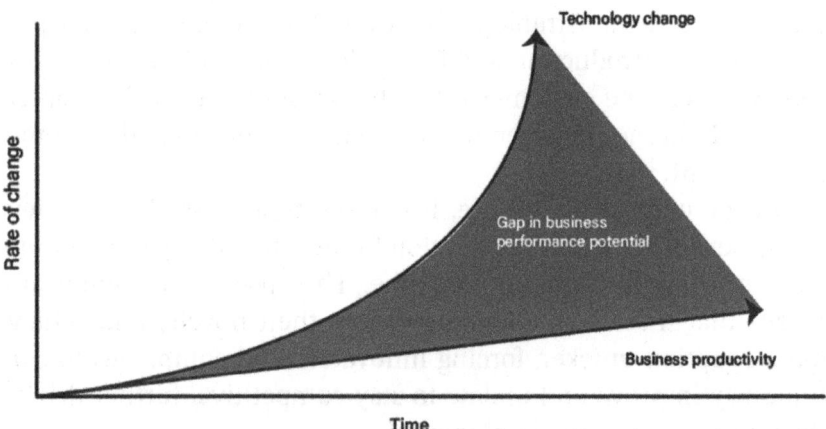

What is really happening

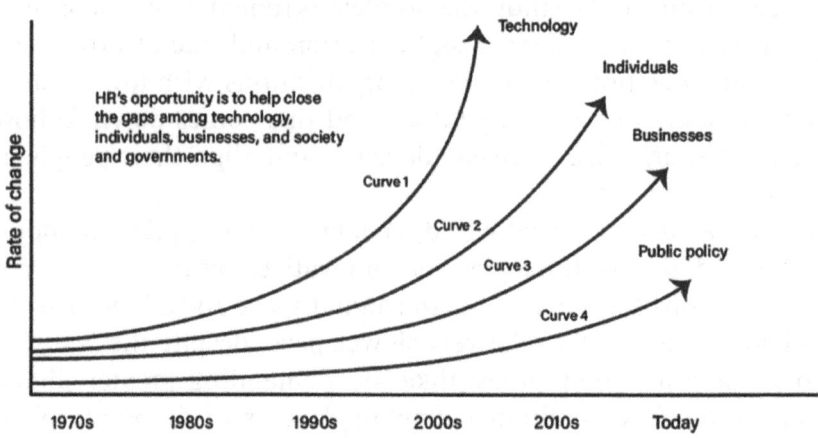

Figure 2.3 Business productivity has not kept up with technological progress.
SOURCE: Adapted from Deloitte University Press, 2017

Future-of-work strategist Heather E. McGowan indicates that work–life balance will be one of constant adaptation, as highlighted in her most recent book, *The Adaptation Advantage* (McGowan and

Shipley 2020). In it, McGowan describes the changes that rapid technology advancements are bringing to the business landscape and society in general. She also warns that each time human skills or capabilities are replaced by technology, for the sake of prioritizing efficiency and speed, we need to be cognizant of reskilling or upskilling ourselves to remain competitive and relevant in the workforce.

Technology is now deeply engrained in our daily lives, transforming almost every aspect of our personal and professional journey, soon even converging with our physical beings. Consider the rapid acceleration of human–machine integration and interfaces. For example, bio-printing human organs with the aim of manufacturing fully biocompatible human organs that will make organ transplants accessible to people around the world. Or even Elon Musk's Neuralink, aimed at implanting devices in paralyzed humans, allowing them to control phones or computers.

As automation takes on more significant roles in our daily lives, an increasing number of actions and decisions will be taken over by automation and autonomous technology. For example, the deployment of autonomous vehicles (AVs) is being explored in dense urban cities such as New York, San Francisco, Tel Aviv, London, and Beijing. Most of the current pilots are limited to expansive urban landscapes, like in Phoenix Arizona or the Bay Area (excluding San Francisco), that allow easier testing conditions, and the ability to cover longer mileage. However, suburban areas alone cannot maintain a profitable AV market due to limited demand and lower economic incentives. There is an urgent need for policy frameworks and legislation to enable the safe experimentation and development of the autonomous technology. Many industry experts agree that there is a need for defining ethical guardrails between society and autonomous technology.

As we progress deeper into the digital future, technology is becoming increasingly engrained in our psyche, embedding more deeply in our sense of value, purpose, and self.

Rise of the Gig Economy

There are an increasing number of people, in fact millions across the globe, who are assembling multiple income streams and supplementary independent work, rather than choosing to remain within a structured salaried job. The steady rise of the gig economy, an independent labor market that includes freelance work and limited or short-term contracts, has been evident across several industries such as transportation, accounting and finance, legal, IT, as well as professional advisory services. Based on a study conducted by Mastercard (Mastercard Thought Leadership 2020), the estimated wage disbursement volumes in the global gig economy are projected to grow to $298 billion by 2023. The study also indicated that a significant portion of the gig workforce was connected to customers and job opportunities by digital platforms, such as Uber, Upwork, Etsy, and Airbnb (see Figure 2.4).

The gig economy has been further accelerated by the coronavirus pandemic, although the impact has not been uniform across all industries. Low-touch sectors that have been able to maintain social distancing requirements, such as food and goods delivery, have undoubtedly experienced a surge in demand. Other sectors that require social proximity, like asset-sharing services, have declined in demand.

Additionally, there has been a progression from narrow skills to a diverse and highly skilled gig workforce. The gig economy was initially the focus of people with specific skills, such as

Gig platform type (2018 data[2])	Description	Illustrative players
Transportation-based services ($61.3B disbursements)	On-demand platforms for sourcing ride-sharing, carpooling, restaurant, and goods delivery services	Uber Grab lyft Instacart POSTMATES
Professional services ($6B disbursements)	On-demand platforms for sourcing business-related services and other high-skilled services	Upwork 99designs GFREELANCE guru
Household services and handmade goods ($14.1B disbursements)	On-demand platforms for sourcing household services and custom handmade crafts	Etsy Care.com TaskRabbit iona
Asset-sharing services ($52.7B disbursements)	On-demand platforms for sourcing home-sharing and other property-sharing services	airbnb boatsetter yourparkingspace

Figure 2.4   Gig platforms by type of industry being serviced.
SOURCE: Mastercard Thought Leadership, 2020

technical developers, physical workers, or app-based skill offers such as Task Rabbit or Uber. However, as organizations worldwide faced headcount freezes and layoffs, there was an increase in demand for highly skilled remote and virtual workers. Not surprisingly, business and professional employment platform LinkedIn launched a dedicated search filter for remote jobs on their platform in a bid to cater to the rising demands of job seekers and companies alike.

The Mastercard study estimates that by 2023 total disbursements are expected to more than double to nearly $300 billion, while the number of gig workers will reach almost 80 million globally. This expected growth will be driven by accelerating adoption within relatively new gig sectors, traditional gig sectors expanding into new markets, and secular changes reshaping the way people choose to work and to live. If we delve deeper into the demographics of the independent workforces, there is significant diversity across the four segments (McKinsey Global Institute 2016), including free agents who proactively choose gig work as their main source of income; casual earners who choose gig work as their supplemental income; reluctants who prefer traditional jobs but make independent work as a primary income; and finally the strapped, who need gig work out of necessity to supplement their income (Figure 2.5).

	Primary Income	Supplemental Income
Preferred Choice	FREE AGENTS	CASUAL EARNERS
Out of Necessity	RELUCTANTS	FINANCIALLY STRAPPED

Figure 2.5 Segments of independent workers.
SOURCE: Adapted from McKinsey Global Institute, 2016

Digital platforms and online channels have contributed significantly to the rise of the gig economy by creating efficient marketplaces that offer scale and facilitate direct matching to potential customers and independent work. Although payment service providers are still exploring how best to serve the gig workforce, the growth in this sector will continue and is further fueled by the interests and aspirations of the global workforce. As we further consider the generation shifts from the previous section, Millennials and Gen Zers are increasingly participating in the gig economy, and may prefer it to full-time employment in a more traditional office environment. This would offer several advantages including flexible work hours, improved work–life balance, and access to an alternative income stream to supplement their interests or personal goals.

As we move into the post-pandemic era, businesses are faced with the great resignation—a new challenge that reflects the millions of people around the world who are quitting their stable jobs voluntarily to re-assess their own personal journeys and purpose. The attrition rates increased from 10% in 2020, to over 20% in 2021 (Gartner 2021). In the United States alone, it is recorded that 47.4 million people left their jobs voluntarily in that same year (CNBC 2022). The pandemic triggered a shift in mindset, as people across the world faced existential questions and re-evaluate their priorities. Waking up to a situation that questions their sense of value and belonging in companies, many are choosing to leave situations that do not align with their needs. The availability of alternative income sources, such as gig work, has made this decision to leave full-time positions even easier. The mass exit has created a surplus of open positions that businesses need to fill, and has leadership teams in a scramble to retain their highly skilled employees.

Undoubtedly, the gig economy is increasingly becoming a fixed element in the global business landscape due to the tangible economic benefits derived, for example raising labor-force participation, alternative working models, increased innovation, crowdsourced skills and capabilities, opportunity for reduction of unemployment, and increased productivity. The ultimate outcome will be that individuals will seek to have more proactive control in managing their work and income sources, and the gig economy, coupled with platform technology, will truly enable this reshaping of the world of work.

Search for a Higher Purpose: Sustainability, Climate Change, and Green Economy

Purpose is the core element that provides orientation and binds individual motivations with the daily work that people perform in an organization. Over the years, there has been a significant shift in motivations and personal interests, with each new generation of workforce prioritizing different values. For example, salary is still one of the most important factors for Gen Zers in deciding on a job, but it has become less of a consideration compared to previous generations (Gen X and Millennials). Increasingly, new generations of employees are looking to be part of organizations driven by purpose and core values that align with their own. The aspirational aspects of brands that highlight societal commitments such as sustainability, climate change, diversity, and inclusion, as well as behaviors and characteristics of leadership teams that align to these, appear more attractive to the new generation of employees. And as a new generation of consumers, these Gen Zers are prioritizing these same elements when figuring out their brand loyalties and spending patterns. Companies are compelled to demonstrate their commitments to higher purpose and values, not only in their product and service offerings, but also their brand message, business practices, and leadership teams.

I would personally suggest that the purpose-driven Gen Zers have been able to influence previous generations of people, pushing them to assess their contributions to the world and alignment with future values. A great example is the Swedish environmental activist on climate change, who has gained international recognition in recent years—Greta Thunberg. As a quintessential Gen Zer, Thunberg has triggered an unprecedented level of activism that has managed to mobilize cross-generational support from across the world. Global climate strikes led by Thunberg have attracted hundreds of thousands of people from around the world to voice discontent with government inaction and a slow response to the climate crisis. Moving forward, companies will need to transform their business models to integrate sustainability principles in daily operations, and showcase a higher degree of responsibility towards the welfare of the global society.

Chapter 3 delves deeper into how organizations define and demonstrate their core values to position themselves as purpose-driven companies for the future.

Chapter 3
A Tale of Two Start-up Cultures

In February 2017, Susan Fowler, an ex-employee at Uber, wrote a blog post about the negative culture at the company that eventually had worn her down, forcing her to leave. Uber had already been struggling with reputational issues relating to female passenger safety; several lawsuits had been filed against the company, and there had been several rounds of bad press. However, the blog post triggered a media firestorm that eventually resulted in the company's CEO and founder being forced to resign.

Uber Technologies, Inc., more commonly known as Uber, is a "mobility as a service" provider with operations in over 900 metropolitan areas worldwide. The company was founded in 2009 and quickly grew to become one of the world's most valuable start-ups. However, in addition to facing fierce resistance from the taxi industry and government regulators during its expansion, Uber's corporate culture was reported to be highly hostile, sexist, and quite offensive to many people.

The company's values, as well as the actions and decisions that reinforce them on a daily basis, become a critical element of the culture. In the case of Uber, the founders had infamously defined a list of 14 values emphasizing meritocracy and fierce competition to deliver growth and revenue targets as a priority, including making bold bets, winning champion's mindset, and "always be hustlin'." Although these values contributed to the company's meteoric success, they also resulted in the emergence of a reported "A-Team" that delivered high results in the company and were given a free hand to act without consequences.

Following an investigation and the messy departure of CEO Travis Kalanick in June 2017, the CEO of Expedia, Dara Khosrowshahi, was appointed to take on the mammoth task of turning the culture at Uber around. Over the past four years, Khosrowshahi has made efforts not only to drive financial success for the company, but also to repair reputation and transform its culture. These included efforts to redefine Uber's corporate values based on feedback from employees and drivers, addressing the legal and security issues that were left unregulated over the years, and creating a more transparent communication and reporting structure that focuses on building trust in the company.

In addition to this, Uber has launched a corporate education program with classes in leadership and strategy, taught by Harvard professors. The education effort, spearheaded by Frances Frei, SVP of Leadership and Strategy, aims to fill the gap in formal leadership training among the management level in the company, as well as empower employees with understanding of business strategy and collaborative culture.

In 2021, Uber (along with its service Uber Eats) launched a new slew of ads featuring a new slogan: "Go Get It." On their website, the company's mission statement still highlights a focus on achieving results with the statement "We are Uber. We are go-getters", still highly focused on the technology that enables mobility. The company has made headway in the right direction; however, it is clear there is still a long journey ahead.

On the flipside, another start-up that has capitalized on the sharing economy is Airbnb, a platform for individuals to rent out their primary residences as lodgings for travelers. Since its founding in 2008, the company quickly grew and expanded internationally, reaching a total revenue worldwide of $3.38 billion in 2020. Similar to Uber that was founded on the idea of requesting a ride from your phone, the idea for Airbnb was born out of necessity when the founders were struggling to pay their rent and came up with an inventive way to make some extra money—they put down air mattresses and offered a bed and breakfast for nearby conference attendees.

Since then, the company has grown exponentially. Airbnb had over 7.9 million active listings as of December 2020 in over 190 countries and 34,000 cities, which generated $26.8 billion in gross revenues (Revenues for Airbnb + Hosts).

Airbnb faced many challenges, including pushback from the trillion-dollar global hotel industry that feared competition from long-term rental units being converted into de facto hotels. Also, cities started to reject Airbnb rentals, triggering an ongoing regulatory battle for the company across regions. For example, as reported in *Business Insider*, New York threatened to ban Airbnb and short-term rentals in 2014, as well as fine every host. Many city laws also made it illegal to rent out units for less than 30 days.

The company also faced issues with poorly behaved renters who damaged host properties, as well as negative guest experiences due to bait-and-switch scams (i.e., a network of fake accounts advertising stays at dozens of properties across cities that once booked were said to be unavailable at the last minute), poorly kept lodgings, and discrimination by hosts. In 2014, when the company relaunched its logo as an amalgamation of people, places, love, and the "A" of Airbnb, it was faced with backlash on social media for the design's sexual connotations and uncanny similarities to another company's logo.

Every organization faces challenges, but the measure of a strong culture is in how they respond to these challenges and deal with them. A major part of Airbnb's immense success has been the company's ability to maintain a positive culture, even in the face of challenges. In order to address host and renter issues, the company quickly launched coverage policies to help protect hosts, as well as security checks to ensure renter safety and security. Airbnb has shown a similar kind of positive initiative in responding and largely collaborating with cities to ensure that regulation regarding short-term rentals is respected by their hosts (however, we should also note that Airbnb has involved itself in a range of legal battles with cities and governments that are perceived as wrongfully regulating or restricting short-term rentals).

In contrast to Uber, the founders of Airbnb prioritized building a positive culture at the start-up. Airbnb invested significantly in its corporate culture, focusing heavily on creating a community and establishing partnerships. They facilitate their host groups for knowledge sharing, integrated into a host application that also embeds hospitality standards, and meetups for hosts to exchange information. The company's emphasis and facilitation of community and connectedness are very visible in their brand strategy—"Belong Anywhere."

In addition, the company focused on creating a corporate culture of transparency—employees are not only invited to share their experiences, but also feel safe to do so knowing their feedback will be actioned. According to Melissa Thomas-Hunt, Global Head of Diversity & Belonging at Airbnb, the mission of the company is to create a world where anyone can belong anywhere—an environment of connection not only for hosts and guests but also for employees. She highlights that Airbnb works to understand the challenges of its hosts, community, and employees to foster greater belonging in the workplace, as intended by the company's founders.

The contrast between the companies is striking given that both Uber and Airbnb were crucial organizations that triggered disruption in the global business landscape. According to an article in the *Harvard Business Review* (Sundararajan 2014), although both companies are market leaders with flagship platforms in the sharing economy, each has taken a distinct approach to organizational culture with vastly different results. According to Sundararajan, each company facilitated the digitally mediated "peer-to-peer" provision of a service rooted heavily in real-world assets, and regulated by city and local (rather than federal) government. Each raised massive amounts of venture capital, sustaining a market capitalization in the double-digit billions while facing tremendous pushback from regulators and incumbent stakeholders. Each company also invested heavily in government relations, hiring high-profile industry veterans to aid their causes. Both companies developed into leaders in their respective markets, resulting in globally recognized brands that have inspired countless new ventures and permeated new cultural dialog—Airbnb when we travel, we Uber to our meetings or desired locations.

As both companies are built on the premise of a high-quality customer service experience based on a business model that does not own assets or employ any of their providers, it would have been critical to develop a culture that drives the appropriate behaviors and values through the organization. However, as Table 3.1 shows, Airbnb took the approach of creating a strong community with a focus on partnership and sharing of best practices, while Uber placed distance between the platform and its providers (drivers).

Table 3.1 Comparison of Uber and Airbnb values under the company's original founders

	Airbnb	Uber
Tagline	"Belong Anywhere"	"Go Get It"
Brand mission	Connecting and belonging	Reimagine the way the world moves for the better
Values	Community and partnership Collaboration Positive flexibility Loyalty	Meritocracy and toe-stepping Confrontation Competitive Be an owner, not a renter
Founders/ leadership	Involved and engaged Prioritize culture Built personal relationships with initial hosts (e.g., approached hosts directly, personally took pictures of lodgings)	Masculine, "Bro" culture Prioritize growth and financial achievement Poor accountability Distant (CEO has one-to-one relationship with senior execs only)
Employees	Able to provide feedback in a safe space Feeling of community and belonging resonates in the organization	Competitive and cut-throat Non-diverse teams with distinct biases

Uber is not an isolated example. There are numerous examples of start-ups that focus on technology development, growth and scale, as well as market disruption, rather than people. Time and again, we see demonstrations that the human element makes or breaks the organization and plays a crucial role in driving sustainable business success.

Over the years, I have gained in-depth personal experience in mentoring tech start-ups. As a mentor over several years with the F10 Incubator & Accelerator (a global innovation ecosystem with offices in Zurich, Singapore, Madrid and Barcelona, founded by SIX Swiss Stock Exchange) and CV Labs (a hybrid Blockchain incubation program located in Zug Crypto Valley Switzerland), I have had the unique opportunity to engage and advise some amazing companies at their nascent stages. At the forefront of innovation, these start-ups expertly leverage emerging technologies to create solutions that have the potential to transform industries and markets.

As expected, the start-ups that I have worked with consisted of what I would refer to as innovation rockstars—(usually) young people who were not afraid to challenge the status quo and break traditional boundaries of businesses. Apart from sharing my insights and experiences from the business world, I also gained tremendous learnings from these start-ups, particularly on abundance mindset, breaking limitations, and staying current with technology advancements.

However, something I repeatedly observed, and warned against, was an uncanny lack of focus on the people element of business, i.e., building culture and establishing the basics of human capital in the company. These elements seemed to fall in priority next to technology solution development, as well as growth targets. However, as we saw with the example of Airbnb, as well as other companies renowned for their positive and engaging culture such as Zappos, REI, Adobe and Gravity Payments, building the right values, actions, and behaviors should start early at the founding stage. The values established at the start will grow exponentially in alignment with the company's growth.

Culture as a Driving Force for Business Leadership

Every organization has a culture, whether the leaders in the organization build and maintain it purposefully or allow it to breed on its own. An organization's culture defines how individuals work and function, making it a crucial element of a company's success. In the previous section, I illustrated how the root culture created by founders can make or break even the most successful start-ups in the market. Similarly, in incumbent organizations, culture plays a critical role in determining whether the organization sustainably thrives or even survives the next decade in the digital economy.

This became apparent during the coronavirus pandemic, when companies across the globe were collectively exiled to remote working during physical lockdowns. It quickly emerged that the organizational culture was being amplified by the unprecedented situation. Companies with a strong positive culture bound their people together in solidarity. These companies were able to adapt more quickly and pivot as required to enable business continuity faster. However, companies with dysfunctional culture struggled to adapt and suffered a heftier economic impact from the pandemic.

So what is organizational culture and how does it fit into digital business transformation? Organizational culture is the collection of values, expectations, and practices that guide and inform the actions of all members in an organization. It encompasses the foundational values of a company and drives the way people work and function on a daily basis. It also reflects an organization's expectations, philosophy, and the experiences of the employees and leaders within it, often determining the group's future direction.

The culture of an organization governs many things, from how decisions are made to the way employees interact with one another. Although top leadership may create and communicate the culture of the business or company, individuals at all levels of the organization must support and maintain those values. An established culture shows how people in the workplace should behave. A positive, healthy culture that is deeply embedded in an organization's identity can help accelerate sustainable transformation in the digital economy.

The culture of the organization affects all aspects of a business, from punctuality and tone to contract terms and employee benefits. When workplace culture aligns with its employees, they are more likely to feel comfortable, supported, and valued. Companies that prioritize culture can also weather difficult times and changes in the business environment and come out stronger. Airbnb co-founder and CEO Brian Chesky relayed the following: "If you break the culture, you break the machine that creates your products."

At the core of any successful company is its corporate culture. Computer software company Adobe demonstrates this principle in their daily business. The company, recognized on *Fortune Magazine*'s list of 25 World's Best Workplaces for the sixth year in a row (Adobe Team Life 2021), was assessed based on surveys representing 19.8 million employee opinions worldwide. Adobe Systems Inc. was founded in 1983 by computer scientists from Xerox Palo Alto Research Center (PARC) John Warnock and Charles Gescheke. The pair developed multimedia software based on research related to computer graphics systems and printing, revolutionizing visual communication. Since its founding, the company's revenue has grown to over $12 billion with over 24,000 employees worldwide. The company is renowned not only for the employee perks, for example, onsite yoga and cafes, paid family vacations, and health care, but also for the diverse and inclusive working environment, encouraging creativity and innovation, and dedication to career development and well-being. The four core company values are the backbone of Adobe's award-winning culture (Clarke 2017):

Genuine: "We're sincere, trustworthy and reliable" Integrity and sincerity is central to Adobe, and the company takes great pride in their commitment to developing products and services in an ethical way, as well as supporting staff by taking time to listen and care for their concerns. There is a strict code of ethics adhered to throughout the large multinational. Senior officers ensure full, fair, and accurate disclosure of information, while staff are provided with ample opportunity to question and report possible violations of these policies. Despite the large size and global reach, Adobe has created a working environment that provides a sincere and reliable level of care to its employees. In addition, employees are frequently recognized for their contributions and achievements, showcased on the Adobe Life Blog.

Exceptional: "We are committed to creating exceptional experiences that delight our employees and staff" Since its inception, Adobe has always exemplified excellence by creating the industry standard for programs in digital media and content. This is also seen in the Adobe Research program, which brings together researchers and top university students to crowdsource ideas, explore and test new ideas in the industry. Employees are encouraged to contribute to innovation in the company through education and learning opportunities, including education reimbursements, mentorship, on-demand online courses, and leadership development programs.

Innovative: "We are highly creative and strive to connect new ideas with business realities" Innovation is a priority for Adobe and a driving force in keeping the company at the forefront of the industry. Employees are empowered to explore new ideas and, more importantly, given the opportunity to fail as part of the exploration and learning process. The launch of Kickbox, Adobe's award-winning program that invests in their employees' potential, offers a red cardboard box filled with stationery, snacks, and a $1000 prepaid credit card to explore their idea, no questions asked. The initiative is seen as an investment in people, and of the over 1000 employees who have participated, 23 new ideas have been identified for further investment.

Involved: "We are inclusive, open and actively engaged with our customers, partners, employees and the communities we serve"   Renowned for philanthropy and corporate social responsibility, Adobe has actively contributed to community and social causes. Employees are also encouraged to participate by matching time and donations to eligible charities and schools, and providing 15,000 non-profit organizations worldwide free access to Adobe products and services. Additionally, programs such as Project 1324 and Youth Coding Initiative were launched to support the next generation of creatives with scholarships and internships. The company promotes diversity and inclusivity across all its activities through active sponsoring and recruiting in underrepresented minority communities.

As a front-runner in business, Adobe leads by example through these four core values, creating a sense of shared purpose in the organization and encouraging employees to get involved in societal issues to create a better world. The company lives its award-winning principle "People are our greatest asset," winning *Fortune Magazine*'s 25 World's Best Workplaces repeatedly since the launch of the award. This is a testament to the corporate culture that has taken root in Adobe and prevailed during an unprecedented global crisis.

By articulating these core values, Adobe has been able to create a sense of community and responsibility, and encourage a positive and authentic culture that helps the company stand out easily in the global market. The sidebar "Adobe—Leading with compassion" provides some additional examples of how Adobe lives its core values (Forbes 2021).

According to authors of *The Culture Puzzle* (Moussa, Newberry, and Urban 2021), human beings have the uncanny ability to form a culture, adapting the way we think and act to cope with everchanging conditions. This has enabled us to accomplish astonishing feats. Any powerful leader can command transformations in a business. However, they will find themselves mired in a minefield of resistance and even sabotage unless the organization culture is managed appropriately.

The book highlights that most company cultures revolve around the central notion that people are motivated primarily by the immediate need for money, security, and stability. However, most successful companies not only fulfill these basic needs, but also the need to do meaningful work. The authors likened this approach to tending a garden, where the leaders of an organization play the role of the gardener. The garden will require constant nurturing (water, sunshine, fertilizer) to enable it to flourish and thrive, even in the harshest of weathers.

Similarly, an organization needs to fully respect the essential needs of human beings in the workplace in order to fully achieve its strategic goals, namely physiological, safety, love and belonging, esteem, as well as self-actualization.

Adobe: Leading with Compassion
Source: Forbes, November 2021

Understanding how important compassion and empathy are today, Adobe led its pandemic marketing efforts with these sentiments at the forefront. This strategy ultimately helped the digital experiences company better connect with customers during trying times.

(continued)

(continued)

The company took an open-hearted marketing approach that was apparent in several initiatives:

- In May 2020, Adobe launched a one-minute #Honor-Heroes video featuring digital portraits from the community of everyday people doing extraordinary things—a grocery store manager framed by stained glass in a saintly fashion, chefs selflessly presenting their food, a chemist, a doctor, a celebration of mothers, and more. The video garnered over 52 million views, resonating powerfully with global audiences craving a healthy dose of compassion.
- The company launched an entire campaign focused on connection and compassion. In addition to the video, more than 100 #HonorHeroes portraits were displayed online and via social media #honorheroes posts. Adobe also donated over $6 million to organizations providing vital Covid-19 assistance to communities around the world, and Adobe employees gave over $9.5 million in matching grants to local and global nonprofits.
- In support of students and workers suddenly forced to work remotely as a result of the pandemic, Adobe taught classes to kids on illustration, helped small business and enterprise customers maintain their business continuity, and granted access to Creative Cloud to 30 million students.
- The company's Diverse Voices initiative amplifies underrepresented voices by giving them a platform to share their stories with the world.
- The Women Create Wednesday program promotes the stories of women illustrators, entrepreneurs, photographers, advocates, and more, giving them a high-profile signal boost.

Maslow's Hierarchy of Needs in the Modern Workplace

In 1943, American psychologist Abraham Maslow published *A The-ory of Human Motivation*, introducing the hierarchy of needs often depicted as a pyramid, as illustrated in Figure 3.1. This now famous framework describes five levels of human needs, that allow for an individual to feel fulfilled.

The levels describe interdependent elements of basic human needs, from the bottom level referencing fundamental elements for survival and progressing to higher pursuits of the human experience at the top level. Decades later, Maslow's Hierarchy of Needs is still relat-able and provides a deeper understanding for what motivates people:

Physiological   This level refers to meeting the basic requirements for the survival of individuals and communities, including food, water, shelter among others.

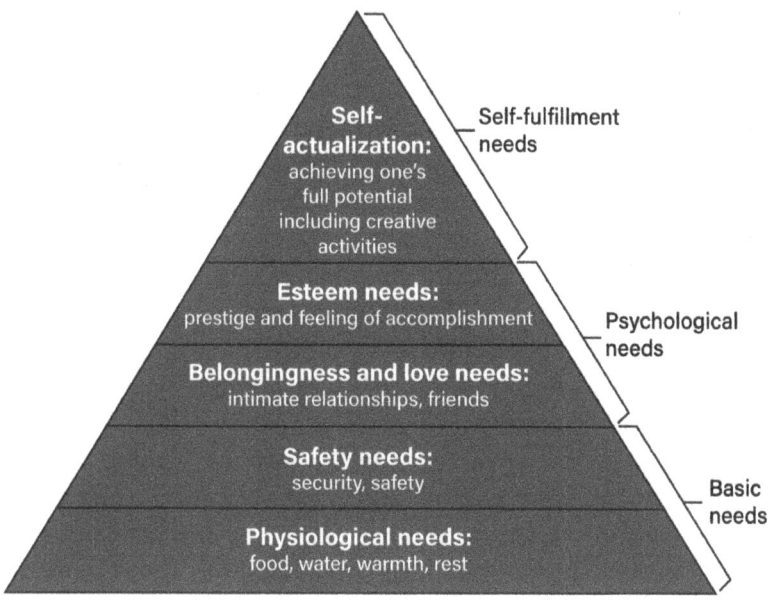

Figure 3.1   Maslow's Hierarchy of Needs.
SOURCE: Adapted from Maslow, A. H. 1943

Safety   This level refers to creating a feeling of safety and security, providing an environment that will allow individuals to survive.

Love & Belonging   This level refers to creating a sense of belonging and acceptance, where individuals are able to thrive in the community and environment they live or work in.

Self-Esteem   This level refers to providing a sense of accomplishment, achieving recognition, and gaining the respect of those in your community or environment.

Self-Actualization   The final level at the top refers to reaching a sense of fulfillment and achievement, relating to the deeper purpose as a human being. It relates to developing an awareness of one's true potential and consciously using it for self-fulfillment and personal growth.

In 1969, Clayton Alderfer updated Maslow's original theory with a more condensed and flexible version which he called Existence, Relatedness, and Growth (ERG) theory. This revision groups the levels into simpler categories, and accepts that humans are not as rigid as described by Maslow's original theory. In modern times, we acknowledge that these needs may blend into one another and that people have the ability to temporarily put aside lower-level needs in the service of higher ones. During the coronavirus pandemic, many people found that their basic needs came under threat due to economic uncertainty, and the survival of many companies came into question. However, companies with strong cultures that contributed to the fulfillment of the psychological and self-fulfillment needs seemed to weather the tough times better, even when basic needs were not a certainty.

Applying the theory of needs in the business context may help leadership teams identify gaps and areas for improvement in the corporate culture. Organizations can strive to provide ways to fulfill these needs. However, it is also important to understand how the types of needs impact the overall success in certain roles. For example, people who struggle with rejection might find a career in sales particularly demotivating. Ideally, a healthy and engaged workforce is filled with individuals who have reached the top level of Maslow's pyramid. Creating a work environment that not only provides for the basic needs, but offers a sense of safety, support, belonging, and contributes to a higher purpose (self-actualization) will greatly influence the sustainable success of an organization.

As described in Chapter 2, the younger generation of people, namely the Gen Yers or Millennials, Gen Zers, and Alphas, will be increasingly looking for a work environment that aligns with and fulfills the upper levels of the hierarchy of needs. They will seek meaningful work that offers them recognition, autonomy, and flexibility, as well as a chance to learn, grow, and better themselves personally and professionally. Additionally, as the first generation of full digital natives who grew up fully immersed in technology, Gen Zers will demand a working environment that aligns with their daily experiences. Organizations that want to engage and attract this younger workforce will have no choice but to offer more than the bare minimum. This means creating working environments, structures, and roles that offer a sense of belonging, accomplishment, recognition, and align with purpose and value.

Digital business transformation offers organizations an opportunity to understand and deliver on the hierarchy of needs. Considering the role that digital technologies play in the lives of people today, providing the right amount and quality of digital tools could significantly impact employee engagement, morale, and productivity, as well as retention. As a basic need (physiological need) in any business environment today, providing the right equipment and tools to effectively perform a job is a given. These may include office space, computers or laptops, access to good internet or Wi-Fi connections, and clean facilities. These needs shifted during the coronavirus pandemic, where physical access to the facilities became mostly impossible and companies needed to rapidly deploy digital collaboration tools. Similarly, the pandemic threatened the security and stability of jobs (safety need) and, in many cases, forced people to work under uncertain conditions.

Moving up the hierarchy, it becomes increasingly critical to meet psychological needs in the workplace. For example, implementing digital solutions to optimize day-to-day job functions could free up employees' time to make more meaningful connections and increase a sense of belonging in the organization (love & belonging need). Additionally, recognition and reward (self-esteem need) are closely linked to job satisfaction and positive self-esteem, where individuals gain more confidence in their ability to succeed. For example, implementing learning and education programs to upskill employees and develop digital skills required in the transforming work environment. An organization that has developed a clear and distinct purpose, aligned with core values and contributing to societal needs, will create a deep and lasting connection to its employees. During the pandemic, it became clear that companies that had already developed these upper level needs were better positioned to deal with the uncertain situation. In many cases, employees were willing to forgo the lower level needs (physiological and safety needs), as their upper level needs were met (love & belonging, self-esteem, and self-actualization).

Joie de Vivre Hospitality, or JdV, a boutique hotel and restaurant operator, is a great example of how Maslow's Hierarchy of Needs can be applied to produce a sustainable and profitable corporate culture. In his book, *PEAK: How Great Companies Get Their Mojo from Maslow*, Chip Conley describes, "How we set up our workplace mirrors our assumptions about human behavior and the world we want to create. As employees, most people have little direct say about this, often to their disappointment. Those of us who are managers or leaders, however, have a great deal of influence on how our workplace is created. Mostly these assumptions are unconscious or at least unspoken. Unfortunately, most work mocks human capacity" (Conley 2017, pp. 19–20).

Conley utilized Maslow to build JdV into the second-largest boutique hotel operator in the United States, before leaving to join Airbnb as their Head of Global Hospitality and Strategy. Referring to the expression "karmic capitalism," where businesses can have a transformative impact on people's lives and the society in general,

Conley encourages leadership teams to consciously self-analyze. Understanding the organization's habits or values practiced in daily business, as well as its alignment to human motivation, will have a sustainable impact on business.

In applying Maslow's Hierarchy of Needs to build an engaging corporate culture, JdV also found it to be a helpful tool to understand customer needs. Businesses worldwide have spent millions of dollars on digital business transformation efforts, only to hit roadblocks or failure due to implementing solutions that do not align with customer needs and wants. By applying the five levels to the customer experience, organizations will be able to identify, develop, and implement transformative solutions that meet unrecognized needs with unique experiences to create long-term brand affinity and loyalty. In the current digital age, where people have become accustomed to having basic access to online and digital capabilities (e.g., Wi-Fi access, connected devices, instant information, immediate post-sale services, frictionless experience across channels), it becomes more challenging for companies to stand out in these areas. Consumers have higher expectations and demand for these capabilities to "just work."

The global business landscape now exists in an expectation economy, where stakeholders including customers, employees, and partners within the business ecosystem are all expecting everything to not only work, but also to be simple, intuitive, predictive, and hyper-personalized. In implementing digital business transformation initiatives, organizations need to focus on delivering the upper level wants of these stakeholders.

The Impact of Culture on the Business Ecosystem

A thriving corporate culture helps to "humanize" a brand, and it also provides customers with a sense of unity with the business. Zappos.com CEO Tony Hsieh took this concept a step further by saying "Your culture is your brand." Every piece of content that an organization creates should reflect its culture, as having a strong culture is an affordable way to promote your organization and gain a following. Organizations can utilize traditional advertising channels, as well as social media and digital marketing channels, to market their culture.

Customer service and interactions are a telltale sign for how effective the corporate culture is. It is almost always a reflection of the organizational culture when something goes wrong with customer services. In order to effectively manage this, leadership teams need to set the right tone for culture throughout the organization and lead by example. A customer-centric culture is reflected in the priorities set within the organization in terms of the way work is done, how people are measured for success, the incentives that have been put in place, as well as the authenticity demonstrated by each individual towards offering great customer outcomes.

Organizational cultures that empower their employees are those in which people are given the knowledge, skills, and opportunities to succeed, as individuals and within the collective of the company. This is one of the primary aspects of building a positive and engaging culture. In today's world where digital technologies are embedded in our daily lives and the rising gig economy creates boundless opportunities, people are looking for jobs that offer freedom, autonomy, engagement, and empowerment. This has a direct impact on how employees serve customers—organizations that are able to empower employees have demonstrated a 50% higher customer loyalty as an outcome (Wagner and Harter 2006).

Digital Culture as a Driving Force for Digital Transformation

Digital transformation is usually triggered by organizations to identify and drive initiatives to generate increased revenues via digital channels, identify opportunities to streamline processes, facilitate improved communication and collaboration between functions, as well as create new digital products and services. Over the years, as I have advised companies in the development and implementation of transformation strategies, I have become increasingly aware of how much digital transformation is really about behavior change within an organization. It is about changing how we behave when addressing challenges or opportunities, as well as operating in our daily business functions.

At the core of successful digital transformation is resilience—delivering sustainable changes within the organization by leveraging the capabilities of new technologies to improve the way the company interacts, operates, and creates value in the market. This requires a cultural shift of collaboration to understand the needs of the customer before delivering on change. When it comes to digital transformation, it is really about changing behaviors about how to collaborate, to use technology to drive value for the business, as well as learning from customers and adapting to their changing needs.

It goes without saying that a shift in organizational culture is almost always more difficult than a change in technology. There are no user manuals or installation guides! A shift in culture requires teams to coordinate and collaborate in new ways, and requires leaders to be more intentional about those changes and embrace digital culture—all while changing legacy systems, technologies, processes, and structures that may prevent the organization from fully transforming. When technology and business leaders understand what makes people tick, they can create more meaningful digital transformations, engaging experiences, and valuable disruptions.

What Is Digital Culture?

Due to the widespread use of mobile and connected devices, as well as the Internet as a mass form of communication, digitalization has become a particularly pervasive influence on culture. The omnipresence of digital technologies in the modern world means that the study of digital culture is not restricted to the Internet or modern communication technologies. Digital culture in an organization is described as the actions, behaviors, mindsets, and values shaped by the emergence and use of technology. Basically, it refers to how digital and online technologies are shaping the way we behave, think, interact, and communicate in the workplace. It defines the relationship between people and technology, and is a product of the boundless persuasive technology that constantly exists around us today.

According to the *World Economic Forum Digital Culture* guidebook (June 2021), an organization with a strong digital culture uses digital tools and data-powered insights to drive decisions and customer-centricity while innovating and collaborating across the organization. When implemented purposefully, digital culture can drive sustainable action and create value for all stakeholders. Although it is clear that culture in itself cannot be "digital," the adoption and use of technology has proven to be a significant driver for human behavior and action, and embodies shared values in the organization.

A digital organization refers to more than just having digital products, services, and customer interactions. It also includes powering core business operations with technology for higher efficiency, digital skillsets and capabilities of the people in the organizations, as well as building digitally enabled business models that prepare the company for the future. Therefore, becoming a digital organization requires fundamental change in the activities people perform, their individual behaviors, as well as the interactions with others across the business ecosystem. Digital business transformation is a strategic paradigm shift and, like any major transformation, it requires creating a culture that supports change while enabling the strategic direction for business. Embedding a digital culture within an organization requires a combination of methodology, discipline, and a human touch.

Ignoring or neglecting corporate culture risks the failure of digital business transformation initiatives. A higher number of companies going through digital business transformation report breakthrough outcomes or strong financial performance when there is a high focus on managing the culture (Hemerling et al. 2018). Over 80% of companies that focused on digital culture reported sustained strong or breakthrough performance as a result of the transformation efforts. This creates a strong case to continuously foster digital culture in an organization. Empowering people during the transformation journey can drive faster results overall. Breaking down hierarchical structures in favor of flatter ones with more distributed control and decision points will enable increased agility and a sense of ownership and buy-in to the change process. The digital culture also serves as a code of conduct, providing employees with clear guidelines and boundaries on what is expected of them during the change process. Additionally, the digital culture acts a magnet for the new generation of workforce and fulfills the basic needs of the younger generation of people. It also prepares leadership teams to motivate, lead, and manage this generation of digitally savvy employees who favor greater autonomy, collaboration, and creativity in their working environment.

Organization culture shows itself in behaviors, mindsets, and values of people in their daily practices—how they do things, make decisions, as well as communicate and interact with one another. Behaviors are more tangible and readily visible. Mindsets and values, on the other hand, tend to be more hidden, comprising of expectations, beliefs, and deep-rooted assumptions that are far less visible and obvious.

Companies are able to influence digital culture by implementing and embedding specific organizational practices to drive targeted actions. For example, a company that wants to promote innovation could put in place simple systems to capture ideas and reward contributions. This approach has been employed successfully by organizations such as Walkers and Lego, for both internal and external stakeholders. Walkers Snack Foods Ltd, a British food manufacturer famous for their potato crisps and snack foods, launched a "Do us a flavour" campaign in 2008, in an attempt to completely overhaul their digital marketing strategy and source new flavors that would excite customers. The campaign attracted 1.2 million entries and winning flavors were selected through a public vote for production and sale. The campaign triggered a new way of working in the organization, where digital platforms were embedded in the daily business to capture a deep level of consumer ideas and interaction.

The digital initiative was highly successful and outperformed category year-on-year sales growth by 68%.

Behaviors are more readily influenced by organizational practices than mindsets and values, which are deeply embedded into the individual psyche and developed through lifelong experiences and beliefs. Mindsets and values are also closely aligned to regional and cultural elements. A company that has cross-regional presence or a global employee base will need to take into account the cultural and regional differences that play a role in the way the people work. In order to successfully implement any change or transformation initiatives in an organization, it is important to gain a deep understanding for the values of individuals and teams, as these influence sustainable behaviors. When individual values are aligned with the values embodied in organizational practices, it creates an environment with strong psychological safety and a feeling of belonging.

Digital transformation or any form of change that is introduced in the organization acts as a threat to the psychological safety that may exist within the organization and will be met with resistance. This is clearly described by the analogy of the human body when a foreign element, such as a virus or even a new transplant organ, is introduced. The human body will shift into survival mode in order to protect the equilibrium that exists in the current environment, and releases antibodies to fight the foreign element. This may manifest itself as fever and, in some extreme cases, result in cancer where the white blood cells falsely attack the healthy red blood cells. This phenomenon is known as the amygdala response, which is described in more detail in Chapter 2. Similarly, an organization is a living system that functions based on the existence of elements that interact and engage to keep the system going. A foreign element, such as major change or organization-wide transformation, introduced into the system will be met with resistance, even if the potential outcome could bring benefits or prevent the extinction of the system in the longer term (Ismail et al. 2014).

Maslow's Hierarchy of Needs offers effective guidance on how to influence behaviors, mindsets, and values of internal and external stakeholders in the business ecosystem. As discussed earlier in this chapter, people are motivated by satisfying their needs and wants. Essentially, by gaining a deeper understanding for people's lower level needs on the pyramid (namely physiological and safety needs), organizations will be able to shift behaviors. For example, implementing digital business transformation initiatives and addressing the uncertainties and changes impacting roles, job structures, or even ways of working will influence behaviors in a positive way.

Similarly, addressing the upper level needs on the pyramid (love & belonging, self-esteem, and self-actualization) will effectively influence mindsets. Aligning digital business transformation initiatives to core values and a shared purpose will go a long way in rallying the internal stakeholders towards the strategic change. This will also be reflected in the way the organization and its people interact with external stakeholders—customers, partners, and suppliers.

Building an Ecosystem Culture That Supports Digital Business Transformation

Digital transformation is not for the faint of heart. All the critical elements of digital transformation—from creating a compelling vision, developing a roadmap of initiatives, continuous communications, to development and implementation, as well as ongoing refinement—require people. However, the success of digital transformation goes beyond simply assembling the right team of people to execute initiatives. Based on my personal experience, true success in digital business transformation can only be achieved when all stakeholders in the business ecosystem are engaged and involved in the journey.

This is easier said than done, according to Mark van Beuningen, Group Chief Executive Officer of CIM Financial Service Ltd. The company offers non-banking financial solutions to over 270,000 consumers, SMEs, and large corporates, and employs over 800 people in the market. Since 2019, I have advised and supported CIM on their digital business transformation journey, from strategy to execution.

As a key player in the Mauritius and Kenya markets, the company aimed to develop a digital business transformation strategy to reinforce its position and grow in the digital economy. The business ecosystem consists of various key stakeholders that contribute to and impact the transformation strategy. According to van Beuningen, developing a strong culture of collaboration and communication, as well as ensuring the right skills and capabilities are involved in the transformation process, is critical for success. In addition, he says that to garner buy-in and support, leadership teams need to prioritize keeping key stakeholders in the ecosystem engaged and informed of the roadmap, journey, and outcomes achieved.

A business exists, and thrives, in an ecosystem—a network that includes internal and external stakeholders involved in the delivery of product or services through cooperation or competition. Each stakeholder group plays a specific role in the business network, and contributes to the way the organization creates, captures, and delivers value to the market. A symbiotic relationship exists between the stakeholders in the business ecosystem—coexistence and interaction that impacts the well-being and generates mutual advantage. In the increasingly digital global business landscape, we are observing more symbiotic relationships develop. Companies are choosing "coopetition," as opposed to competition, where competing companies and peers are cooperating to create greater mutual value in the market. Companies, particularly incumbents, are realizing that it is challenging to keep up with rapidly developing technology and consumer trends on their own, and building strategic or cooperative relationships in the business ecosystem offers access to innovation, technology solutions, customer segments, or even new markets.

These symbiotic relationships may take various forms and structures, and may involve stakeholders from the same industry, adjacent, or even completely new industries. For example, Airbnb partners with Flipboard, a news and social network aggregator app that aggregates content from various sources, such as social media, news feeds, photo sharing sites, and other websites, and presents it in magazine format. The app allows users to "flip" through the articles, images, and videos being shared, hence the name. The partnership between the companies resulted in the creation of Experiences—a collection of lifestyle content designed for Airbnb users that is tailored to their interests and shared by other people who have similar interests.

Digital business transformation initiatives enable business ecosystem stakeholders to build connections, drive change, and improve business outcomes (Figure 3.2). The business ecosystem recognizes that each stakeholder group must work with and around each other in order to keep the overall system stable and optimize the collective benefit. Digital transformation initiatives not only explore the best ways to tap into these collective benefits, but also

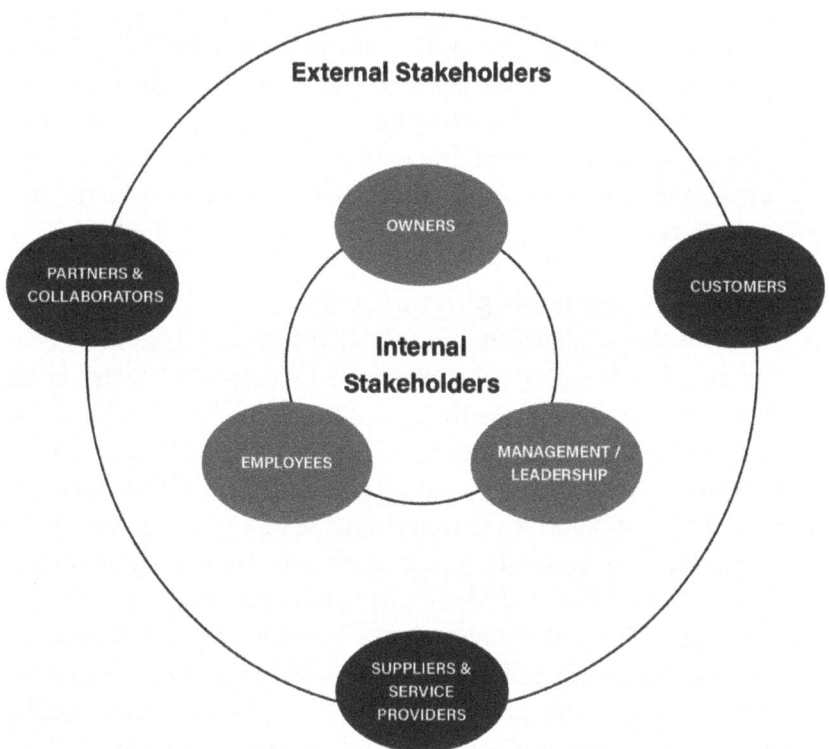

Figure 3.2 Internal and external stakeholders of a business ecosystem.
SOURCE: Kamales Lardi, 2018

enable better interaction, engagement, and collaboration between stakeholders in a trusted way through the application of digital solutions.

Internal Stakeholders

Owners   In the business ecosystem, owners may include any individual or group that owns asset in the organization and profits from it. The owner can be the same person who directs the business and controls its day-to-day processes, for example, in a start-up or small–medium business, or they can choose to have a management or leadership team for that purpose. The owners may also broadly include investors or private equity firms that have invested in the organization's development and growth. Within the context of digital business transformation, owners may have a heavy influence on the strategic direction of business, level of investment, risk appetite, as well as the culture perpetuated in the company. This level of influence may depend on how involved owners are: in smaller organizations where they are actively involved, the influence is greater, and vice versa.

Management/Leadership   The management or leadership team in the business ecosystem includes a range of stakeholders from the board of directors, the executive management team, to the transformation team leading the change journey. These stakeholders have deep and direct influence on the digital transformation journey, and drive the success or failure of initiatives. As a strategic imperative, management teams are responsible for developing the plan and roadmap that the transformation team must execute. The role of the board is to determine if the transformation plan will deliver on the business goals and strategic direction required within a set time frame. This includes assessing the risk appetite (too aggressive, or not aggressive enough); investment plan (realistic, too high or low); and whether the transformation initiatives touch the market and customer in a meaningful way. The executive management team also plays a critical role in developing the right culture and shared purpose that will engage and guide the organization towards transformation success.

Employees Digital business transformation is all about change, and people are pivotal to any change process. Transformation needs to take an employee-first approach to create trust, buy-in, and engagement. Today, the employee base may include a range of different models that transformation initiatives need to account for. The organization's workforce may include freelancers, gig workers, staff on demand, remote and virtual workers, as well as temporary roles, all of which has an impact on transformation and the approach leadership teams take to engage through the change process.

External Stakeholders

Customers The customer plays an essential role in digital business transformation of an organization. Innovation and improvements in customer experience pave the path for change and contribute to the strategic direction, as well as initiatives implemented. Gaining the right level of insights and understanding for what customers need and want should be prioritized. In the current business landscape, digital platforms and tools are able to capture and analyze customer data at a deep level of granularity, potentially creating insights on a personal and individual level. Feeding these insights to the digital transformation strategy and ensuring initiatives are developed to cater for the current and future needs of the market will be essential to sustainable success.

This stakeholder group may also expand beyond the traditional definition to include communities and crowds (Ismail et al. 2019). Community is made up of a large global group of individuals who are loyal to the shared purpose of the organization, and passionate about the brand and product offerings. Crowds on the other hand are an even larger global group of individuals who may have a passive interest in the shared purpose of the organization, but are not directly connected to the brand or product offerings. The community and crowd play a vital role in the current business landscape, as they dominate the online channels and social platforms that influence consumer opinions, buying decisions, brand loyalty, as well as impacting societal causes. They are also valuable for ideation and validation of new ideas, as well as accessing new segments of customers.

Suppliers and Service Providers Successful organizations adopt digital transformation programs by leveraging and aligning their strategic competencies with new digital capabilities, rather than simply replacing the old with the new. The emergence of new technologies has, however, resulted in more uncertainty and confusion about which digital investments are the most strategic for the company. In the world of multi-supplier managed services, it has become especially critical to make sure that companies leverage the right providers for maximum benefit and access to the right technology solutions. Suppliers and service providers bring specialized knowledge and expertise, and are able to build the required capabilities that help drive transformation. These may include algorithms, interfaces, or dashboards that accelerate automation and connect the internal business environment with external meaningful information, tools, and platforms.

Partners and Collaborators The business ecosystem is powered by collaboration, constituting a range of strategic partnerships that create new solutions and opportunities. Organizations need to work together to identify emerging needs in the market, access new segments, or develop new products and services for real business scenarios. Partners and collaborators may be diverse, coming from other industries or companies of various sizes, as well as contributing specializations or broad capabilities. They may even include educational or research institutions, or community and crowd mentioned earlier in this section. The true value of partnerships and collaborations comes in the ability to offer a range of benefits, such as learning opportunities, sales opportunities, and growth opportunities—to all participants.

Companies that have clearly defined purpose and core values will find that they not only achieve continued loyalty, consistency, and relevance with customers and employees, but will also attract stakeholders in the business ecosystem that align with their values. Together, these stakeholders will contribute to accelerating the digital business transformation in the organizations.

Leadership Essentials for Digital Business Transformation Success

In 1984, Zhang Ruimin took over the Qingdao refrigerator factory as director. The company was facing existential challenges, with significant debts and frequent leadership changes (Ruimin being the fourth director appointment that year). The employees, just over 800 at the time, were awaiting several months of back pay, and unsurprisingly turnover was high. Fast forward to 2021, Haier's operating revenue is worth €26.5 billion and the company employs approximately 100,000 people (Haier, LinkedIn 2022). The company was named the Number One Global Major Appliance Brand in volume sales in the world—for the 12th consecutive year (ERT 2021). In March 2020, when the pandemic brought the global business world to a screeching halt, Haier's domestic factories' production returned to full capacity, and was able to fulfill 99.8% of their orders (Lu and Mu 2020). How did Ruimin transform this dying organization into one of the world's most innovative and valuable brands?

Leadership teams in the current business landscape are under tremendous external and internal pressure to deliver similar transformations, outcomes within a much shorter timeframe. The extraordinary journey of Haier, spanning over three decades, provides crucial lessons in leadership that could help accelerate digital business transformation in any organization. I had the opportunity to delve deeper into the Haier's transformation journey, organization culture, and leadership styles with Vincent Rotger, Chief Strategy Officer Haier Europe and President of Haier France. A full overview of this interview is available in Chapter 9.

Maximizing Human Value

At the center of Haier's success is the ability to engage people and motivate them to create the best value for themselves. The company successfully applies the "Rendanheyi" model, a core idea that human values come first. The core idea by Zhang reinvents the traditional hierarchical organization structure to create an environment where all employees are best able to create value for themselves, the company, and its customers. Haier achieved this by building self-managing microenterprises (MEs), where employees behave like entrepreneurs and engage directly with consumers to create the best user experiences based on their needs.

Rendanheyi breaks the boundaries of traditional organization and industry, creating an ecosystem where all stakeholders are able to benefit, cocreate, and evolve together. Zhang has famously shared his belief that employees need to be allowed to make decisions for themselves in order to perform at their best, quoting sixteenth-century Chinese philosopher Lao-Tzu in saying "A leader is best, when people barely know he exists."

At Haier, employees are given sufficient autonomy to create an impact, rather than be treated like cogs in a machine. Leadership teams may fear that such autonomy may trigger chaos, poor productivity, or inconsistent outcomes from each individual employee. In his experience of building up MEs in Haier France, Rotger shared that, at first, employees new to this system were confused and hesitant to take risks. However, they quickly became comfortable in the autonomous working model and consistently outperformed. Each ME consisted of a mix of capabilities, enabling the team to leverage on each other's knowledge and experiences to deliver outstanding performance. In such an environment, the leaders need to provide guidance, act as a sparring partner and advisor, creating a safe and innovative space for employees to develop and deliver results. For me, this was reminiscent of the start-up incubator environment, where mentors played a similar role. This approach provides positive reassurance that everyone in the ecosystem is trusted to perform at their best.

Creating a Shared Purpose

The autonomous structure that Haier has built works well due to the established purpose, values, and culture that are shared by all stakeholders. The structure of the organization today appears as a collection of small pieces, loosely joined together to function as one. It works because purpose and core values are not only clearly defined and shared, but are also visible from all aspects of the business ecosystem. The principles of Rendanheyi drive the company's culture and even play a key role in attracting stakeholders with a similar belief to the ecosystem. Rotger admitted that this was a key attractor for him to join Haier's leadership team. There is no formal training for the management team but a leader must live the philosophy, allowing it to guide them in their daily actions and decisions, to give it credibility and engage their team.

Additionally, change is part of the Haier ethos and has become a constant for employees. While, for most organizations, this uncertainty may be considered unsettling, Haier has done a good job of building a "social architecture" within the organization that reduces the fear associated with such change (Neelima 2015).

"Zero Distance" to Customers

In order to develop "zero distance" to customers, where everyone in the organization would be directly accountable to customers, Zhang divided the organization into MEs, of which a majority are market facing, while the rest provide support and services. Each ME consists of 15–20 employees, working together as entrepreneurs to build and scale (refer to Figure 3.3 and Figure 3.4).

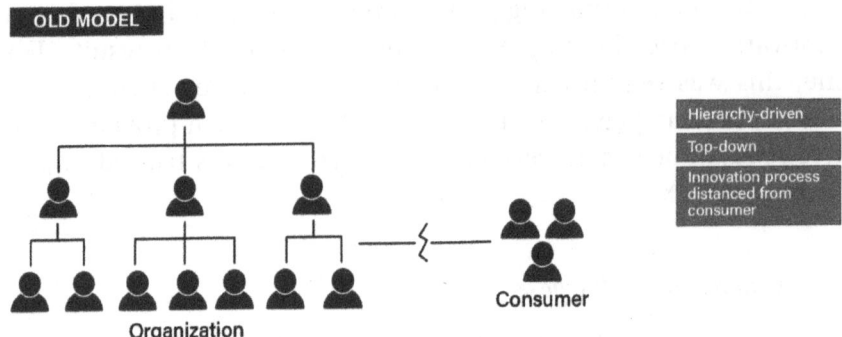

Figure 3.3   Traditional organization structure at Haier.
SOURCE: Chao Fansen/CKGSB Knowledge, 2015

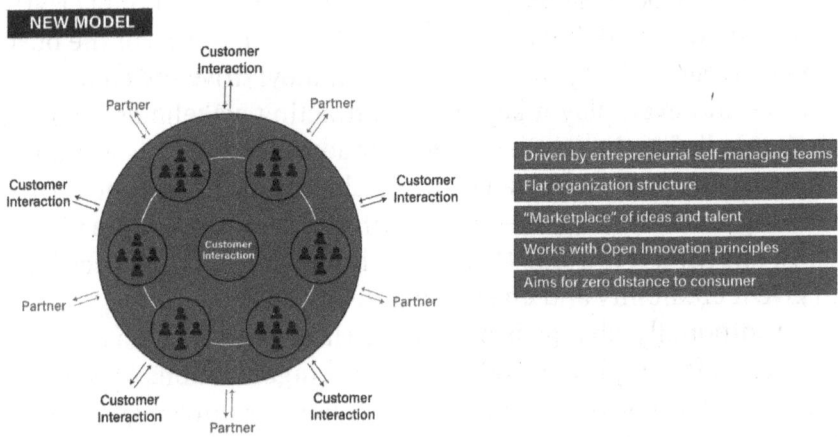

Figure 3.4   Reengineered Haier organization structure.
SOURCE: Chao Fansen/CKGSB Knowledge, 2015

The market-facing MEs have different focus, for example transforming MEs that prioritize reinventing the core business; incubating MEs that explore innovative new business opportunities; and node MEs that offer design, manufacturing, human resources, and other support services. Microenterprises are given "leading targets," market-facing revenue and profit goals for growth and transformation, set at four to ten times faster than industry average. Rotger explained that the autonomous and innovative environment often resulted in MEs achieving and exceeding the targets set for them.

This environment creates internal competition, which helps to filter out the "low-efficiency projects"—and people. As in any entrepreneurial environment, individuals who are not able to adapt or change will end up leaving.

Leveraging the Business Ecosystem

Haier sees itself as a hub in a larger network, where new products are developed in the open with feedback from customers gathered directly on social media networks such as Baidu. Responses come in the millions, as potential users share their needs, preferences, pain points, and top concerns. The company has assembled a large network of institutions and technical experts from around the world to crowdsource solutions and address challenges in some 1000 domains (Hamel and Zanini 2018).

In addition, Haier leverages a network of institutions and technical experts from around the world to address challenges across a range of domains. The Haier Open Partnership Ecosystem (HOPE) platform acts as an active outreach to the broader innovation community. The company shares the innovation fields being explored, the recommended solutions and resources to fulfill these needs, enabling the collective knowledge of a "hive mind" to work on its behalf. Business partners are able to confidentially share their patents and receive rewards if the technology is used. Suppliers are able to contribute in the initial design phases, and receive preferential consideration during vendor selection.

These online platforms also offer access to a talent pool, as outstanding contributors are often recruited into the company. Haier's purpose and culture attracts ecosystem partners with shared values, ensuring these collaborative relationships work in a trustworthy way.

Understand the Motivations of People

In the early years of taking over Haier, employees were owed several months of back pay. Zhang understood the urgency of ensuring employees received their salaries for basic necessities and borrowed money to pay them. As the company developed and grew, morale improved, and he adopted a task-centered and authoritative leadership style to drive productivity and standardized working approach across the organization. Eventually, as the company achieved bigger successes, Zhang shifted his style once again, opting to create a shared responsibility and ownership with the employee base through a new organization structure. Employees were given sufficient room to create value and achieve self-realization, ensuring that compensation provides incentive to behave in a market-driven way. For example, people are not paid based on positions, which is the standard practice in the corporate world. Haier employees are rewarded according to the performance of their teams—if a task is accomplished or goal achieved, every member of the team gets a bonus in line with their respective contributions.

Referencing Maslow's Hierarchy of Needs, the needs and motivations of employees shifted higher up the pyramid as the organization evolved, developed, and matured. Haier's leadership was able to recognize this shift and create motivating factors that suited the specific needs. As I understand from Rotger, this approach has been highly effective and people are fully committed to delivering on the ambitious targets, beyond simply completing a job for salary. Every employee is given a shot at becoming an autonomous entrepreneur, which makes meaningful explorations for value co-creation and common prosperity.

Six Essential Leadership Traits

Haier has created an adaptive strategy over the past three decades that has been the foundation for its success and unique organization structure. Although it has been proven highly effective, I believe this is a key competitive advantage for the company as it would be difficult to replicate. Learning from Haier's journey, organizations and leadership teams will need to forge their own path, taking into consideration their unique purpose, culture, values, and business ecosystem.

To survive and thrive in the current business world, leaders need to be more than high-performing and demonstrate a willingness to experiment with new strategies and techniques during the transformation process. This means being able to connect organizational change to the fundamental values, abilities, and aspirations of the people who are involved in it. Recognizing that large-scale transformation is a gradual process that can be a difficult and painful experience for many people, leaders need to be patient in bearing the pressures that come with it.

Business leaders managing the transformation process will need to acknowledge that the process is painful and it should be a priority in their role to help people through the uncertainty. This was key advice from Nazim Ünlü, Head of People and Organization at data42, Novartis. In our conversation, he shared that as a leader during the transformation process, he was unclear on what to expect, making the journey more complex and challenging. However, leaders need to focus on creating trust through open and honest communication. In addition, the traditional corporate culture in business views vulnerability in leaders, especially during transformation and change journeys, as a weakness. Contrary to this, being able to demonstrate vulnerability takes strength and creates opportunity to approach the uncertain situation in solidarity with employees. Nazim shared the positive impact of this approach in the transformation journey at data42, a program initiated at Novartis to harness the wealth of data and insights through the digital research and development platform. Nazim also emphasized that in the digital world, being in a senior position did not mean being the most knowledgeable person in the room. Often, he found that younger people in the team were naturally more digitally savvy and adapted to changes more quickly. Senior staff were now in a position to learn from them, creating a greater balance in authority and increased collaboration. Novartis has invested significantly in culture, focusing on driving increased collaboration and transparency in the corporate environment. People were encouraged to bring their lessons learned from past experiences, as well as to learn from failures.

The people in the recently established data42 team were not the typical corporates; they were considered to be the "black sheep" of the corporate teams—more agile, open, and innovative. Often the traditional corporate environment views forward thinkers as misfits, but Nazim described his role in leadership as an umbrella for the forward thinkers, shielding them from the constraints of the traditional corporate world, giving them an opportunity to thrive in this new unit. Nazim says the most important element in transformation is for leadership teams to be able to "lead with your heart," focusing on understanding the people and creating a psychologically safe environment for people to be vulnerable and create trust that challenges will be faced together in a human way. The role of leadership has shifted from hierarchical, authoritarian, and directive, to being comfortable with vulnerability and uncertainty.

Leadership is not based on seniority anymore, as business environments like Novartis are becoming multidisciplinary, where seniority in various areas and expertise are varying—some people may be experts in technology, while others might be experts in clinical trials. Good leaders must know how to lead people in these various disciplines and with different areas of expertise. My full conversation with Nazim Ünlü is available in Chapter 9.

Leaders who are digitally ready lay the groundwork for digital business transformation and streamline their organizations in a way that allows them to reap the greatest possible benefits from the change process. These leaders encourage and support their employees in their efforts to change the way they work, resulting in the transformation of their processes, the increase of profits, and the extraordinary growth of their organizations. Figure 3.5 shows the six leadership characteristics that are essential for achieving success in digital transformation.

These six leadership traits are described in the following sections.

Abundance Mindset

Leaders with an abundance mindset believe in the exponential opportunities of business and understand that there are enough

Key Leadership Traits for Future Organizations

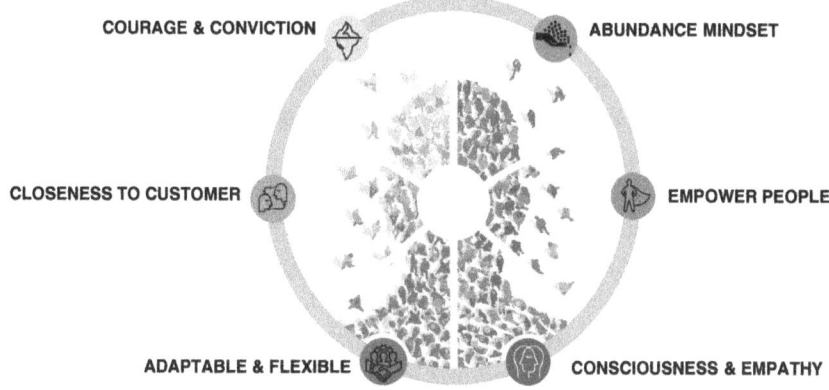

Figure 3.5 Six leadership traits for digital transformation success.
SOURCE: Kamales Lardi, 2020

resources and successes for all. Due to this belief, they have a tendency to take a positive and confident outlook to the transformation process. This is in contrast to a scarcity mindset, often present in the competitive business world, based on the foundational idea that another (person or business) has to lose in order for one to achieve success. Scarcity thinking frames the world in terms of what is missing or insufficient. Fear or the belief that nothing is ever enough and never will be enough are the motivating factors for leaders with this mindset, and they are often wary of anything that does not appear to be realistic or doable to them. An abundance mindset creates empowered leaders who see the opportunity in change, rather than challenge or defeat. This is not to say that they are unaware or blind to the risks and challenges faced during the digital business transformation process, but rather approach it differently. An abundance mindset leader approaches difficulty by first identifying the skills that they need to develop in order to make their desires a reality, and then taking steps to develop those skills as quickly as possible.

The digital business transformation process aligns closely with the abundance mindset, as emerging technologies create the opportunity for exponential growth and scale, with the need for far fewer resources than traditional businesses. For example, in a scarcity environment, companies looking to expand into new regions or markets would traditionally need to establish a physical presence. In the current business landscape, any organization would be able to gain access to a global marketplace through digital channels and platforms, irrespective of physical assets or presence. By cultivating an abundance mindset, leaders will be able to break away from traditional, limiting business thinking and leverage digital transformation for exponential results.

It is common for business leaders to become caught up in the day-to-day operations of the company. However, during the transformation process, leaders need to consider the future and keep a vigilant eye on new opportunities. Uncertainty and change are an unavoidable part of the business world. The response of a leader to change is frequently a reflection of the mindset that they have adopted. Leaders who are confident and adaptable lead with abundance, whereas leaders who are scarcity-minded often anticipate the inevitable "failure" that is to come, calculating all the resources, time, and money they lack to achieve success. In the aftermath, scarcity leaders may find themselves in a downward spiral that drains them of the confidence they require to face a challenge or take a necessary risk—in fact, it may frequently result in the very thing they fear the most: failure. Leaders who have scarcity mindsets have a negative impact on their organizations' work environments. When leaders believe in abundance, they make investments in themselves and in the people on their teams. Individual development is valued, and they make a conscious decision to provide as many opportunities for growth as they are able to their employees. Their support for professional development is not limited to job-related skill training, either. It encompasses aspects of emotional and mental well-being, as well as physical health and fitness. A sense of self-worth develops among team members, allowing them to devote their time and efforts toward the company's success.

Empower People

Sustainable success in digital business transformation requires a shift in organizational behavior, focusing on increasing collaboration and customer-centric thinking, as well as openness to innovation and exploration. In order to achieve this, leaders will need to create an organizational environment that empowers employees to embrace change. Start by establishing formal mechanisms that reinforce new behaviors and ways of working that support organizational change. For example, open forums to encourage engagement, interaction, and ideation, as well as digital learning platforms to support upskilling and continuous learning. Such initiatives enable employees to proactively share their experiences of the transformation journey, as well as contributing to the improvement of their daily work environment.

Organizations need to put in place processes and policies that enable employees to be more self-sufficient. At the same time, leaders must facilitate this process by providing the support and feedback that instill confidence in employees to act independently and participate in the decision-making process. Employees who are given the tools, resources, and ability to make decisions and participate in the digital business transformation journey are more loyal, committed, and potentially more productive.

Consciousness and Empathy

In recent years, consciousness and empathy have taken a more central role in corporate leadership. Companies have started to recognize the value and positive impact of leading people in a radically responsible, self-aware, and authentic way. Consciousness refers to the state of being aware of our surroundings while also being aware of our inner landscape. Conscious leaders put themselves under a microscope and venture into all aspects of their thinking, feeling, choices, and decisions, creating a deeper understanding of why they do what they do. This inner exploration helps to understand how their beliefs and perspectives influence the view of the external world and drive leadership style. It uncovers blind spots and develops a leadership style that connects with people in a more authentic way.

Empathy has always been a critical skill for leaders, but it is taking on a new level of meaning and priority in the digital era. Empathy is the ability to recognize and share in the feelings of others. As companies increasingly adopt technology solutions to drive productivity, innovation, and revenue, the risk of losing touch with the employees who drive business success grows. Trust is most fragile during organizational transformation and change. Empathy builds trust and respect, which in turn creates a healthy foundation for digital business transformation. Leaders can demonstrate empathy through cognitive or emotional empathy. For example, cognitive empathy considers how others might think in a certain situation. Conversely, emotional empathy focuses on understanding the feelings of others. Effective leaders will be able to develop cognitive and emotional empathy for employees through proactive listening and honest engagement.

Identifying and communicating the pain points that organizations are experiencing while also developing actionable solutions is essential when defining a digital transformation roadmap for a business. It is necessary to conduct an honest assessment of the digital maturity and capabilities of the organizations in this situation. Business leaders must understand developing technologies, their impact on the business, as well as the gaps that exist within the organization, in order to transform the organization effectively. As trust is maintained throughout the transformation journey, empathy, honesty, and open communication are essential. This is especially true when confronted with difficult situations such as skill gaps or new ways of working. In addition, actions speak louder than words. When there is alignment between what a leader says and what they do, people are more likely to trust them and to feel a greater sense of engagement and commitment. Understanding and offering to assist an employee who is experiencing difficulties is an example of empathy in action. It is recognizing and appreciating another's point of view, as well as participating in a constructive debate that leads to a more satisfactory solution. It is taking into account the perspectives of employees and developing a new recommendation that will assist in achieving greater success.

True success in digital business transformation does not come from holding positions of authority or power; rather, it comes from guiding people through times of fear and uncertainty, encouraging them to adapt to new circumstances while still performing well in the old. This is a significant challenge for any business leader; however, leaders who are compassionate and understanding will be better able to understand and manage the human side of transformation effectively. The ability of the organization's people to collectively drive change is critical to the success of digital transformation initiatives.

Adaptable and Flexible

An adaptive leader is defined as someone who is capable of altering their behavior in response to changes in a given situation or situational context. It is in their nature to be adaptable, demonstrating resilience when things do not go as planned, and bouncing back from failure, seeing it as an opportunity to learn. While they may employ past knowledge and experience to approach a problem, they are realistic in their understanding that what has worked in the past may not work in the future and vice versa.

Adaptability is a critical capability for any employee, but it is especially important for those who are responsible for leading others and an organization through constantly shifting environments. We have seen firsthand from our clients and their leaders the need to adapt to changing contexts within their roles, as well as when moving from one leadership role to another, with a need for leaders to adapt their influencing skills and become more strategic and empowering as they progress through their careers.

Closeness to Customer

Successful leaders in digital transformation always ensure that customers are at the heart of the business. In many organizations, leaders were often kept at a distance from the customer by hierarchical structures, as well as daily business operations. As a result, leaders often lose touch with customer needs and preferences, and the real value that the business is able to create in the market. We often see this reflected in communications and marketing promotions that focus on the products and services, rather than customer needs. In order to cultivate a customer-centric culture in the organization, top leadership team members need to build a deeper appreciation for customers, understanding their needs, predicting their behavior, as well as creating engaging experiences that build loyalty.

The digital business transformation journey presents an opportunity for organizations to leverage integrated data, technology, and content to create hyper-personalized and unique customer interactions across all available touchpoints—from the initial search through pre-sales, purchase, and post-sales support through to self-service platforms. These components offer in-depth, actionable data and information about customer needs, preferences, and the values that are important to them. Business leaders will be able to interweave these values into the core of the digital transformation strategy.

Courage and Conviction

In order to make transformational change in an organization, leaders need to be bold and aspire to do things differently, in order to drive fundamental change that transforms the organization for the better. For leaders to thrive during the digital business transformation journey, they will need to demonstrate courage, guide the organization towards a future direction, and think beyond the status quo. It is also essential for leaders not to wait for the perfect solution. While getting lost in "analysis paralysis" can slow down the change process, making snap decisions can also prove detrimental. Bold leaders are also willing to stand out and persevere in the face of failure, driven by their conviction for the strategic direction and purpose. When faced with a period of change or prolonged uncertainty, courageous leaders manage transformation effectively and transparently.

Bold leaders recognize that people are our most valuable assets and are committed to assisting others in growing and developing new skills. Successful leaders place a strong emphasis on teams, rather than hierarchies, as well as on developing the abilities of high and solid performers to work together to achieve better results. In some cases, leaders will need to take tough decisions relating to resources, skills, and roles in order to achieve the goals during the transformation journey. In addition, people are motivated by recognition for their efforts and want to feel good about the difference they are making. Bold leaders develop opportunities that allow strong and high performers to accelerate their performance even further, thereby feeding the recognition cycle even more effectively.

Chapter 4 explores purpose and values in an organization, as well as the benefits: how clear purpose-driven organizations are able to successfully drive the digital business transformation journey.

Chapter 4
Influencing Digital Business Transformation

Back in 2008, I was part of a Big Four consulting team engaged to implement a core system replacement for a multinational consumer business brand based in Geneva, Switzerland. The large project team, consisting of over 25 people deployed from various parts of Europe, was split into several workstreams including functional and technical implementation teams, and project management office (PMO). I was a manager at the time, leading the business intelligence module implementation alongside a small team of data analytics specialists, including a German senior manager who constantly impressed me with his ability to balance technical prowess with empathy and people skills. I remember the project fondly, despite the long hours and months of spending weekdays away from home (I lived in Zurich at the time, about three hours away, and spent weekdays in a Geneva-based hotel with other team members).

Overall, the project ran rather smoothly, despite facing its fair share of typical implementation challenges. For example, as with any large system implementation, the existing process landscape of the company needed to be mapped clearly, which involved analyzing process and operations documentation, as well as uncovering hidden processes developed by people over time. This was a mammoth exercise and took several months to complete considering the size of the organization and scope of business functions. As our team moved on to the blueprinting phase, we focused on designing To-Be processes that combined the new system workflow with the existing business requirements. This involved numerous discussions during blueprinting workshop sessions with the teams and stakeholders from the company. In addition to project challenges, the consulting team, people from the Big Four consulting company offices across Europe including Switzerland, the Netherlands and Germany, faced challenges and culture clashes. Despite sitting under the same global brand, the country teams had very different ways of working, cultures, and practices.

One thing that I remember vividly was the lack of a workstream or team leading culture change management for the project. Needless to say, the project was a large undertaking, both for the client company and the consultancy. Many of the issues faced during the project could have been addressed effectively if some focus had been put on managing the people side of technology implementation. To clarify, the project teams had enough forethought to propose a change management workstream, but it was a matter of budget scoping. The key stakeholders decided that it was a "nice to have" element and carved it out of the project scope to save costs.

This situation is not unique, as transformation leaders will attest—the "people" elements of technology project implementations are often viewed as non-essential and oftentimes become the subject of cost cutting and scoping. Managing change tends to be placed on the back burner for many organizations. At the end of the day, that perception hurts the transformation agenda and ultimately the bottom line of the business. Data repeatedly shows that implementing change management strategies can enable organizations to successfully complete more projects. Prosci, an independent research company in the field of change management, gathered data from over eight years and found that initiatives with excellent change management are six times more likely to meet objectives than those with poor change management. In the 2000s, a McKinsey study based on 40 large-scale industrial change projects found that the return on investment of large projects was 143% when an excellent change management program was used but only 35% when there was a poor change management program, or none at all (LaClair and Rao 2002). Another 2004 PricewaterhouseCoopers study of 200 companies also found a clear link between change management, high performance, and a high project management maturity level (Nieto-Rodriguez and Evrard 2004).

Despite an abundance of research, data, and insights that have been available over the years, companies still spend a considerable amount of time and money on project management methodologies and tools training for staff, but rarely invest in the same way for change management.

Undoubtedly, the effectiveness of the organization's change management strategies dictates to a large degree the success or failure of technology initiatives. A significant challenge that the core system project faced was the friction that had developed among key stakeholders, which led to resistance across the functional teams. Eventually, the project team realized that the underlying assumption that all stakeholders would be on board was a mistake. The need for change management techniques to manage the teams, the interactions between client and consulting teams, as well as guide the transition to the new system was crucial. The project leaders had not made a planned, cohesive effort to fully understand the changes they were asking everyone in the organization to make. Eventually, the system was successfully implemented, and I believe a key factor that contributed to the project execution was the efforts of individuals in the functional teams who were able to influence and generate enough trust to enable the transition.

I took away a lot of key learnings from that project experience. For example, as a transformation leader, one of the first tasks on an engagement is to assess the key stakeholders, business leaders, and department heads, mapping out where each one stood in terms of accepting the digital business transformation. Subsequently, I develop actions and tactics to bring these leaders on board, utilizing strategic communication and messaging designed to address each specific concern. I have found this strategic communication approach effective in building trust and giving stakeholders more confidence in supporting the transformation initiatives.

How Change Management Falls Short for Digital Business Transformations Today

Traditionally, change management applies methods to define and execute change within the organizational processes, both internal and external. This approach includes preparation and support before the change, establishing the necessary steps for the change, and monitoring pre- and post-change activities to ensure successful implementation.

Change management of organization culture refers to the process designed to shift an organization from one state to a potential future state in terms of culture—pattern of values, norms, beliefs, attitudes, and assumptions that may not have been articulated but shape the way in which people behave and things get done in the organization.

Organization culture and change management processes are closely interrelated. The culture of each organization is unique, and any change process will affect the culture, i.e., working models, management practices, and organization structures. This means that, without proper management of culture change, any transformation or major change in the organization will face significant barriers and resistance. Significant organizational change can be challenging. It often requires many levels of cooperation and may involve different independent entities within an organization. As such, it is critical to develop a structured approach to change in order to ensure an effective transition while mitigating disruption.

Changes usually fail for human reasons, such as leaders of change did not account for the real and predictable reactions of people to disturbance of their routines. Effective communication is one of the most important success factors for successful change in an organization, in ensuring all stakeholders understand the reasons and direction of change, as well as progress through the various stages and results achieved. However, organizations tend to presume that change management relates mostly to executing a communication plan surrounding a change or transformation initiative. In practice, it is critical to assess the organization's culture and dynamics as well, through specific touchpoints and techniques such as interviews, focus group observation, or surveys, as well as developing a roadmap of initiatives that drive and manage the change process.

Digital business transformation is probably one of the biggest transformation or change initiatives an organization will face. This is because real sustainable transformation will require organization-wide change that impacts every aspect of the business. In order to influence digital business transformation success, a deeper level of change management that takes a holistic view of culture and transformation is required.

Kelly Campbell, a trauma-informed conscious leadership coach, refers to this as transformation that involves "being" and "doing," a reference to mindfulness leadership practices based on the underlying concept of the Buddhist noble eightfold path to happiness. Change management is the process of doing—the framework or scaffolding for how we are going to make these changes over time. How will this be communicated? What are the logistics pieces? Who needs to be involved in the preparation, execution, and ongoing monitoring of the changes? What are the roles and responsibilities? Campbell refers to these as the operational elements of the change management process.

However, before advancing on a path of execution, organizations need to define the purpose, goal, or intention of the transformation or change that will take place—the "being" part. This involves identifying why the transformation needs to happen and, more specifically, the direction to head towards. What needs to change in order to bring sustainable returns and align with the vision and goals of the business? How do employees feel about the transformation? What do they value and how can this be incorporated into the transformation process?

The work that Campbell does leans closer to this part of trans-formation, an area she calls the "beingness." Both elements—the being and the doing—are critical to digital business transformation in an organization and should be addressed sequentially. However, in many organizations, business leaders tend to jump directly into the doing or execution aspects. According to Campbell, based on her work with organizations across various industries, this approach fails to hit the mark and falls short of achieving what is needed for transformation. This is because internal stakeholders are not able to rally behind initiatives that do not align with their values and motivations. As a result, change management initiatives are often cut out for not delivering results.

Driving Business Transformation Through Purpose: Start with Why

During a digital mindset coaching session with the C-level man-agement of a financial service company, I was leading a discus-sion on the customer value proposition. As a team, we were trying to pinpoint the reasons why a specific target customer group (in this instance professional women) would select the product range offered by the brand. As the team went back and forth trading ideas—including one suggestion that the products could be offered with free gifts such as handbags or pink pens!—I paused the discus-sion to ask a basic, yet essential question. In order to determine the value that the company brought to the market, I asked the team to describe their purpose. The responses varied from "to make money" to other more altruistic responses such as "to drive change in the way people exchange value." At this point, it became clear that the leadership team was not aligned in their purpose.

The Golden Circle is a concept presented by Simon Sinek in *Start with Why* (2009). What I find fascinating about the Golden Circle is that it provides a simple and clear explanation for the com-plexities of human behavior. It tells us why we do what we do. And in terms of transformation, this is essential.

"If we don't understand people, we don't understand business."
Simon Sinek, 2012

The Golden Circle provides compelling evidence of how much more we can achieve if we remind ourselves to start everything we do by first asking why. The Golden Circle is an alternative perspective to existing assumptions about why some leaders and organizations have achieved such a disproportionate degree of influence. In the book, heralded as the "best-selling leadership book" of its time, Sinek describes two fundamental ways leaders are able to influence change—to manipulate or to inspire.

Manipulations (e.g., tactics that include dropping prices of goods, launching a promotion, or an event using a scare tactic to quickly force customers into action) can be very effective, but the gains are usually short-term. Over time, manipulations tend to get expensive—businesses must keep coming up with bigger and better manipulations, sometimes at the expense of profits and always eventually sacrificing loyal relationships with customers. In the context of digital business transformation, the manipulation tactic manifests itself as the "shiny new thing" that leadership teams want to have.

For example, a global insurance company CEO I was working closely with to develop a digital strategy came in one Monday morning with an intriguing announcement—the company was to implement an AI-based dashboard for management decisions. The announcement surprised the entire management team, including me. I had developed a deep understanding of the data and information landscape of the company. An AI-based dashboard would require a data strategy and several months of data clean-up to ensure accuracy, source credibility, and alignment of structured and unstructured data formats. So where had this idea come from? It turned out that the CEO had played golf over the weekend with peers from other companies, one of whom was currently implementing an AI-based decision system. Once I understood his motivation, we were able to openly discuss if this was the right initiative to focus on, and if so, how to go about successfully implementing it.

The Golden Circle
Start With Why, Simon Sinek, 2009

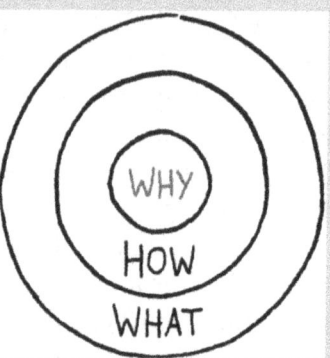

WHAT: Every single company and organization on the planet knows WHAT they do. This is true no matter how big or small, no matter what industry.

HOW: Some companies and people know HOW they do WHAT they do. Whether you call them a "differentiating value proposition," "proprietary process," or "unique selling proposition," HOWs are often given to explain how something is different or better.

WHY: Very few people or companies can clearly articulate WHY they do WHAT they do.

If most companies don't really know why their customers are their customers or why their employees are their employees, then how do they know how to attract more employees and encourage loyalty among those they already have? People don't buy WHAT you do, they buy WHY you do it.

The second approach, inspiration, focuses on creating loyalty and is triggered by a shared purpose or vision—the WHY factors described in the Golden Circle. Within an organization, this shared purpose will inspire employees to rally behind a transformation roadmap and, when reflected effectively in your organization's communication and portfolio of offerings, will drive customer loyalty.

Although it could take many forms, one of the most effective ways of inspiring is leading by example to drive change within an organization. For example, leadership teams who want employees to adopt a new system or alternate way of working should live what they preach and naturally inspire change. At the core of creating inspiration is understanding people. According to Sinek, when companies or organizations do not have a clear sense of why their customers are their customers, they tend to rely on a disproportionate number of manipulations to get what they need.

Both strategies have a place in the business toolbox and, when used authentically, could be effective in continuously engaging employees, fostering customer loyalty, and driving increased profits. However, at the core is a deep and steadfast understanding of the purpose of your organization in the market.

Purpose-Driven Organizations Built for Success

A purpose-driven organization is one that stands for and takes action based on something greater than its products and service offerings. The purpose provides a guidepost for decision-making to demonstrate commitment to responsible business leadership, including defining the broader strategic direction; opportunities the organization decides to pursue, or not to; and conduct of the daily business operations. A well-defined purpose sets the organization apart in the competitive landscape and proactively attracts people and customers who share the same values and beliefs, and ties them to the organization in the long term. Irrespective of the company size, stage of business maturity, or industry focus, purpose-driven organizations have one thing in common—a clear understanding of what they stand for, and the willingness to make decisions that align with that purpose.

There is often a misconception that focusing on a purpose may compromise the commercial aspects of the business. Although leadership teams increasingly understand that purpose is central to business success, the focus remains on defining and communicating purpose for commercial success (PwC 2016). Purpose is also often not referenced as a guidepost for decision-making—an authentic indication of a purpose-driven organization. Contrary to this, research has demonstrated that purpose-driven organizations are far more profitable, simply because the business direction and decisions taken produce outcomes that are aligned more closely to the needs of the consumers and the market.

The current global business landscape is crowded and noisy. Over the last decade, consumers have shifted to digital, spending more time on mobile devices and online channels. It is now easier than ever for brands to access and engage with consumers. Direct-to-consumer brands are appearing everywhere due to lower entry barriers, making it easier for consumers to find and try alternative or new products and service options. The coronavirus pandemic has further accelerated this shift in consumer behavior and consumption patterns, forcing even mature, more established brands to compete for attention and loyalty. Organizations that demonstrate a clear alignment with purpose across customer-facing activities, including brand strategy, marketing and communication, and product offerings, stand out from the crowd and achieve continued loyalty. Consumers today are spoilt for choice and often seek to align who they are and who they want to be with a brand's purpose on a deeper level. Based on a global consumer pulse survey (O'Brien et al. 2019), respondents indicated that their decisions point focus on how brands treat their workforce, demonstrate care for the environment, as well as supporting communities in which they operate. Purpose-driven organizations are able to build deeper connections with consumers and amplify the brand's relevance in their lives.

Employees are also seeking deeper meaning and value in the work that they do. When an organization and its leaders focus on connecting people to their purpose and build this perspective into daily business activities, a transformation will take place. A workforce that is aligned to a shared purpose and highly motivated will be able to bring more creativity to their work, as well as demonstrate more loyalty in the long term. With a clear, shared purpose, the individual drive and collective good will align, creating positive peer pressure, reenergized workforce, and a sense of closeness and belonging in the organizations.

In his best-selling book *Drive* (2011), Daniel Pink highlights that people do their best work when their intrinsic motivation is awakened. In past decades, organizations depended on the traditional "carrot and stick" motivation tactics, fueled by the assumption that employees are mainly interested in fulfilling the contractual requirements of their positions at minimum personal cost and effort. This belief aligns with previous generations of workforce, who were motivated by a drive to survive or external rewards and punishments for the work done. We explored these generational motivations and reasoning in detail in Chapter 2. However, current and future generations of workforce are becoming increasingly sophisticated, enabled by the instantaneous access to information, technology, and people from across the globe. Technology-based solutions are also enabling the automation and digitization of repetitive and mundane tasks, creating a greater need for more creative and heuristic work. External motivations and rewards may motivate people in doing routine work, but effectively dampen creativity, enthusiasm, and engagement. Alignment with purpose triggers intrinsic motivation, as it is less to do with external rewards and more connected to inherent satisfaction of the task itself, resulting in better performance in the long run.

Unsurprisingly, purpose-driven organizations with satisfied, loyal customers and highly motivated employees will inevitably deliver better business outcomes. The Global Leadership Forecast 2018, a survey of 1500 global C-level executives, found companies that defined and acted with a sense of purpose outperformed in the financial markets by up to 42% (DDI 2018). A clear purpose contributes to building organizational resilience and improves long-term financial performance and shareholder value, acts as a unifier that raises employee engagement, and increases customer loyalty and commitment (see Figure 4.1).

These real benefits are only realized when organizations are business leaders and management teams demonstrate behavior that exemplifies the shared purpose in their daily business and decision-making. In addition, organizations that effectively and consistently articulate their core business purpose will not only attract talent with a shared mindset, but also partners, suppliers, and collaborators to create a greater impact in the business ecosystem. When an organization embraces purpose, it becomes better positioned to confront and address uncertainty, disruption, and transformation. A higher purpose and shared values bring key stakeholders together and form a unified approach to making key decisions and setting the direction for digital business transformation, and the expected outcomes from these efforts.

Business leaders need to do more than talk about the purpose in order to fully leverage a purpose-driven organization. They need to demonstrate passion and commitment to the purpose, implementing and embedding the necessary elements in daily business, and make it easier for people to deliver on their promises to customers.

> Impact of purpose on Financial Performance

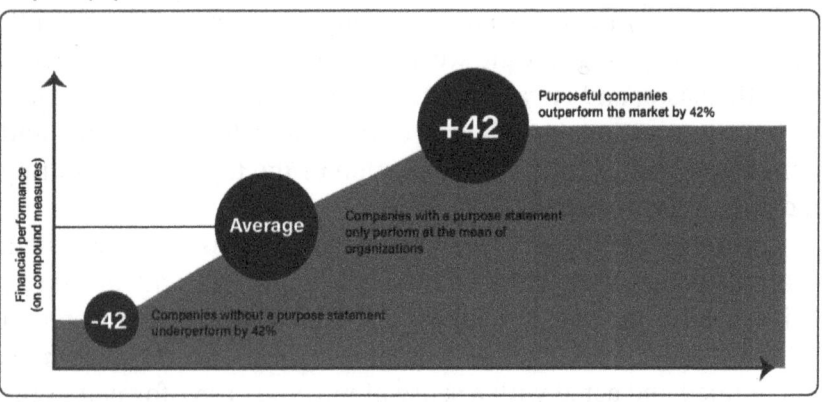

Figure 4.1   Impact of purpose on financial performance.
SOURCE: Global Leadership Forecast 2018, DDI

Three principles are at the core of building a purpose-driven organization:

Define the purpose with clarity Articulate a clear purpose and shared values by addressing existential questions around why the company exists and what key internal and external stakeholders truly care about. These questions will put a spotlight on the business and its daily activities, as well as guide decisions on how to move forward strategically. It is important to validate the defined purpose with broader groups of stakeholders, and, once finalized, embed it across various business communications and interaction touchpoints.

Integrate purpose and values into the core business strategy Reinforce the purpose across daily business operations and treat it as a commitment to shareholders by publicly communicating and reporting on its progress. Highlight to employees how their daily work contributes to the shared purpose and value to end customers. In a recent conversation with a R&D business leader in the textile manufacturing industry, I realized that he was deeply embedded in research and had lost sight of the impact of the team's work to the end customer and market. By creating a touchpoint to the sales team, we were able to not only highlight how their work impacted people all over the world, but also inspired new innovative ideas to be explored.

Create measurable goals to embed purpose in business In order to make the purpose more concrete, develop and set clear measurable goals to put their purpose statement into action. Identify the business impact metrics that flow from the enactment of the purpose, and align both business and individual performance metrics to these to give it gravity.

An organization will not be able to achieve long-term profits without embracing purpose and considering the needs of a broad range of stakeholders in the business ecosystem. In the course of our lives in these modern times, people will spend an average of

90,000 hours at work. Our self-identity is closely linked to the work that we do on a daily basis, and our sense of purpose is intertwined with it. Commitment to an organization is experienced as a psychological attachment, making it all the more critical for leadership teams to define and develop a purpose, or north star, that will not only boost employee motivation and overall job satisfaction, but also speak to the shared values of the customers.

In 2015, Dan Price, founder and CEO of Gravity Payments, made global headlines when he announced a commitment to pay every employee a minimum wage of $70,000. The credit-card processing company received mixed responses, with many critics calling Price's commitment a "socialist" act that would leave the business in financial turmoil. When the coronavirus pandemic hit in March 2020, many of their small-business clients were forced to close or cut back services. As Gravity Payments' revenue fell by 55%, Price estimated that they would be out of business in a few months. Most organizations chose to lay off staff to keep their businesses running during the height of the pandemic. Price chose a different route, by meeting with his employees to explain the company's situation, and nearly every one of the 185 employees agreed to a voluntary pay cut of between 5% and 100%. Collectively, they also agreed not to jack up payments for their 200,000 customers, which would have yielded an extra $2 million a month, choosing instead to endure the pain internally. This was a demonstrable example of how a shared purpose and human-centered approach in the organization helps to weather disruptions and uncertainty. Gravity Payments was able to not only keep its track record of never having laid off any employees, but also pulled together as a solid team to attract new business by 31% during the pandemic. The company has now restored employees' full salaries, and also paid them what they lost in July from the pay cuts.

In Price's own words, he describes how "the purpose of an organization is to make the humans' lives better. It's not the purpose of humans to make the organization better. That is 100% backwards with how most of us look at companies and organizations. It's always company first, and I'm going to sacrifice myself, sacrifice my colleagues, sacrifice my integrity, sacrifice my loyalties, in the name of supporting the almighty organization, and that's really wrong. People should come first."

Setting Your "North Star" to Drive Organizational Purpose

In recent years, a new breed of organizations has emerged that are responding to the transformations of the digital economy and future of business. Exponential organizations—as referred to by Salim Ismail (2014) in his best-selling book of the same name—grow at an above-average rate. These companies are not only able to grow up to ten times (10x) faster than comparable companies in the industry, but can make do with considerably fewer resources thanks to new forms of organization and the application of emerging technologies.

Ismail, the former Head of Innovation at Yahoo and founder of Silicon Valley innovation hub Singularity University, explains that rather than increasing human capital or physical assets, the most successful twenty-first-century companies leverage information and technology to achieve rapid expansion in pursuit of a "massive transformational purpose" (MTP). In doing so, they are able to scale their business strategies, culture, organizational frameworks, and purpose at the same rate as the technology—one that follows an exponential curve.

Ismail now runs OpenExO, a global community of more than 17,000 certified coaches, investors, consultants, and innovation experts. I joined the OpenExO community as a certified consultant several years ago as I recognized the exponential organization framework as one of the most powerful tools to allow companies and businesses to thrive in the future digital economy. With this framework, companies will be able to implement new organizational techniques that leverage accelerating technologies solutions to create disproportionately large impact or output—at least 10 times larger—than their peers. This means organizations will be able to grow faster, bigger, and cheaper than the competition, and scale as quickly as digitally enabled companies and rapidly developing technologies do.

A core element and starting point of the ExO Framework is the MTP, meant to be the north star for the organization that provides direction when key choices are required. It helps to build a purpose-driven organization with a higher aspiration to achieve radical transformation and a distinct focus on abundance. Exponential technologies enable abundance, and exponential organizations are built to connect with this abundance. The focus in every industry today is shifting from a scarcity environment, where there are intrinsic limitations relating to physical assets, geographic boundaries, and narrow mindsets, to one of abundance and exponential capabilities.

Massive transformative purposes are not vision or mission statements. A vision statement describes what an organization wants to become, while a mission statement describes how they will achieve the vision. Conversely, an MTP does not address how the purpose will be achieved, but what the overarching purpose is. This allows your organization to modify the approach or even pivot, over time, staying dynamic and agile with the rapidly changing digital times. For example, global media organization TED Talks has developed an MTP that provides a reference for keeping the organization's activities focused, while achieving exponential growth and scale across the world—"Ideas Worth Spreading." In the same way, Swedish furniture conglomerate IKEA has developed an MTP that goes beyond furnishings and addresses a broader purpose and value for the market—"To create a better everyday life for the many people."

There are several methods to help organizations craft an MTP (Ismail, Palao, and Lapierre 2019). The approach that I have applied repeatedly for client engagements is the WHY/HOW/WHAT approach, designed to frame your thinking according to these three categories and help separate the MTP from execution. In my experience, this approach works well for incumbent organizations that are typically constrained by the need to take into consideration existing offerings and operations (conversely, start-ups and newly founded companies may have the opportunity of starting with a blank slate and define their MTPs from scratch).

The WHY/HOW/WHAT approach brings together key individuals from across the organization, including hierarchies and functions, to brainstorm three main questions:

- Why does your organization exist?
- How will your organization address the need or opportunity?
- What will your organization deliver?

At the core of this session is defining the purpose through an iterative process of sharing ideas and selecting one to develop further (up to five or six iterations until a version of the MTP that resonates with the group is identified).

Peter Diamandis, cofounder and executive chairman of Singularity University, often says "Find something you would die for, and live for it." Employees and stakeholders within the ecosystem of purpose-driven companies that are organized around a unifying massive transformative purpose will work harder and are more dedicated, and most importantly, feel more fulfilled about the work that they do.

Driving Digital Empathy Through Purpose

In an increasingly crowded digital landscape, companies find it difficult to stand out and gain the much-needed engagement and attention from their customers. However, purpose-driven organizations are able to do just that—stand out in a unique and differentiated way, as opposed to becoming a part of this sea of sameness.

Approximately 5 billion internet users exist across the globe and the coronavirus pandemic in 2020 has further accelerated their activity online. An annual infographic by Domo (Domo, Inc. 2021) captures the essence of how much activity is going on in any given minute on the Internet. At the heart of the world's digital activity are the everyday services and applications that have become staples in our lives. For example, in a minute on the Internet, 6 million people shop online, 5.7 million Google searches are conducted, and YouTube users stream 694,000 videos.

To get a glimpse at just how much data was created every single minute across high-traffic platforms and apps in 2021, check out the infographic shown in Figure 4.2.

Considering that the amount of data and information available in the digital universe is effectively doubling every two years, it is fair to say that companies today not only need to have a strong presence online, but also face daunting competition to stand out and get noticed by customers. Consumers have now become accustomed to engaging with digitally enabled businesses seamlessly across

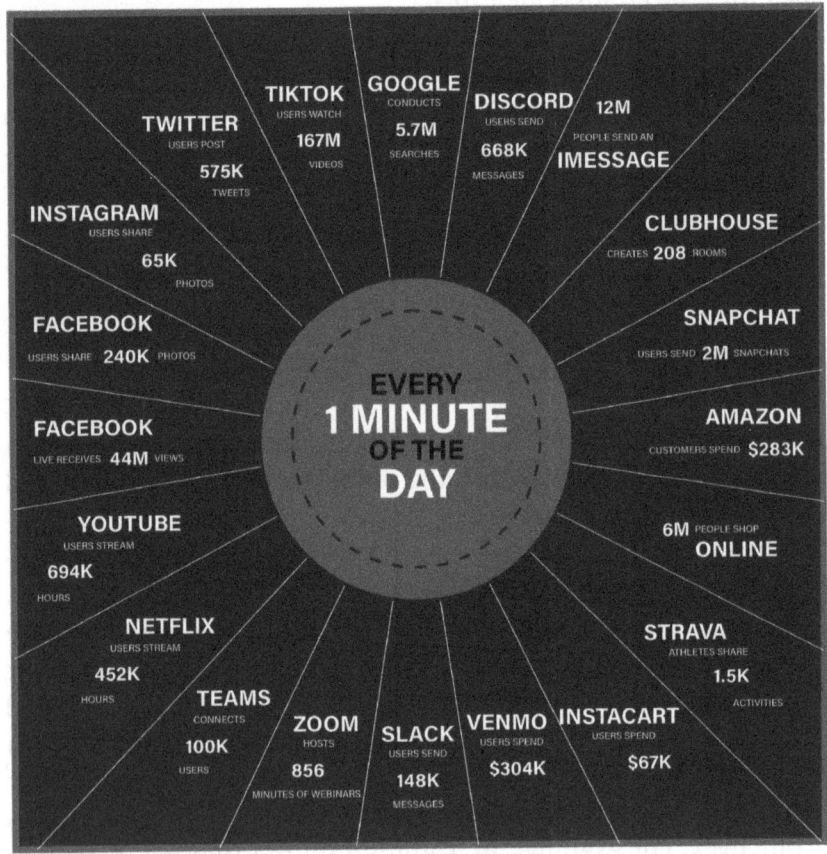

Figure 4.2 Data Never Sleeps 9.0: How much data is generated every minute?
SOURCE: Adapted from Domo, Inc., 2021

channels and touchpoints, as well as accessing hyper-personalized product and service offerings that meet their specific needs. As the coronavirus pandemic accelerated digital interactions and online acquisitions, companies across industries implemented digital strategies to keep up with the demands.

Covid-19 has also accelerated the transformation of business practices and processes. For example, the rise of remote work offered a glimpse into hybrid working—home office, digital meetings, and online collaboration tools—further blurring the lines between digital and physical boundaries. This is the new normal, and companies that want to thrive going forward are going to have to continue to reimagine the use of technology to bring those new cadences to life faster and more easily.

In order to succeed in these digital interactions, companies need to ensure that they build empathy into transformation solutions and customer journeys that are implemented online. A shared purpose helps motivate and drive people towards a common direction that they believe in, while empathy moves them towards each other in a helping and healing capacity. Digital empathy builds on this concept further by connecting people in realizing the full potential of technology and understanding how human users interact with platforms, systems, and processes. This new approach to building relevance in the digital age applies to both employees using technology in their daily work lives, as well as customers who experience an organization's product and service offerings, and interact across channels and touchpoints in the market.

Mastercard provides a good example of how empathy and purpose steered the brand's online strategy and helped it stand out during the coronavirus pandemic (Rozen 2021). The global financial services giant was just as shocked by the worldwide pandemic as any other company, however Mastercard was relatively better prepared to quickly shift to a fully digital working model. This enabled the company to shift their focus on ways to demonstrate empathy and prioritize supporting their customers and communities. According to Raja Rajamannar, Mastercard's Chief Marketing Officer, it was important for the company to demonstrate digital empathy and lead through the lens of "to serve and not sell," both for consumers and for society at large.

As a global brand, Mastercard had already defined clear commitment to social causes that align with its purpose. During the pandemic, the brand made efforts to keep these existing commitments. For example, Mastercard continued its partnership with Stand Up To Cancer, an organization that was instrumental in getting seven drugs discovered and approved for cancer patients. As part of its commitment to support diversity and inclusion, Mastercard launched the "True Name Card" credit card in 2019, specifically developed to support the transgender community. The card incorporates both the name that the person identifies with, as well as their "legal" name in small type on the back to fulfil regulatory requirements. Additionally, Mastercard is vocal in supporting the Black Lives Matter movement following the tragic death of George Floyd, and had pledged $500 million to help close the racial wealth and opportunity gap for Black communities and businesses.

During the coronavirus pandemic, Mastercard continued to support and engage, as well as demonstrate empathy, for these social causes through digital channels and interactions. The company believes that organizations have the resources, network, and power to shape perception, beliefs, and mindset, and need to make an effort to create greater impact in society.

In the current business landscape, organizations are expected to demonstrate a certain degree of empathy across channels and touchpoints to the market. Building digital relevance through empathy involves implementing communication approaches that leverage technology solutions to gain a deeper understanding for people's values and priorities, and responding in alignment to this. The practice of building trust through authenticity and transparency will help drive digital empathy for any organization. This is described in a structured approach as follows:

Active listening Active listening involves a deep commitment to seeing the world through the eyes of customers and key stakeholders. Online channels and technology solutions that exist today make it easier than ever to gather data and generate insights to better understand consumers. A great starting point is to set up digital listening capabilities to find out who is influencing the discussions or topics of interest in your industry, and what is being shared. Analyze the content to explore what people think, feel, say, and do, to proactively build empathy with stakeholders.

Integrate insights   The insights gathered from the active listening phase should feed into the organization's communication and engagement activities. Focus on developing a narrative that describes the purpose and value your organization offers and how it aligns with the values of customers and key stakeholders.

Shared experiences   Consumers today are not satisfied with one-way interactions, where companies bombard them with content, announcements, and promotion. People want meaningful communication where they are seen, heard, and valued, especially with the brands they interact with. Create shared experiences by exploring interactive channels that give customers and key stakeholders the opportunity to respond, interact, and engage with your channels and touchpoints. For example, the increasing user adoption of augmented reality (AR) devices provides an opportunity for companies to create experiences that engage people's emotions. The ultimate aim is to establish trust and a shared space where companies and people are able to interact, engage, and build resilient relationships.

Evaluate, measure, and refine   Establish a continuous evaluation and measurement to determine the impact of the communication and engagement activities, ensuring demonstrable progress in building digital empathy. For example, user adoption is a key metric that indicates that the engagement strategies are being used across the channels and touchpoints.

Consumers want human engagement, that is, to interact with brands in the same way they interact and engage with family and friends. They want to be seen, heard, and valued as humans through personalized interactions, and not to be reduced to a cluster of data points. And, most importantly, consumers now expect brands to showcase their humanity through empathy, regardless of the channels or touchpoints used.

Influencing Digital Business Transformation with Culture Change

An organization that has a clearly defined purpose and developed capabilities to demonstrate deep empathy for internal and external stakeholders will be able to better navigate uncertainty, disruption, and transformation. As leadership teams gain a deep understanding for how purpose and empathy overlap with change, they will be able to build long-term, trusting relationships with their stakeholders, be it employees, customers, or collaborators and partners in the wider business ecosystem. A humans-first approach to communications, engagement, and interaction will mean taking additional effort to explain the overarching purpose through the lens of

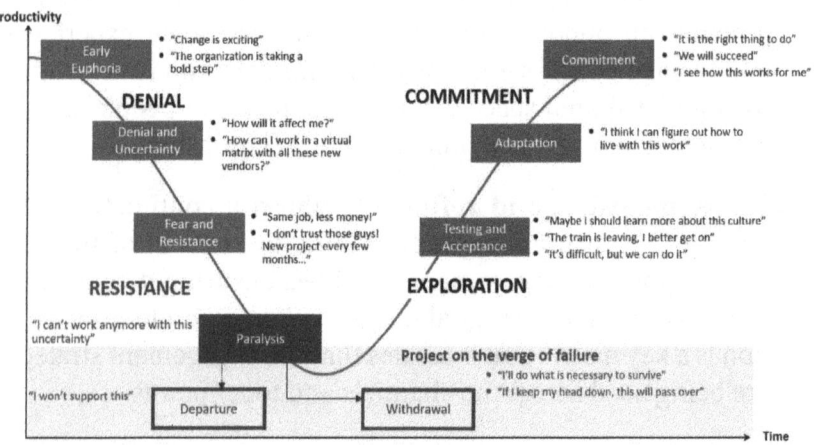

Figure 4.3 Change curve: how people go through change in different phases.
SOURCE: Elisabeth Kubler-Ross, 1960

stakeholder needs and values. In a letter addressed to employees of Microsoft during the pandemic, Satya Nadella wrote: "It is in times of great disruption and uncertainty that our ability to stay grounded in our sense of purpose and remain true to our identity is of the utmost importance" (Nadella 2020).

Digital business transformation is a process that needs to be proactively managed. It involves organization-wide change, triggering a range of emotions including excitement, anticipation, fear, loss of control, anxiety, and anger, among others. Organizations that do not proactively manage transformation will face resistance that results in productivity loss—lack of support, low morale, initiatives running over budget, unplanned increase in scope, compromises in quality, or rejection of initiatives entirely. Figure 4.3 illustrates the Change Curve, the four phases that people usually experience in any change or transformation process.

The Change Curve is a powerful model that helps predict how people will react to change, providing organizations with guidance on how to support and drive the transition from one phase to the next. The model was initially developed by psychiatrist Elisabeth Kubler-Ross in the 1960s to explain personal transitions in grief and bereavement. However, the model is often used in modern business to manage major organization transformation that could be genuinely traumatic for the people undergoing it. Digital business transformation, although occurring over time, may be described as major change as it involves adopting new ways of working, engaging, and governing within the organization. The Change Curve model describes the four stages most people go through as they adjust to change:

Stage 1: Denial   When digital business transformation initiatives are first introduced, the initial response in the organization may be shock or denial, as people react to the challenge to the status quo. Key stakeholders may choose to avoid the topic and even continue doing things like before. At this stage, stakeholders may consider the new initiatives or solutions as unnecessary hype and believe that people will roll back to the old standards eventually.

In the denial stage, clear, transparent communication is essential to counter the shock or denial that people may face. Apart from enough time to adjust to the transformation, people need frequent, consistent, and continuous information to understand the change, how it will affect them, and what is expected of them throughout the journey. Create a transformation communication plan that incorporates multiple channels and touchpoints, as well as formats of communication that will reach the target audiences. Utilize stories and narratives that will provide required information in an engaging way that is easy to absorb.

Stage 2: Resistance   Once the reality of the transformation hits, people will start to show their reactions to it. This initial reaction may range from negative to positive, depending on the level of transformation and type of change. Employees may show fear, feel anger, or event resist the transformation completely. Managers may fear the loss of control, new levels of transparency, or skills requirements. If not addressed in a timely manner, it will impede the transformation efforts and keep the organization in the resistance stage of the Change Curve.

In the resistance stage, it is important to set up appropriate methods to listen and observe the impact of the change. Consider the impact of the transformation efforts and the reasons for resisting the change. For example, someone who has built up expertise in a certain "old" way of working may fear losing their position or not being able to learn the skills required for the new post-transformation environment. By gathering insight through listening and observation, the true motivations behind resistance could be identified and addressed effectively.

Stage 3: Exploration   This stage brings some relief as people start letting go of the old environment and begin to accept the transformation initiatives. Curiosity and exploration kick in, allowing them to try out the new solutions or embrace new ways of working. As people start to adapt, the reality of what works well and what does not will start to emerge. Leadership and transformation teams will have to address these to keep the momentum of change.

The exploration stage requires focus on upskilling people in preparation for the transformed business environment. This stage incorporates skills and capability assessments to develop training and education plans, as well as sufficient opportunity for people to try, test, and provide feedback on solutions that may be implemented. This is vital to encourage learning and acceptance, which will result in buy-in and support for the transformation efforts.

Stage 4: Commitment In the commitment stage, employees and stakeholders will have accepted and embraced the transformation initiatives, allowing the organization to finally realize benefits and desired outcomes. The Change Curve offers organizations the opportunity to identify ways to move people through the stages more quickly, as well as make the curve shallower and narrower.

A key way to do this would be to share and celebrate successes. As the organization starts to reap benefits and teams become increasingly productive and efficient, it is important to share these successes and provide the opportunity to celebrate them. Recognize key people at every level of the organization who have helped drive the transformation, and showcase outcomes that have been achieved. Digital business transformation is an ongoing journey, and celebrating successes will make it easier to gain support when more transformation or change efforts are required.

In reality, it is critical to understand that transformation does not take place only through implementation of new systems, processes, or structures, but occurs when people in the organization adapt and change along with it. By observing people's reactions in relation to the Change Curve, leadership teams will be able to help accelerate the movement along the curve towards more positive emotions. Organizations will truly be able to realize the benefits of change when its people are able to make their own personal transitions. In my personal experience of implementing digital business transformation in organizations, it can be an intensely traumatic experience for many people. The easier that leadership teams can make this journey for their people, the more quickly success can be realized.

Influencing People for Transformation

Successful and sustainable implementation of digital business transformation strategy is as much an art as it is a science. Those who lead transformation efforts in an organization must find a balance between a structured approach to define, develop, and implement change initiatives that will move the business towards future readiness, and the fine art of influencing people in the organization to adopt and live these changes in the long term.

This brings to mind a story of the Trojan War in Greek mythology, illustrating how creative methods are an essential component of the strategic toolkit. The Trojans and Greeks faced off in a war for over ten years, without a clear winner in sight (McInnis 2020). The Trojans were known to favor Ares, the god of war, tactics, and brute force, while the Greeks favored Athena, a goddess recognized for her strategic and creative affinity. The Trojans held up behind a strong wall, successfully fending off attacks, pushing the Greeks to try an unconventional, creative approach to shift the balance of the outcome. The story goes that the Greeks built a giant horse filled with soldiers and convinced the Trojans to bring the massive statue through the gates of Troy. This gave the Greeks the opportunity to gain access through the impenetrable walls, and as a result, beat the Trojans to win the war. There has been much debate about the historical evidence for the Trojan War. However, the story offers a reminder that a successful strategy implementation requires a combination of structured and creative components.

In my personal experience, developing creative strategies to influence and drive transformation in an organization is essential. Unlike the Greeks who tricked the Trojans with misinformation, leadership teams need to take an authentic and empathetic route to engage, communicate, and lead people through the transformation process successfully. This approach may include several effective human strategies to gain buy-in and accelerate the journey. Harrison Monarth, executive coach, leadership consultant, and the *New York Times* best-selling author, describes how principles of human behavior that generate buy-in will generate more respect and honest effort for long-term sustained organizational success. I first came across Monarth's executive development service several years ago, as I was growing my consulting firm and in need of a business coach. In engaging with him, I gained insights not only into understanding what motivates people, and how to inspire and motivate people towards change, but also an understanding of my own leadership style and how best to utilize it for the digital business transformation work that I do.

In his book, *Executive Presence* (Monarth 2010), Monarth describes the distinctions between compliance and buy-in. In essence, compliance is rooted in traditional, hierarchical systems with defined roles and organizational structures. Compliance is linked to authority and fear, where people may be forced to carry out instructions even if these contradict their personal beliefs. Over the years, I have observed numerous teams work in compliance that is perceived to be buy-in. The outcome is low commitment and short-term success.

In the context of digital business transformation, where initiatives or changes may be complex and with significant impact, buy-in is necessary to achieve long-term sustained success. According to Monarth, buy-in is an alignment of thoughts and beliefs that drive people to work together towards a common goal to achieve a win-win outcome for all parties. There are a few creative strategies that can effectively gain buy-in and influence people to shift their attitudes and behaviors. At the root of these strategies is trust – the foundation element that builds teamwork, as well as effective and ethical buy-in. The role of the leadership team shifts from directive to one that promotes a safe and trusting environment, where employees are empowered through informed and team-driven decisions, open communication and collaboration, as well as showing vulnerability and empathy.

Apart from the essential element of a shared purpose that we have already covered, I have found a few strategies immensely effective in gaining buy-in through the execution of digital business transformation, irrespective of the maturity, readiness, or existing culture in organizations:

Focusing on adding value Always add value first. This lesson has stuck with me through the years as a consultant and transformation leader. It is human nature to look for personal benefit in any situation, be it an intellectual or an emotional outcome. Tap into this by focusing on how the transformation relates to the people and what they may gain from it. For example, a new technology solution implementation may result in the ability to quickly complete tedious tasks, or even eliminate this completely through automation, hence taking away a specific pain point for employees. Being able to find the value for employees or stakeholders rests on listening attentively to their motivations, challenges, fears, and optimism.

Strategic storytelling Stories have the ability to pull people in, gain their attention, and engage with them on a deep personal level. Use strategic storytelling to share visions of the future, purpose, and meaning of the digital business transformation work that is being executed. Storytelling is also a powerful tool and, when used effectively, can influence thoughts, demonstrate credibility, and create an emotional link to the content and presenter. Leadership teams that use strategic storytelling to drive change are able to gain buy-in and influence employees' reactions to change.

Simple message, continuous communication   It is known that communication is a critical element of any change journey. However, crafting a simple message and sharing it in a phased manner that builds knowledge and understanding over time will distinguish successful transformations from all others. Develop simple key messaging to describe the vision, purpose, and direction of the digital business transformation strategy, ensuring anyone across the entire organization will be able to understand and absorb it. The communication should be authentic and human, designed to connect on both intellectual and emotional levels, and take advantage of the range of channels available in the organization.

Chapter 5 describes the digital business transformation journey, starting with a digital maturity assessment and key insights on tackling complex change.

Chapter 5
Foundation Elements of Digital Business Transformation

November 2021 will be remembered as an iconic month. It is not often that we hear global conglomerates announce serious restructuring, and that month three such organizations announced the transformation—General Electric, Toshiba, and Johnson & Johnson. These companies join the long list of conglomerates that have made the radical decision to dismantle their business empires in the name of unlocking potential hidden value in the complex corporate structure.

General Electric (GE) is splitting up into three public companies focused on growth sectors of Aviation, Healthcare, and Energy. As described in a Forbes article (Fischer 2021), the repeated efforts at downsizing, divestitures, leadership changes, and the constant pressures for improved operational excellence over the past few years have fallen short of the intended outcome. This led to the drastic decision to split the multi-dimensional conglomerate into more manageable "mini" corporate structures.

Similarly, Toshiba faced a trying journey into decline. Following over seven years of challenges, Toshiba has been unsuccessful in managing market disruptions, rapid technology developments, financial under-performance, internal conflicts, and governance failures. Abruptly in November 2021, the board proposed to split the 140-year-old company into three standalone companies—one with an infrastructure focus, the second focused on devices, while the third company includes memory chip pioneer Kioxia Holdings Corp. and Toshiba Tec Corporation. The separation plan, the result of five months of work by the Strategic Review Committee of Toshiba's board of directors, represents a significant inflection point that hopes to look beyond the confines of past Japanese business practices. Several other Japanese conglomerates have already faced calls for restructuring, and will be under pressure to forge ahead in the wake of Toshiba's plan.

Johnson & Johnson (J&J) announced its intention to create a new publicly traded company for the Consumer Health business. According to reports, the separation would create two global leaders that are better positioned to deliver improved health outcomes for patients and consumers through innovation, pursue more targeted business strategies, and accelerate growth. The 135-year-old company, recognized in global health care R&D and innovation, faces a myriad of legal challenges across products, as well as rapidly shifting consumer health care demands and diverse pharmaceutical and medical devices markets. By separating the consumer health business from pharmaceuticals and medical devices, J&J hopes to become better positioned to address the distinct segments through innovation and targeted strategies and to potentially accelerate growth.

These companies, as well as others like Siemens, DowDuPont, and United Technologies, are dismantling their long-standing business empires in the hopes of addressing a looming decline—stagnant growth rates, lack of innovation, shifts in the global industries, evolving consumer behaviors, an increasingly competitive environment (including big tech players and start-ups muscling their way into the traditional industries), and poor governance, among others. These restructuring efforts seek to break the large complex structures into smaller and focused entities that will be able to address dynamic market segment needs in a more agile way. In addition, these companies are positioning the restructuring efforts as major transformation initiatives to better create value in the market and circumvent limitations of complex corporate structures. However, from the outset, it appears that the companies are merely creating more of the same, with little evidence of innovation, agility, new skills, or shift in mindsets.

Based on a report by strategytools.io (Rangen 2020), there are fundamentally three scenarios that trigger transformation, as depicted in Figure 5.1.

- **SHOCK:** This involves a shock or surprise triggered by outside events or external pressures that force a company to transform, or at least attempt to transform. This is typically portrayed in terms of a "burning platform" and is the most difficult to deal with. Due to the external triggers, the journey is largely out of the company's hands because of lack of awareness and preparation or simply due to hesitation and delay. Typically, they are behind the change curve, and scrambling to retrieve some semblance of continued relevance. A great example of the "shock" scenario includes brands in the broadcast and entertainment industry that have been either driven out of business or forced to explore

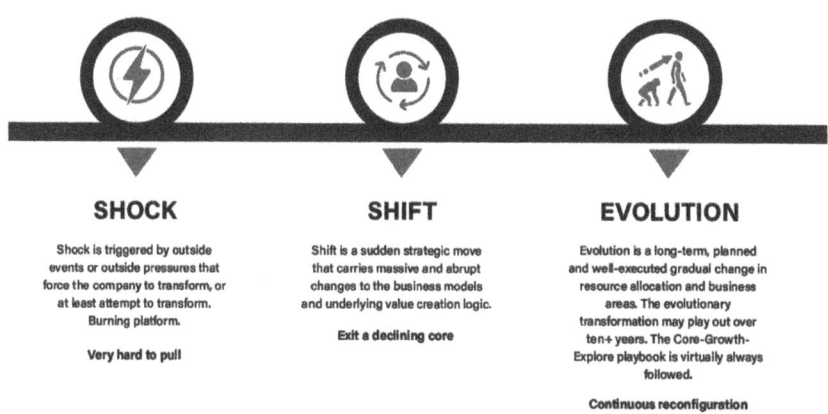

SHOCK

Shock is triggered by outside events or outside pressures that force the company to transform, or at least attempt to transform. Burning platform.

Very hard to pull

SHIFT

Shift is a sudden strategic move that carries massive and abrupt changes to the business models and underlying value creation logic.

Exit a declining core

EVOLUTION

Evolution is a long-term, planned and well-executed gradual change in resource allocation and business areas. The evolutionary transformation may play out over ten+ years. The Core-Growth-Explore playbook is virtually always followed.

Continuous reconfiguration

Figure 5.1   Three types of transformation.
SOURCE: Rangen, C. 2021 / StrategyTools.io

new offering and business models, following the popularity of Netflix streaming among viewers.

- **SHIFT:** Triggered by a sudden strategic move that carries massive and abrupt changes to the business models and underlying value creation logic. These transformations are commonly referred to as pivots, and often represent jarring changes in status quo, as a result of late awareness of external market and technology changes that have been in motion without being recognized. These preemptive, internally authored transformation journeys are often built around major business-model shifts, leading to a scramble to bring together talent and resources needed to pursue a new strategic path. During the Covid-19 pandemic in 2020, there were many examples of such business pivots, where companies were forced to very quickly find alternative business continuity strategies to overcome global physical lockdowns. One great example is Emi Controls, an Italian company that offers custom-made solutions for fighting fires, dust, and odors with the help of water mist. During the pandemic, the company was able to tweak their product line to offer disinfection solutions for large indoor and outdoor industrial areas.

- **EVOLUTION:** This involves long-term, planned, and well-executed strategic responses to a recognition of unfolding external conditions. The evolutionary transformation approach could play out over a longer term, in excess of ten years, and follows a traditional business strategy playbook. A great example of the evolution scenario is Microsoft, as the technology giant develops products and solutions that build on its strengths while taking advantage of emerging trends over time.

Based on this framework, it is clear that the restructuring approach taken at J&J and Toshiba has been triggered by SHOCK, while GE has made a long-term, attempt at the EVOLUTION transformation. Essentially, these organizations are responding to their triggers with restructuring, not the true transformation that will be required for sustainable success in the future.

In the report, Rangen distinguishes between transformation and digital transformation, referencing the former as "a change in value creation logic," and the latter as "a change in operating logic." My own view here differs, as I believe that in the current digital economy it is difficult to distinguish digital from organizational transformation. Digital and technology solutions are a key enabler for value creation, as well as a trigger for transformation in any organization, as they have become embedded in almost everything we do in business. There are few transformation initiatives that are not impacted by technology solutions and, in most cases, technology offers rapid and sustainable results across value creation, capture, and delivery.

For the most part, what we are observing is a simple dismantling, rather than transformation change. As a result, these organizations risk creating smaller replicas of their former larger selves, effectively just shifting the problems, not addressing them. This scenario may create less bureaucracy, but without a different way of working, distributed leadership autonomy, or mindset shift, it will be difficult to garner sustainable results.

What Is Digital Business Transformation?

Digital business transformation is not just about restructuring complex organizations or digitizing the existing business. Nor is it about implementing new technology solutions such as artificial intelligence or blockchain, or utilizing digital channels to access customers. Digital business transformation is an organization-wide change that requires a structural redesign of the company and its value chain. This can be a massive undertaking for any organization, particularly if it is not approached in a structured and focused way. At its core, digital business transformation is about changing how your company operates and delivers value to the customer, in order to keep up with the rapidly changing world.

Many organizations have either initiated independent digital ventures, for example, digital business units, incubators, innovation hubs, or start-up collaborations, or launched new technology-based solutions, for example, digital products or services, digital marketing, and communication channels. An effective digital transformation strategy focuses on leveraging new technologies to understand the evolving needs of connected consumers and deliver experiences that exceed expectations. In other words, organizations that are able to look deeper into critical business dimensions such as strategy, operations, people, and technology will effectively succeed in the future.

An organization-wide transformation of this magnitude requires significant adjustments to traditional business and operating models, including operations, resources, physical assets, processes, and customer value propositions. This process can be complex and challenging, but the results can be quite dramatic. Digital transformation goes beyond updating technology implementation or engaging with customers on digital channels. It drives organization-wide change that impacts revenue, operations, culture, and people. Many organizations understand the need to change how they work and have embarked on numerous initiatives, yet few have been able to go beyond isolated success cases or marginal benefits. Many leadership teams are still hesitant to invest in digital transformation without clearly defined returns on investment.

In a typical business environment, concerns over daily operational challenges take precedence over new or innovative solutions. This is further reinforced by top-level communication and organizational metrics. Traditional strategic planning approaches lead executives to view disruption in a binary way—to assume that the world is either certain, and therefore open to precise predictions about the future, or uncertain, and therefore completely unpredictable. Many companies are still locked into strategy-development processes that churn along on annual cycles. Executives are quickly realizing that traditional strategic planning processes that align to annual business cycles are not able to address the high levels of uncertainty created by digital disruption. Conversely, knee-jerk reactions based on current trends may result in companies investing in technology solutions that are the latest hype.

Digital business transformation initiatives are often complex projects. The complexity increases significantly for organizations that span across regional or geographical boundaries, as the specifics of the various markets will need to be considered in developing strategic direction, defining transformation initiatives, and implementing the solutions.

What Is the Difference between Digitization, Digitalization, and Digital Transformation?

One thing I frequently observe when advising companies is the diverse understanding or misalignment on what digital business transformation truly is. This is usually the starting point, even in organizations that are further along their transformation journey or that have demonstrated higher digital maturity and readiness.

The terminology used has various implications relating to the scope, depth, and impact of change required (see Figure 5.2). Each stage is necessary in the journey to becoming a digitally enabled organization that caters to the needs of the consumers. Often, in discussions, I have heard the terms digitization, digitalization, and digital transformation used interchangeably. Each stage is necessary in the transformation journey to becoming a digitally enabled organization that caters to the needs of customers.

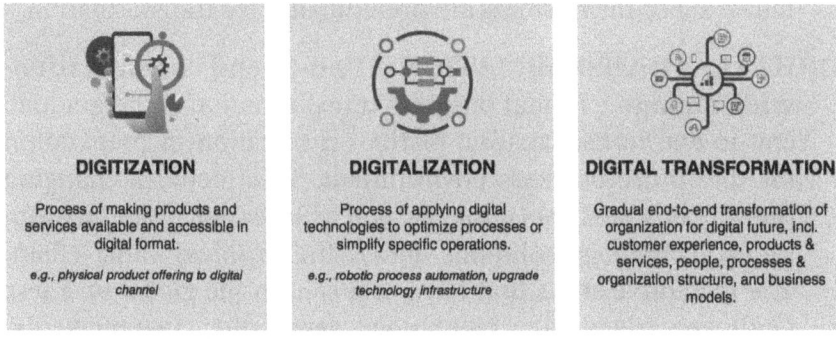

DIGITIZATION	DIGITALIZATION	DIGITAL TRANSFORMATION
Process of making products and services available and accessible in digital format.	Process of applying digital technologies to optimize processes or simplify specific operations.	Gradual end-to-end transformation of organization for digital future, incl. customer experience, products & services, people, processes & organization structure, and business models.
e.g., physical product offering to digital channel	e.g., robotic process automation, upgrade technology infrastructure	

Figure 5.2   Differentiating digitization, digitalization, and digital transformation.
SOURCE: Kamales Lardi, 2015

DIGITIZATION: Shifting from analog to digital Digitization refers to the process of making products and services available and accessible in the digital format. For example, developing an e-commerce platform to offer physical products, or switching from paper-based record-keeping to digital. Most incumbent organizations have surpassed the digitization phase, however there are still some industries or business functions that are trailing behind. In recent years, I developed a blockchain-based traceability solution for agriculture, and was a little surprised to find that manual or paper-based record keeping was still a prominent practice across the industry. As a result, digitization of the existing environment was the first challenge that I needed to tackle, before new technology solutions could be deployed.

DIGITALIZATION: Utilizing digital solutions for optimization Digitalization, on the other hand, focuses on applying digital technologies to optimize processes or simplify specific operations. For example, implementing robotics process automation to optimize processes or even upgrading technology infrastructure. In recent years, I have engaged with several organizations in the financial services industry, many still operating with legacy technology systems that were over two or three decades old. Proactive efforts to replace the core systems and accelerate digitalization of the business are prerequisites for transformation.

DIGITAL TRANSFORMATION: End-to-end organization-wide change Digital business transformation is the gradual, end-to-end transformation of the organization in preparation for the future business environment. This includes changing the way business gets done, as well as leveraging and incorporating technology solutions across the business value chain. The incredible shifts that have occurred in the global business landscape, triggered by technology, demanding customers, disruptive entrepreneurs, the environmental crisis and social climates, as well as unexpected shocks and uncertainties have forced organizations to transform themselves to survive into the next decade.

Traditionally, a "transformation" implies there is a start and an end point, with specific changes occurring to achieve the end result. In reality, the digital business transformation is a continuous journey that occurs over time. As the journey progresses, and organizations achieve higher digital maturity, the transformation objectives will also mature and evolve. As such, digital business transformation of an organization will need to be an ongoing process—an evolution. There are three levels of the digital business evolution that organizations will experience, as illustrated in Figure 5.3.

ACCESS   This level includes all external touchpoints and interactions with customers. Change at this level enables companies to better understand the needs and behaviors of digital customers, as well as improve the way they access and interact with these customers. Over the last few years, companies have focused their digital activities on the Access level. Initiatives at this level tend to be less complex and provide quick results, for example, using social media channels as new customer access points, launching apps for e-commerce, or online communities to interact with customers.

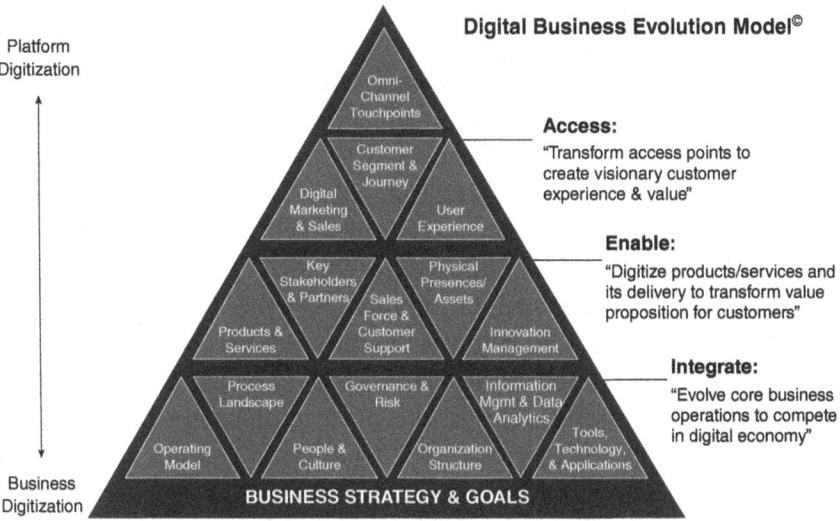

Figure 5.3   Digital Business Evolution Model©.
SOURCE: Kamales Lardi, 2017

ENABLE   This level involves elements that make up the value proposition an organization offers to customers, for example, product or service digitization, as well as incorporation of digital elements to physical locations. Changes at this level are a little more complex to implement, but bring demonstrable benefits.

INTEGRATE   The Integrate level includes elements that trigger evolution at the core of the business operating model. It involves understanding how the organization needs to evolve in order to succeed in the increasingly digital business landscape. Changes at this level impact the company operations, people and culture, infrastructure, and technology platforms.

Digital evolution could be triggered at any level, however the impact will eventually involve all levels over time. As an example, Nike started their digital evolution by implementing social media and digital marketing efforts (Access level), and eventually launched the Nike+ digital product suite that includes shoes, mobile device such as iPods, and an online community (Enable level). As customers adopted these products, the demand for customized shoes increased, resulting in Nike offering mass customization for shoes that involved modifying their business model (Integrate level).

With this model, companies will be able to maximize on the investments that have already been made, for example, new technologies or channels that have been implemented. In addition, business leaders will have the option to trigger organization-wide change or identify specific building blocks to initiate long-term change. Either way, the process is a journey over time, rather than a one-time transformation initiative.

A key challenge organizations face, in the context of digital evolution, is thinking beyond the existing business model or operations. I usually combine the Digital Business Evolution Model© with business model design thinking principles to enable companies to define potential future scenarios. This enables companies to explore the impact of digital technologies and digital consumer behaviors on the existing business model. Design thinking in this context is useful because it involves reimagining the business environment with digital economy elements (e.g., technology developments, digital entrants, customer behavior, regulatory requirements, etc.) and the potential impact on the business. In a way, it allows companies to disrupt themselves, instead of being disrupted by external drivers.

Digital Transformation Building Blocks

True digital transformation involves organization-wide change to achieve sustainable value in the digital economy. I developed the Digital Transformation Building Blocks© to break down the effort into smaller, more manageable parts. The building blocks provide a holistic structure for thinking through, managing, and delivering large-scale transformation programs, as illustrated in Figure 5.4.

This approach enables organizations to address initiatives across four key focus areas in the business, tackling these in a phased and pragmatic way to ensure sustainable return on investments. The digital business transformation roadmap and initiatives may be grouped in alignment with the building blocks:

Digital transformation is a foundational change in how an organization delivers value to its customers. There are several fundamental building blocks that need to be addressed for successful implementation of digital transformation in an organization.

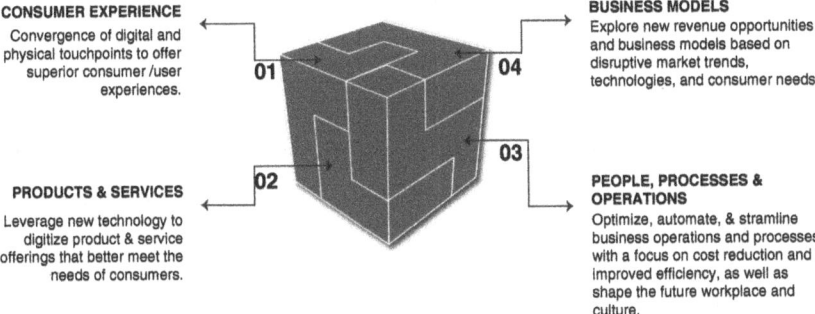

CONSUMER EXPERIENCE
Convergence of digital and physical touchpoints to offer superior consumer / user experiences.

BUSINESS MODELS
Explore new revenue opportunities and business models based on disruptive market trends, technologies, and consumer needs.

PRODUCTS & SERVICES
Leverage new technology to digitize product & service offerings that better meet the needs of consumers.

PEOPLE, PROCESSES & OPERATIONS
Optimize, automate, & stramline business operations and processes with a focus on cost reduction and improved efficiency, as well as shape the future workplace and culture.

Figure 5.4   Digital Transformation Building Blocks©.
SOURCE: Kamales Lardi, 2015

Customer Experience   Convergence of digital and physical touchpoints to offer superior consumer or user experiences.

Products & Services   Leverage new technology to digitize product and service offerings that better meet the needs of consumers.

People, Processes, & Operations   Optimize, automate, and streamline business operations and processes with a focus on cost reduction and improved efficiency, as well as shaping the future workplace and culture.

Business Models   Explore new revenue opportunities and business models based on disruptive market trends, technologies, and consumer needs.

This approach makes it easier to align initiatives to specific strategic objectives and link the outcomes of the digital business transformation initiatives to success measures and business metrics. Additionally, initiatives in each building block may be organized as workstreams, with teams of people allocated to manage and deliver the workstreams. The ultimate aim of the building blocks approach is to break down transformation efforts into smaller, more manageable parts. Companies will still need to address initiatives across all building blocks and prioritize according to value and impact for the business. The guiding principle is that eventually, over time, all building block areas will need to be addressed. Due to the dependency across all building blocks, organizations will see sustainable results from digital business transformation once all areas are tackled.

For example, an organization may focus on developing and implementing digital acquisition channels for customers in order to increase revenue potential, as well as leverage technology solutions to offer personalized touchpoints at scale to increase engagement with customers. These initiatives would clearly fall into the Customer Experience building block. However, these initiatives would bring limited results if the internal process and operational environment are not optimized to deliver on these new demands from the digital channels and touchpoints. Additionally, staff will need to be upskilled and trained to manage these new technology solutions, as well as interact with customers on the digital platforms. Superior customer experience can only be developed when the internal operations and people support the delivery of it. These are initiatives that fall under the People, Processes, & Operations building block.

During the coronavirus pandemic, many companies found themselves in a similar situation. As digital acquisition channels and touchpoints were hastily launched to ensure business continuity, operational environments struggled to deliver on these, particularly if the processes and operations were not already supported by digital and automated solutions.

Building Block 1: Customer Experience

Enabling Superior Customer Experiences with Technology

Gucci is reinventing itself. The luxury fashion house has invested tens of thousands on digital, online, and social media channels in their effort to target, connect, and engage with a new generation of consumers. Kering Group, the parent company of Gucci and several other recognizable luxury brands such as Bottega Veneta, Yves Saint Laurent, Balenciaga, and Stella McCartney, has seen enviable growth in the last few years. Online sales have continued to grow at a steady pace, despite the global pandemic that caused disruptions to most other industries. At the helm, Gucci's earnings, composing 39% of Kering's corporate revenues, grew by 4.5% in 2021 (Kering 2021). This growth aligns closely with the group's strategic direction indicating a strong focus and investment on new market approaches and growth platforms.

Recognizing rapidly growing trends such as the impact of disruptive technologies on the global market and the rise of the "always-on" generation of consumers, Gucci has launched several digital initiatives targeted at Generation Z. Currently, this segment may have a lower buying power than traditional luxury consumer segments. However, they have a high level of influence and reach across digital channels, which translates to real-world acquisitions. Gucci recognizes that this segment is changing the rules by bringing new expectations and desires to the market. They are continually searching for purpose, meaning, and for ways to stand out and be seen—and their behavior influences people of all ages.

In order to engage this segment, Gucci is reinventing itself by launching a proactive strategy to adopt emerging technologies; digital and online tools, such as augmented and virtual reality; AI-based chatbots; mobile applications; as well as collaboration partnerships specialized in delivering digital products, services, and immersive experiences. Augmented reality (AR) in particular has garnered significant interest among the user base, and since the Covid-19 crisis started, many luxury brands have integrated virtual try-on technology into their digital channel offerings. The Gucci app virtual try-on technology enables customers to try products using their mobile device cameras. The AR technology simulates the customer's experience of entering and trying on products in a physical store. Customers are easily able to visualize the style, size, and fit of the product they are interested in, before making a purchase. The Gucci app users are also able to photograph the virtual products, share online, and get feedback from friends, further enhancing the digital shopping experience.

As a result, Gucci has become Kering Group's best performing brand due to incredible sales growth. According to Statista, in 2020 Kering's Gucci brand generated a global revenue of about €7.44 billion, despite the pandemic, due to integrating a strong digital approach with its in-store dominance for an omnichannel strategy that will be definitive for the success of luxury brands in the coming years.

As demonstrated by Gucci, digital transformation in the Customer Experience building block focuses on creating an integrated omnichannel strategy that connects, engages, and interacts with consumers in a unique and compelling way. In the overcrowded online world, it is getting harder for organizations to stand out. As products and services, particularly digital and online offerings, become increasingly commoditized, consumers are shifting away from focusing on products to looking for more meaningful experiences that create a more emotionally fulfilling sense of value. This shift means companies and brands need to focus on identifying moments of truths in the customer journey to create lasting and deeper impressions. "Moments of truth" are instances or moments when a customer interacts with a brand, product, or service to form or change an impression about the company. Digital technologies and online tools today enable companies to create hyper-personalized and engaging experiences seamlessly across touchpoints, at scale, and at a fraction of the cost compared to physical touchpoints. Based on the Salesforce report *State of the Connected Customer*, over half of customers surveyed said that technology has significantly changed their expectations of how companies should interact with them. The research reports that 68% of customers responding to the survey expect brands to demonstrate empathy, while 66% of respondents expect companies to understand their unique needs and expectations.

Repetitive actions or interactions, such as payments and administration of the acquisition, can easily be moved to the background with automation. Uber is a great example of this automation. In the past, payment was a key part of the customer journey, but Uber flipped this by automating the function of payment to the background creating frictionless, effortless, and personalized experiences for customers.

The integration of digital capabilities to the existing physical elements and presences is also considered here. For example, the recently launched Amazon hair salon utilizes AR-powered mirrors in the physical store that allow customers to select from a range of the hair styles and colors. There are also many examples of brands utilizing AR features on printed marketing materials that allow customers to view additional information, live links, and interactive elements with their mobile devices.

Digital technologies and online platforms have also made it easy for companies to draw together large groups of people who share a common value or purpose, and leverage them as resources.

Based on the Exponential Organization context (Ismail 2014), communities and crowds are an essential element of driving exponential properties of an organization. In this context, the community is made up of large groups of individuals who are passionate about the brand, while the crowd is made up of an even larger global group of individuals with some passive interest in the brand but who are not yet directly connected to the organization. Both the community and crowd may be leveraged to gain business value, for example, through peer-to-peer engagement, crowdsourcing ideas or problem-solving, testing product ideas, expanding brand reach, crowdfunding exploration initiatives, as well as creating a pilot group or ready market of initial consumers.

Lego offers a great example of how to utilize the power of the community and crowd through the Lego Ideas platform, where users can share ideas for new products, as well as vote for ideas presented by other users. Popular ideas are taken into production, which not only creates more engagement and loyalty amongst users, but also continuously generates new product ideas for the brand.

Building Block 2: Products & Services

Digitizing Product and Service Offerings

The coronavirus pandemic changed consumer behavior forever, and, in particular, the dramatic increase in online acquisition of products and services is set to stay. As reported in consulting firm PwC's Global Consumer's Insights Pulse Survey (December 2021), mobile or smartphone shopping is the most popular online shopping mode, even gaining ground on in-store shopping. The report also highlights that in order to succeed in a digital world, companies will need to take advantage of new technologies by investing in the differentiating capabilities that allow them to deliver on customers' needs.

There are several ways to approach digital transformation of products and services. A common approach is to make your existing products and services available on digital channels and online platforms. For example, creating an e-commerce presence online or making purchases possible via social media channels. Although this may seem like a logical step in business growth and expansion, I was truly surprised to see the number of organizations that scrambled to set up online acquisition channels and customer touchpoints during the early days of the coronavirus pandemic. This approach simply focuses on creating accessibility to purchase products and services, enabling customer interactions with the company across multiple channels, as well as business continuity.

Another approach is to digitally enable existing products and services. Here, the focus is on modifying existing products and services to make them more suitable for the digital channels and touchpoints. Typically, companies that take this approach want to avoid cannibalizing the existing market, but at the same time would like to generate a new wave of customers not currently purchasing physical products and services. This approach requires modification or customization of the existing products and services to fit the digital and online channels. The banking industry utilized this approach extensively in the early to mid-2000s by introducing online and mobile banking. The features that were being offered were in essence the same as at the physical branches, however modified to suit the online website and mobile phone capabilities.

Finally, new digital products and services can be developed, specifically intended for the digital economy or future of the business. In March 2020, Gucci created a collection of digital sneakers that consumers could try on using AR. Using the "Gucci Sneaker Garage" that is available on the Gucci app, customers are able to purchase and wear digital sneakers. The sneakers, called Gucci Virtual 25, cost $11.99 in the app and are designed with neon colors inspired from the 1980s. Users are also able to customize their sneakers in the Gucci Sneaker Garage to create unique versions that fit their individual styles. In exploring the increasingly popular metaverse, Gucci has developed virtual versions of its collections and other products for e-sports such as Tennis Clash, gaming platforms like Roblox and Drest, as well as virtual reality chat apps where users can dress up their avatars with Gucci products.

At the core of product and service digitization is identifying the real problem that your customer or market faces, and leveraging the capabilities of your organization to resolve it. Technology solutions enable organizations to solve the customer's problem faster, more efficiently, at lower cost, or even to eliminate it completely. A deep understanding of the customer base will enable organizations to quickly respond to growing trends or disruptions that may arise in the market. Stagekings offers a positive lesson for addressing such disruptions. The Australian company designs and fabricates temporary custom physical structures and installations of all sizes. When the coronavirus pandemic halted live events and festivals, drying up steady revenues streams, Stagekings recognized the opportunity to begin constructing home office furniture as a means of ensuring business continuity. Over two years later, the company has successfully pivoted its product and service offerings by launching a range of designer home furniture. Stagekings is worth the mention as it is one of the most successful Covid-19 pivot stories, having sold over 35,000 pieces of furniture since launching its IsoKing At Home product line, a new ultra-modern furniture range that is available online.

Building Block 3: People, Processes, & Operations

Optimize, Automate, and Upskill the Internal Organization

A critical element of digital transformation involves the changes that an organization and its people have to go through in order to achieve the required business outcomes. This is the most critical element, as success depends heavily on being able to leverage existing capabilities, while at the same time developing new capabilities that support the new environment. Although a critical piece of the transformation puzzle that enables sustainable success, the internal organization often does not receive the focus and prioritization that it should.

As organizations leverage technology to transform the front-of-stage interactions, including customer experiences, channels and touchpoints, as well as product and service offerings, the back-of-stage interactions and supporting processes also need to change to enable, support, and deliver the required interactions. Back-of-stage interactions refers to internal capabilities such as operations, processes, support functions, people, and capabilities. I like to use the analogy of a stage performance to illustrate the importance of internal organization transformation in this building block. The audience of a stage performance, the customer, sees the play on stage as the final product—actors, costumes, stage designs, dialogue or script, and music. However, what is not clearly visible is the backstage support that enables the entire performance to run smoothly, from one scene to the next. This involves clear processes, trained people, infrastructure and systems built to support the performance, as well as lots of practice. Similarly, the organization's back-of-stage capabilities need to be optimized to ensure that it can deliver efficient, cost-effective, and well-run front-of-stage interactions that customers will appreciate.

Addressing this building block can be daunting, particularly for incumbent organizations that may hold complex structures spanning functions, regional presences, and heavy legacy systems. Identifying what to tackle first, how much to change, and how quickly can seem like a mammoth task. A key guiding principle is to focus on empowering people to deliver their work effectively and efficiently, anywhere possible. This may involve embracing new ways of working, implementing technology solutions to increase collaboration or turnaround times of activities, optimizing processes and operations through digital and automation solutions, or even upskilling the workforce to increase productivity. During the coronavirus pandemic, for the first time in modern history, a global workforce was enabled through online platforms, including video conferencing, online and visual collaboration, workflow and task management, as well as knowledge and content sharing.

With some organizations, I observed employees and teams struggle to pick up the digital skills that were previously not a necessity for their daily business. Many organizations had underestimated the value of digitizing and automating their business environment, and had to quickly implement patch-work tools to ensure business continuity. The CEO of one company in particular, a technology manufacturer of industrial products, announced proudly that the company had finally implemented Microsoft 365 due to the demands during the pandemic lockdown. There are, however, many organizations that took the opportunity to push boundaries and explore new ways of operating. As a contrasting example, Gucci frequently leverages a "shadow committee" of millennial advisors below the age of 30, that has been established as part of the brand's "bottom-up" management approach. Employees in the committee provide insights and ideas considered outside of the scope of knowledge and awareness of the older generation staff.

For example, in order to keep employees safe and to ensure that travel restrictions were adhered to during the Covid-19 pandemic, food and drink conglomerate Nestlé expanded its use of AR technology for remote support of its production and R&D sites, as well as to connect with suppliers. Utilizing AR capabilities helped prevent needless physical interactions during the Covid-19 crisis to set up and repair production lines, carry out vital maintenance with suppliers, and conduct employee training sessions. Augmented reality-based solutions offer significant cost savings and diagnosing issues remotely allows companies to prioritize operations and reserve their expert resources for AR-assisted service to new technicians and more complex in-person repairs. Augmented reality has been shown to reduce mistakes and unnecessary calls by 90%, achieve 50% faster task performance, and serve as a compliance tool that logs activity in real time, ensuring service calls are properly performed. Going forward, remote assistance will become a new way of working at Nestlé.

Optimizing the operating model and process landscape of business functions are also critical elements that closely align with workforce enablement and leveraging technology solutions. Focusing on deploying technology solutions and upskilling staff brings returns in the mid-term, although sustainable outcomes from digital business transformation are only achieved once the operations and processes have been optimized. In this context, we look beyond typical process improvement efforts that tweak the existing process landscape to achieve a better result, to focus on reengineering. Business process reengineering (BPR) involves remodeling current or As-Is state processes completely to achieve different results and improve the system entirely, to get to the future or To-Be state processes. Typically, the BPR initiative follows the target operating model design stage that addresses how the transformed organization will function.

CIM Financial Services Ltd, a client that I have been advising on digital business transformation since 2019, offers a good example of this effort. Following the development of the company's digital business transformation strategy, I supported the leadership team in developing a target operating model that would meet the future needs of the business. Each element of the target operating model was meticulously redesigned and developed for implementation, including the internal operational landscape which is set to be transformed into a shared services structure. The operating model canvas, as illustrated in Figure 5.5, is an effective way to define the elements of the target operating model.

Based on the operating model canvas, a target or To-Be blueprint for each element was defined and taken into further development as part of the implementation roadmap. The process landscape was assessed in detail to identify opportunities for reengineering and optimization, sampled in the summary Figure 5.6.

Building Block 4: Business Models

Enabling New Revenue Potential with Technology Capabilities

Technologies have triggered significant changes and disruption in the global business landscape. However, technology solutions alone do not transform entire industries. Rather than offer a competitive advantage, technology solutions may be quickly replicated by industry players and even newcomers. Sustainable competitive advantage comes from developing business models that are able to leverage the capabilities of technology to create a compelling value proposition for customers. This is a fine balance between understanding the evolving market needs, leveraging the existing capabilities of the organization, as well as utilizing new capabilities enabled by digital technologies, to create new business models and revenue opportunities (see Figure 5.7).

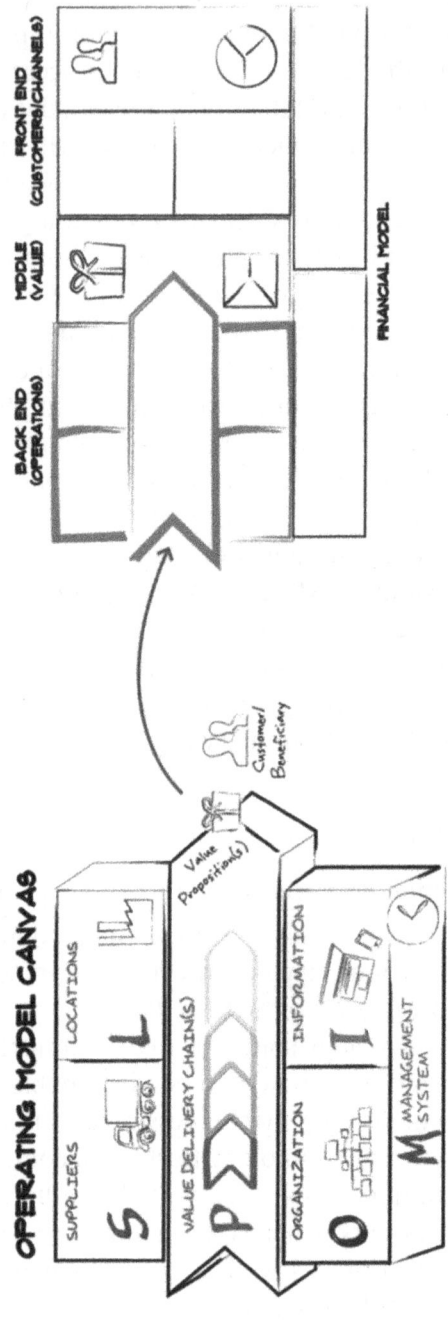

Figure 5.5 Operating model canvas aligns with the business model.
SOURCE: Campbell, A. et al., 2017 / Van Haren Publishing

144

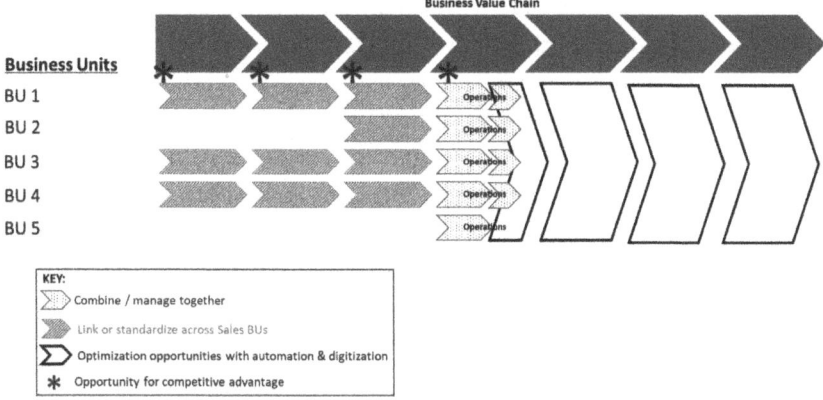

Figure 5.6   Summary business process reengineering, part of the target operating model.
SOURCE: Kamales Lardi, 2019

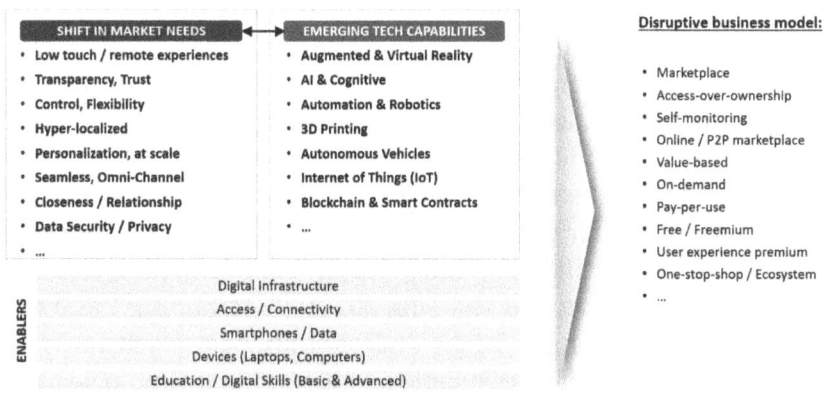

Figure 5.7   Develop business models that link technology capabilities to emerging market needs to achieve transformation.
SOURCE: Kamales Lardi, 2016

Emerging technologies have enabled a range of new business models and revenue streams for companies. Many digital native companies have been able to leverage these digital-first business models to rapidly displace incumbent organizations. For example, Netflix has completely redefined the way viewers access and consume movies and films. In addition, Netflix benefited during the coronavirus pandemic because consumers turned to online streaming as an alternative to cinema and television viewing. However, Netflix's subscription-based business model proved more sustainable than some other newer streaming offerings, such as Quibi, which has been forced to shut down in recent months.

A key principle for successful business model development is to focus the value that can be delivered to the customer and market. Emerging technologies have triggered changes in customer behavior, demanding new business models that meet these needs. Another principle is to understand that business models may be applied in a variety of ways. Many successful companies combine several types of business model and use different models for different parts of their companies. Traditional business models are far less durable in the current environment of rapid technological development, which has transformed the basic rules of creating and capturing economic value. Today, business models are subject to rapid displacement, disruption, and, in extreme cases, outright destruction.

For incumbent organizations, business model transformation is notoriously hard, as some companies struggle to recognize the potential opportunities, while others hesitate in fear of cannibalizing existing profit streams. However, innovative business leaders will be able to trigger this process by identifying and reframing the basic and foremost industry beliefs about value creation, capture, and delivery (de Jong and van Dijk 2015). By reframing these traditional beliefs, business rules, and assumptions, particularly in relation to new capabilities enabled by emerging technologies and disruptive trends, organizations will be able to develop new mechanisms for creating value in a sustainable way for the future.

Widiba Bank offers a great example of this approach (see Figure 5.8). The Italian bank recognized the increasing demand from consumers for a more personalized relationships with financial service providers. As customers' financial sophistication grew, with broader access to financial knowledge and information across the market, customers not only wanted more control of their personal finances, but also personalized interactions via online channels as they would experience in the physical locations.

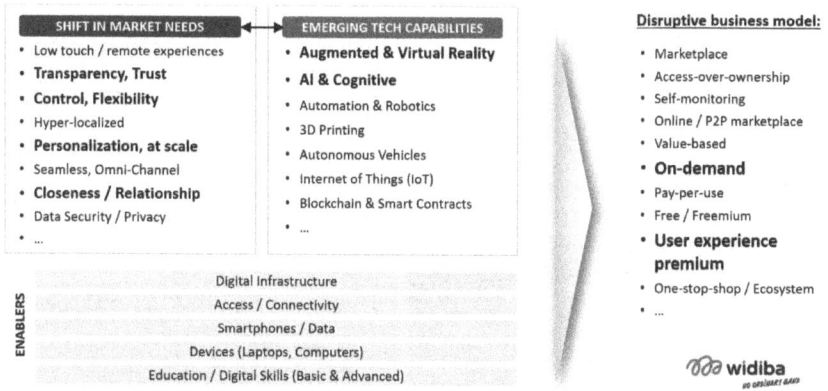

Figure 5.8   Business model innovation—Widiba Bank example.
SOURCE: Kamales Lardi, 2021

In an effort to take the banking relationship back to the customer, Widiba Home was designed to offer the same level of personal touch that customers experience at the physical branches, while at the same time fitting into their busy lifestyles. The virtual reality solution, where customers simply download the Widiba app and wear a pair of virtual reality glasses, offers anytime, anywhere access to a virtual branch. Customers are able to carry out transactions, check their account or card balances, as well as talk to an advisor, a real agent tasked to respond to customers on this platform, see Figure 5.9.

In my eyes, business model transformation is both a science and an art, combining the value of insights gained from data and information analysis, with creativity and open-mindedness that trigger innovation. In his book *Gamechangers*, Peter Fisk describes a range of disruptive and innovative companies that are reshaping the world. These start-ups and corporates capture their higher purpose that resonates with their target audiences, enabled by data and technology, empathetic design, and rich human experiences. Gamechangers, from Alibaba to Zipcars, Ashmei to Zidisha, Azuri, and Zynga, think and act differently, innovating every aspect of their strategy and business model, brand and marketing, process and leadership. This enables Gamechangers to achieve exponential transformation and truly change the game.

Figure 5.9   Widiba Bank virtual reality branch.
SOURCE: Widiba Bank Italy, 2021

Starting Point for Transformation Journey

At its core, digital business transformation is about changing the way your business operates and delivers value to the customer to survive and thrive in the fast-changing world. Failing to transform, or to transform quickly enough, raises existential challenges for any organization. However, as we have observed, many organizations have failed to make sufficient progress in their transformation journey, and end up stalled or running in circles as initiatives do not achieve the intended purpose.

Digital business transformation is a journey, not an end-state design. Often, organizations fail in their transformation effort because it is positioned and managed as a typical implementation project, with a focus on executing a specific tangible element such as a technology solution or channel to market. This limits the scope and potential gain from a true transformation effort due to a poor understanding of the full *scope* of digital transformation.

Research conducted by Boston Consulting Group (September 2020), shows that while digital transformation had already been a priority in recent years, more than 80% of companies plan to accelerate their efforts and 65% plan to increase investments in this direction. There is overwhelming evidence to support these efforts, as digital leaders demonstrate 1.8 times higher earnings growth than digital laggards. Successful digital business transformations set organizations up for sustained returns that are visible in productivity improvements, better customer experiences, new growth opportunities, as well as business model innovation. However, according to the same research, only 30% of transformations succeed in achieving their intended objectives because it involves delivering fundamental changes at scale in large, complex organizations.

According to Westerman, Bonnet, and McAfee (2014), it is not just what the digital leaders or masters invest in, but also how they lead change that makes these companies stand out in successful digital business transformation execution. In my conversation with Didier Bonnet, Professor of Strategy and Digital Transformation at IMD and thought leader in global digital transformation, he described how Digital Masters excel in two critical dimensions—digital capabilities and leadership capabilities—each of which are distinct dimensions of digital mastery. It is critical to know where and how to invest in transformative opportunities that leverage technology to unlock new ways of doing business, get closer to customers, empower employees, and optimize internal processes. Strong, committed leadership capabilities create a clear and broad vision of the future and stay continuously involved to build out the vision over time.

As Bonnet pointed out, although Digital Masters tend to stand out in both these dimensions, many organizations may excel in either digital capabilities, leadership capabilities, or neither dimension, which means they are only at the beginning of their transformation journey. As a logical starting point, it is critical to conduct a digital maturity assessment to understand what your organization's capabilities are, where your business stands out, and what are the biggest gap areas that need to be addressed to achieve sustained success in digital business transformation.

What Is a Digital Maturity Assessment?

Back in 2011, I was staffed on a consulting project that was engaged to increase employee engagement through the application of a digital collaboration platform. The client, one of the world's largest reinsurance companies, based in Zurich, Switzerland, was responding to the workforce requests for a more structured way to engage, interact, and collaborate across organizational units. A key trigger that raised leadership team awareness of the challenges faced across the organization was the result of a free-form feedback collection initiative that allowed employees to anonymously provide opinions and reflections on their experiences in their daily work environment. A digital forum was set up to allow the approximately 12,000 employees to share their points of view, based on several questions posed on the platform. The forum was left open for a limited period, after which text and data analysis produced specific results on the commonalities in the feedback content. Some of the major outcomes identified were the difficulties in collaborating across teams; lack of shared information, content, and knowledge in the organization; as well as few opportunities to engage outside of formal work meetings. The company, known for its focus on people and talent management, prioritized addressing this feedback through the consulting engagement.

As a first step, a special task force was assembled, consisting of several key people from the Marketing and Communications, HR, and IT departments. I was the only external consultant on the task force, engaged to provide advice, guidance, and insights on project approach and solution development. We were immediately confronted with over 300 pages of feedback, content that was extracted from the open forum. Although the data and keyword analysis was helpful in providing direction on key themes to focus on, the depth of information required to take any useful action was missing (note that we were working with still rudimentary analytics capabilities from over a decade ago).

Over the years, I have developed and worked with maturity models on numerous occasions. It is a great way to measure the capabilities of an organization for continuous improvement in a particular area of focus. Maturity models could be developed pretty much for any discipline—people, process, or technology—providing there

Find
- People / Experts
- Content / Information
- Interlinking of Various Information (people, content & organization wide)

Share
- Learning (formal, on-the-job, e-learning, on-boarding material)
- Document & Content Sharing
- Experiences / Lessons Learnt / Opinions (informal, personal level)

Organize
- Communities (informal, e.g. knowledge networks)
- Workgroups (formal structure & ad-hoc, cross-organizational, e.g. deal / project team, line organization, underwriting)
- Culture & behaviour / Performance Management (measure & reward behaviour change)

Communicate (including real-time & time delayed)
- Leadership (1 – many)
- Peer-to-peer (internal & external peers, 1 – 1)
- Team (internal & external team members, incl. virtual teams, 1 – many)
- External (both sharing static information)

Figure 5.10   Maturity model dimensions (example).
SOURCE: Kamales Lardi, 2011

is clarity on themes or dimensions to assess against. The maturity model approach had the appropriate characteristics that would prove beneficial for the reinsurance project engagement. Based on data and keyword analysis, I was able identify four common themes or dimensions that set the foundation for building the maturity model. Each of these dimensions was further broken down into specific sub-dimensions to be measured, and definitions for each developed across maturity levels—basic, advanced, excellent, and visionary (see Figures 5.10 and 5.11).

Dimensions	Basic	Advanced	Excellent	Visionary
People / Experts	I have an individual personal network & individual knowledge of contacts. Basic contact information (e.g. telephone directory).	I have an individual personal network & knowledge of contacts, plus extended network within my contact group. Contact information & skill base made publicly known.	I am able to proactively use a profile directory to create an organization wide network. Leverage on social networks to identify relevant contacts. Integrated into processes / workflow.	I am able to easily find trusted contacts. Leveraging opinions and unstructured information about contacts. Information about contacts is automatically generated. Internal & external contacts are all combined in one network.
Content / Information	I find things in repositories/ sources I typically use. I may need to search multiple times to get information from various sources.	I find things in repositories / sources I typically don't use, but I don't understand the context of the documents. I am able to search through multiple sources in one go.	I am able to find articles / information that are helpful and categorize them for myself. I understand the context of the documents. I am able to subscribe for notifications about new / changed material in sources. I am able to search all sources of information from one single point.	I am able to see which articles/ information are helpful to others and how other users categorize articles. I know immediately which documents will answer my issue /question. I do not differentiate between my own documents and those from others. There is a sophisticated keyword based search, as well as workflow and governance built to support (and encourage) this environment.

152

Dimensions	Basic	Advanced	Excellent	Visionary
Interlinking of Various Information	I am not able to identify the owner / origins of each content.	I am able to identify the owners / origins of each content.	I am able to identify the owner / origin of each content (org unit, location). I am able to understand the context of the person/content because its structure is readily visible. When I search for a person, I immediately see which content he/she recently created.	I immediately know which documents/people will answer my issue/question. I am familiar with the structure of the content/organization and use it actively when identifying people/categorizing content. I can immediately identify subject matter experts in topics interesting for me and see which content they trust/have created.

Figure 5.11 Maturity model sub-dimensions (example).
SOURCE: Kamales Lardi, 2011

153

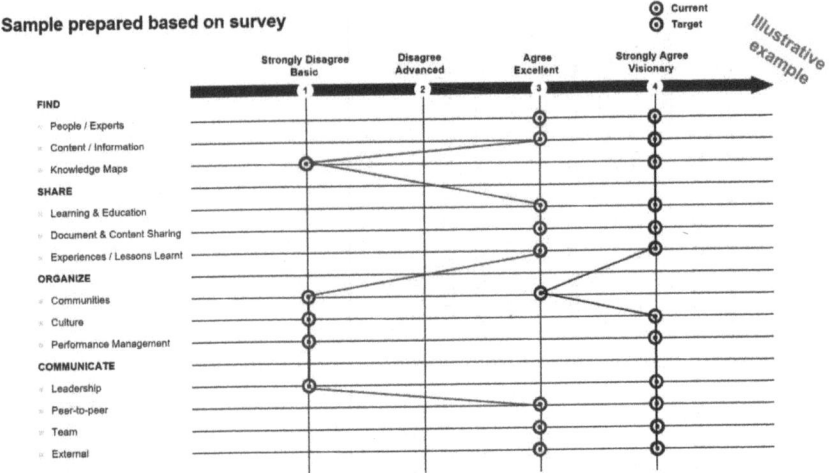

Figure 5.12   Maturity model current and target levels (example).
SOURCE: Kamales Lardi, 2011

Once the dimensions and maturity levels were validated and agreed with internal stakeholders, an assessment or survey was carried out with selected employees from across the organizations to further corroborate the current and target maturity levels (see Figure 5.12). This was used as a basis to define and develop an employee collaboration and knowledge management strategy for the organizations.

The approach not only provided a structured frame over the subjective content that was gathered through the open forum, but also gave the task force a firm foundation to build on. The gap areas, particularly the areas with the largest distance between current and target maturity levels, were used to define specific initiatives and actions that would close the gaps. One key outcome from this assessment was the need for an internal employee collaboration platform. The dimensions and sub-dimensions of the maturity model also provided the basic requirements to assess technology solutions that would be used to build the collaboration platform. The platform was developed and launched, with the aim to foster communication, interaction, and information sharing across geographic and functional locations, increasing productivity and engagement by up to 40% within the first six months of launch. The platform is still in use at the organization.

Digital Maturity & Readiness Assessment

Based on the practical experience of applying maturity models, I realized that this would be a good starting point for digital business transformation as well. The digital maturity model can be used in each phase of the digital business transformation process to help identify where there are gaps, establish key areas to focus on, and define where to start. Although the maturity assessment does not replace the overarching framework, it does serve as a reference guide throughout the transformation process. Several maturity models exist in the market with a range of scope. However, I decided to develop a proprietary model that works in close alignment with the custom-designed Digital Business Transformation Strategy© framework.

The Digital Maturity & Readiness Model©, as illustrated in Figure 5.13, is a pan-organizational maturity framework that covers six core dimensions of business:

Leadership   The leadership dimension assesses the digital mindset and readiness of the leadership team that have been tasked to drive the digital agenda in an organization. This dimension

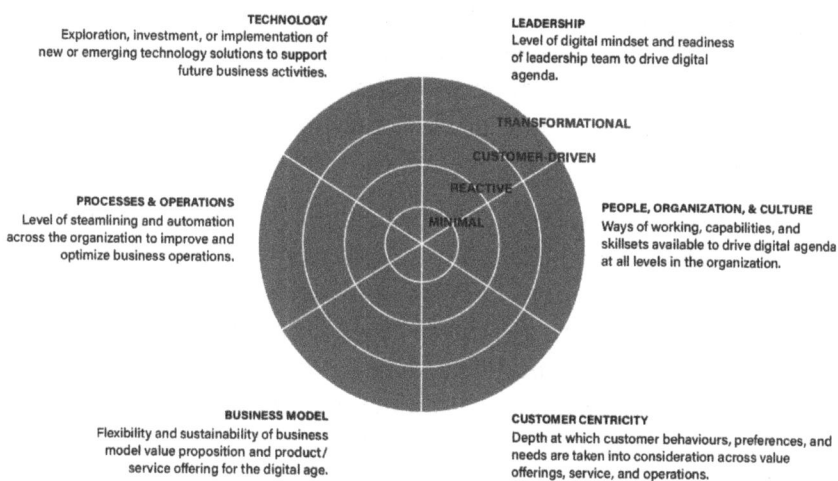

Figure 5.13   Digital Maturity & Readiness Model©.
SOURCE: Kamales Lardi, 2015

could also be applied to board members or owners of an organization to gauge their readiness for transformation and understanding of what is required to achieve change.

People, culture, and organization   This dimension assesses the ways of working, capabilities and skillsets, as well as organization structures that are available to drive the digital agenda at all levels of the organization.

Customer centricity   Many organizations utilize the term customer-centric, but few live this term in daily business. This dimension assesses the depth at which customer behaviors, preferences, and needs are taken into consideration across the value offerings, services, and operations of the organization.

Business model   Sustainable returns from digital business transformation efforts are visible when the business model of the organization shifts in alignment with the organization-wide change that occurs. This dimension assesses the level of flexibility and sustainability of the business model value proposition and product or service offering for the digital age.

Processes and operations   In alignment with value creation and capture transformation, the organization's internal value delivery capabilities also need to change ensuring business continuity and resilience. This dimension assesses the level of streamlining, automation, and digitizing that has been applied to optimize the organization's operations and business functions.

Technology   Technology is a key enabler for transformation and can be leveraged to enable unprecedented scale and growth across value creation, capture, and delivery capabilities. This dimension assesses the level of exploration, investment and implementation of new or emerging technology solutions that have been embedded in the organization's digital strategy to support the future business activities.

As the maturity model indicates (Figure 5.14), transformation is a gradual process that unfolds across the organization over time,

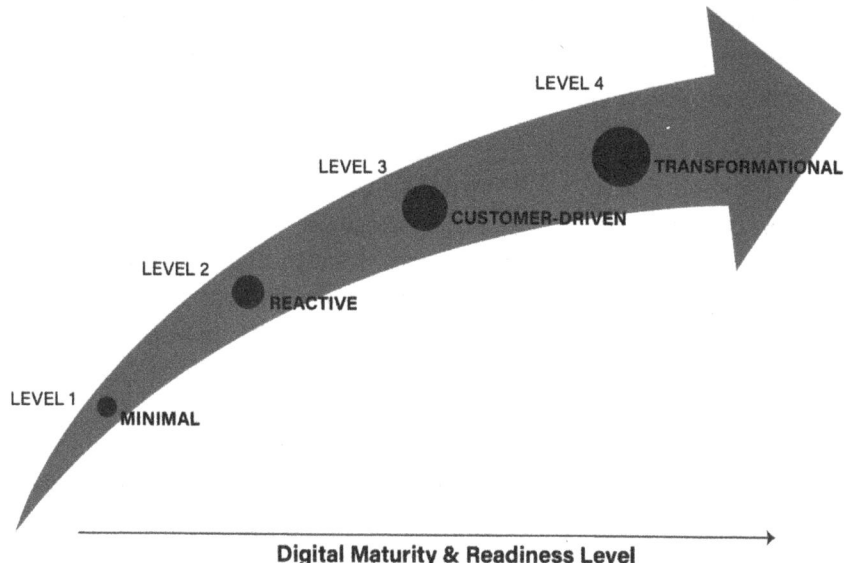

Figure 5.14   Levels of Digital Maturity & Readiness Model©.
SOURCE: Kamales Lardi, 2015

and companies at different stages of maturity can continue to grow and adapt in order to reach a higher level of maturity.

Across the dimension, maturity levels are defined to indicate the overall state of the organization in terms of capabilities and readiness for transformation. The levels are defined as follows:

Minimal   The current business strategy and vision does not sufficiently take into consideration digital as part of its main agenda. The leadership team may be aware of the potential impact of digital technologies in the business, but are not fully aware of its business potential. Few or no digital initiatives are planned and leadership teams are less active users of emerging technologies. Minimal investments are allocated to digital initiatives and efforts are concentrated on traditional IT investments. There are only minimal attempts to explore emerging technologies or how digital solutions might benefit the organization and customers. As a next step, organizations in the Minimal maturity stage are encouraged to focus on understanding the latest disruptive trends and how digital technologies create opportunities for business and revenue generation.

Reactive   The current business strategy and vision takes digital into account in reaction to external drivers, for example, technology trends or evolving competitive landscape. Leadership teams recognize the potential value of digital technologies through exposure from various sources, for example, industry news, expert analysis, peers, or media. Digital solutions are planned or implemented within functional areas that deliver specific technologies. Selected digital initiatives have been planned or will be implemented in response to market trends or competitive landscape. Investment in exploration is limited to selected business areas or functions (e.g., launching a mobile app or exploring a new technology such as blockchain). Additionally, there are some efforts to change the way the business operates due to competitive or business pressures, but still little change to the core business and traditional ways of doing things. As a next step, organizations in the Reactive maturity stage are encouraged to explore the benefits of digital transformation across the entire organization and develop a roadmap of initiatives that span across operations, processes, products and services, as well as business models.

Customer-Driven   The current business strategy and vision includes some digital initiatives in response to customer demands, emerging consumer behavior trends, or increase in adoption of specific technologies. The leadership team may not be using digital technologies themselves, but support or drive the use of digital technologies to engage customers and drive business activities. Digital initiatives are planned or implemented in response to external pressures to transform some areas of business, but this is limited to external-facing functions. Investments in exploration are limited to service offering development and customer feedback may be actively sought to design and develop better service offerings, as well as prototype new products, services, or revenue opportunities.

External-facing functions (e.g., sales, marketing, customer support, and service) utilize digital technologies to improve engagement and are trained to access external digital channels. As a next step, organizations in the Customer-Driven maturity stage are encouraged to explore the benefits of digital transformation across the entire organization and develop a roadmap of initiatives that span across operations, processes, products and services, as well as business models.

Transformational   Digital is deeply embedded as part of strategy and the potential benefits or impact are considered in all strategic initiatives defined. There may already be a clear vision in place for how to bring the company to the digital future. Leadership teams may be digitally savvy and use technology to stay connected and informed, support use of technology to engage customers, and drive business activities. The customer needs and expectations drive transformation in service offerings and delivery, including products and engagement. Core processes in the organization are reviewed, streamlined, and optimized, while digital channels and technologies are integrated. There is a clear investment strategy in exploration, as well as digital skills development, to support the understanding and exploitation of digital technologies for business. Additionally, proactive efforts are made to change the way the business operates and develop new ways to transform the core business operations. As a next step, organizations in the Transformative maturity stage are encouraged to refine the transformation roadmap, as well as define digital business models that can create alternative revenue potential.

Based on the maturity model, an online rapid assessment tool was developed to help assess where you are before developing strategies on where you want to get to, effectively providing an assessment of your organization's strengths, shortcomings, pain points, and barriers that could arise when embarking on the digital business transformation journey. The six dimensions of the maturity and readiness model are further divided into 30 sub-dimensions against which organizations are assessed, as described in Figure 5.15.

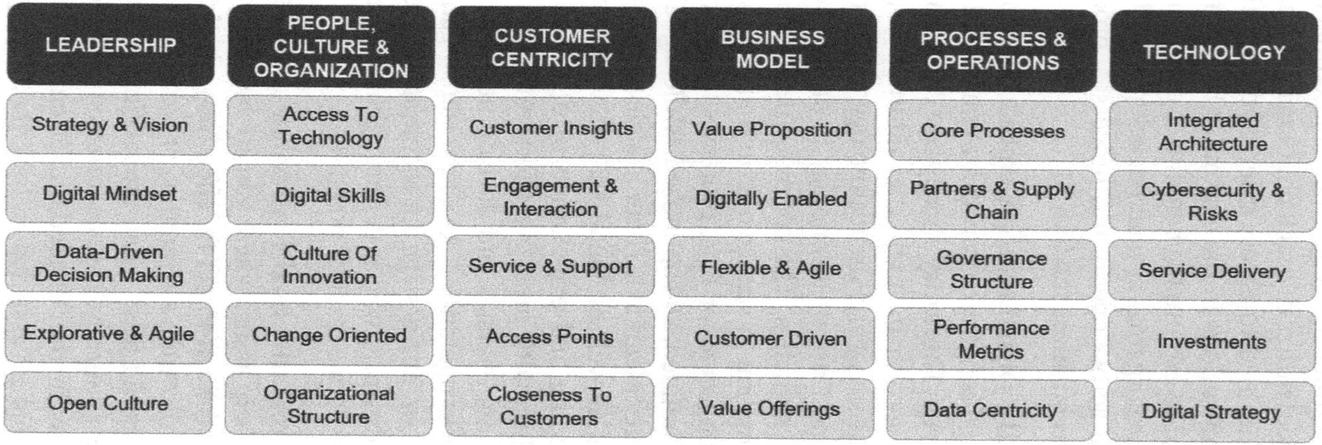

LEADERSHIP	PEOPLE, CULTURE & ORGANIZATION	CUSTOMER CENTRICITY	BUSINESS MODEL	PROCESSES & OPERATIONS	TECHNOLOGY
Strategy & Vision	Access To Technology	Customer Insights	Value Proposition	Core Processes	Integrated Architecture
Digital Mindset	Digital Skills	Engagement & Interaction	Digitally Enabled	Partners & Supply Chain	Cybersecurity & Risks
Data-Driven Decision Making	Culture Of Innovation	Service & Support	Flexible & Agile	Governance Structure	Service Delivery
Explorative & Agile	Change Oriented	Access Points	Customer Driven	Performance Metrics	Investments
Open Culture	Organizational Structure	Closeness To Customers	Value Offerings	Data Centricity	Digital Strategy

Figure 5.15   Sub-dimensions of Digital Maturity & Readiness Model©

SOURCE: Kamales Lardi, 2015

The assessment tool can be completed within minutes, providing a way for organizations to identify gaps in the current business environment across the six core dimensions and determine the best way to move forward as quickly as possible. This uncovering of existing capabilities in the organization is the key to defining a competitive digital business transformation strategy and roadmap.

How to Apply the Digital Maturity Assessment

As I engage with leadership teams, I often ask if they are in alignment in understanding the capabilities of the organization and where to focus transformation efforts. The responses usually contain strong conviction that there is alignment in thinking, priorities, and improvement areas. In 2019, I was invited to conduct an executive briefing for the leadership team at Victorinox AG, a Swiss consumer business organization that is globally recognized. In addition to being the sole supplier of multi-purpose knives to the Swiss army, the brand is the largest manufacturer of pocket knives in the world, and includes watches, apparel, and travel gear in their product portfolio. Participating in their annual leadership strategy session, I conducted a workshop on digital disruption in their market, trends and developments in the industry, evolving customer needs, and transformation the organization may need to compete in the digital future. As part of the workshop, the leadership team was asked to complete the Digital Maturity & Readiness assessment.

The result of the online assessment was a surprise to the leadership team. A family-owned business, Victorinox pride themselves on their people-focused approach to people management. The leadership team are a tight-knit group, each member of the team an essential part of the Victorinox extended family. Still, the results of the maturity and readiness assessment illustrated how dispersed the perspectives of the leadership team were. There were some commonly expected patterns, for example, results from the control functions tended to be more conservative, while sales and market-facing functions appeared overly optimistic. However, across the core dimensions, there was a lack of clarity on where to focus transformation efforts. The session proved to be an eye-opener for the CEO, Carl Elsener, who in his own words agreed that the digital business transformation strategy needs to be clearly defined with the leadership team as a priority:

> [T]he Digital Maturity Assessment, or the picture that emerged from our assessments, was very impressive. Without a common understanding of the questions, the different images are not surprising. Nevertheless, it has shown that it is imperative that we start activities to first get a common understanding on this topic and then jointly start the 'Digital Business Transformation Journey' for our company.
>
> Carl Elsener, CEO Victorinox AG

A critical prerequisite for the successful execution of digital business transformation is the buy-in and commitment of leadership team members. The management team must take the time to make sure that all stakeholders are committed—from board members to interns—or risk jeopardizing company culture and long-term transformation success. However, aligning mindsets and perspectives is not easy, even in organizations with the most open and agile culture. The maturity and readiness assessment offers a structured way to bring people together towards a common understanding for the direction and purpose of transformation. It also highlights misconceptions and differences in perspectives, which can be addressed in an open and objective way.

Maturity and readiness assessments are applied in several ways during the digital business transformation process. At the start of the transformation journey, the maturity assessment offers a snapshot of the current capabilities that your organization could leverage, or helps identify improvement opportunities and actions in the form of key gap areas. In addition, conducting the assessment from two distinct perspectives—current and target—offers organizations a benchmark to work towards. During the transformation process, the maturity assessment offers a methodical way to check the progress of the digital business transformation journey. As you progress along the journey, the direction and goals of the transformation effort may evolve and could look different from where you started. The maturity assessment provides a tangible compass to help stay the course, as well as reset the direction if required. The maturity assessment could also be used to demonstrate the value and impact of initiatives, and gain buy-in, support, or additional investments to continue steering in the right direction of transformation.

The maturity and readiness tool was designed to be versatile, applicable by companies at any stage of the digital transformation journey. For companies at the beginning of the journey or still trying to figure out where to start, the assessment highlights clear gap areas to focus on. For example, a very low maturity in Customer Centricity could mean that executives should focus on transformation initiatives that relate to digitalizing customer access points, improving engagement through online channels, or utilize digital technologies to gain more insights regarding customer behavior and preferences.

Conversely, this maturity tool offers companies already embarking on their digital transformation journey a great way to take stock of their progress and determine if their planned or implemented initiatives are aligned with the strategic direction. The tool not only assesses maturity levels across each sub-category for a company, but also offers an average score or benchmark against other companies.

Leadership teams may choose to deploy the maturity and readiness assessment in several ways, depending on the type and size of the organization. For example, heads of departments could be asked to complete the assessment tool to determine alignment and understanding of the digital business transformation direction. For large organizations spanning various regional locations, each country or location should complete the assessment tool to highlight regional differences and gap areas that may be unique to them.

In smaller organizations, all employees or key stakeholders could complete the assessment tool to take into consideration all voices that impact the organization transformation. The maturity and readiness assessment should not be viewed as a standalone, but in combination with existing initiatives, culture, industry, and emerging trends impacting the organization.

In Chapter 6, we will delve deeper into the step-by-step approach to implementing sustainable digital business transformation for organizations.

Chapter 6
Framework for Digital Business Transformation

I n the business context, there is often a tendency to distinguish between the corporate or business strategy and a digital strategy. Traditionally, the two terms have had a distinct focus. For example, global strategy platform strategytools.io (Rangen n.d.) makes this distinction by describing the core difference in the underlying logic for each—business transformation driving change in value creation logic, while digital transformation triggers changes in operating logic. However, in the current global business landscape, where customers and markets exist in a physical and digital environment that has mostly converged seamlessly, it is unwise to distinguish corporate strategy from digital. Technology and digital solutions have fundamentally transformed the business landscape by shifting where and how companies create, capture, and deliver value.

For example, platform firms like Google, Amazon, Facebook, Apple, and Alibaba (often referred to as GAFAA) have achieved higher market values and even higher margins, with half the employee count, compared to traditional incumbent players, by leveraging the digital ecosystem to orchestrate value creation. These companies create more value in a shared environment enabled by digital platforms, rather the firm's own value created through product and service offerings.

Technology solutions enable significant improvements in efficiency of current operations through automation and digitization, rapid scaling of hyper-personalized customer touch points, digitizing of products and services, as well as new capabilities that suit the hybrid physical-digital environment. Digital business transformation pushes organizations to transform by embracing adaptive cultures, technologies, and business models. Referencing the authors of the book *EDGE: Value-Driven Digital Transformation* (Highsmith, Luu, and Robinson 2019):

> *Digital transformation is not for the timid, but rather for the bold and gritty, hanging out on the edge of chaos. It is a move that forces organizations to build critical capabilities to evolve and continuously adapt to the accelerating rate of change in the global business landscape. A key to success in this space is to have a framework that provides the right guidance and direction to navigate uncertain waters.*

The Power of a Strategic Framework

Throughout my career in business advisory, I have observed the power of utilizing a structured approach or framework to drive the successful implementation of an initiative. When I launched my consultancy in 2012, I quickly realized the need for a structured framework to help navigate digital business transformation in organizations. In conversations with business leaders and senior executives, articulating the scope of change required in order to achieve sustainable return on investments and top line gains was challenging. At that time, we were on the cusp of digital disruption, and digital transformation was still viewed as an "IT-related project" to be delegated to the technology department.

Based on the practical experience that I had gained over the years in implementing business and technology solutions across industries and regions, I began developing a framework that would provide the appropriate guidance and direction to drive digital business transformation, while retaining sufficient flexibility to be applied in organizations of various sizes and stages of maturity, as well as with various business focus. The resulting approach was subjected to many rounds of review and real-world trials in order to ensure that it could be successfully applied in various situations.

I developed the Digital Business Transformation Strategy© framework as a step-by-step guide for companies to understand digital disruption, develop a transformation vision and strategy, as well as implement new target operating models for the digital era (see Figure 6.1). The framework guides organizations in leveraging technology solutions to create value propositions that focus on superior customer experience, commercial profit, and sustainable competitive advantage.

Most organizations across industries now realize the disruptive impacts of emerging trends such as new technologies, evolving consumer behaviors and preferences, digital businesses and expanding competitive landscapes, as well as sifting regulatory requirements. However, companies are still facing challenges on the road to realizing digital business transformation goals:

- Which disruptive elements will have the highest impact on the business?
- How to jump start/accelerate digital business transformation? Where to start the process?

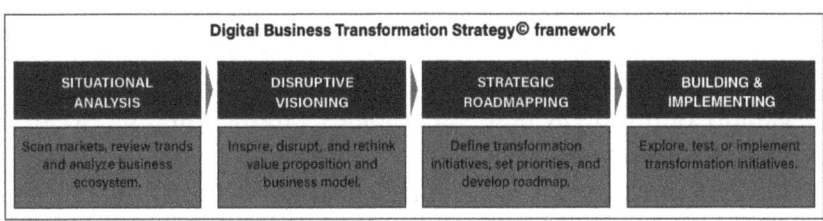

Figure 6.1   Digital Business Transformation Strategy© framework overview.
SOURCE: Kamales Lardi, 2015

- What is the best approach to introduce operational agility in business?
- How to leverage existing business capabilities (e.g., people, processes, and legacy technology) while exploring new solutions?
- Where to focus resources and investments for future growth?
- What are the skillsets/capabilities required?

In essence, the key question that is top of mind for business leaders and management teams is: How can the organization drive transformation from vision to action? Based on my observation of organizations across industries, business leaders approach the digital transformation as a plan, rather than a journey. Such a plan tends to focus on a one-time change or implementation, typically relating to a specific technology solution. In order to be truly effective, digital business transformation needs to be defined as a journey that the organization embarks on with continuous improvement built in to account for the rapidly changing business landscape.

The Digital Business Transformation Strategy© framework offers a pragmatic end-to-end approach to understand disruption and define a prioritized roadmap of initiatives for organization-wide transformation. Additionally, the framework closely aligns to the business vision, mission, and goals of the organization in order to successfully deliver expected returns. This approach helps companies approach digital transformation in a phased, pragmatic way, enabling them to:

- understand emerging trends and top disruptors in the market;
- determine which disruptors will have highest impact on company and business;
- define a vision for transformation and develop a roadmap of transformation initiatives;
- explore or prototype new technologies, products and services, as well as business models;
- identify the best way to leverage existing business capabilities; and
- assess skillsets required to successfully implement digital transformation.

To date, I have successfully applied the framework to guiding cross-industry organizations from vision to action, delivering results not only in creating innovative ideas for the business to move into the new digital economy, but also practical implementation strategies that leverage existing capabilities and infrastructures for organization-wide transformation.

Digital Business Transformation Strategy© Framework: A Proven Guide for Turning Vision into Action

Traditional companies will need to undergo organization-wide transformation that goes beyond implementation of new technology solutions, in order to thrive and remain relevant in the global digital business landscape. Instead of knee-jerk reactions that call for short-term solutions, digital business transformation centers on leveraging technology to understand the evolving needs of digitally connected consumers (i.e., their behaviors, preferences, and motivations), and delivering customer experiences that exceed expectations.

In other words, organizations that are able to look deeper into critical business dimensions such as strategy, operations, people, and technology will effectively succeed in the digital age. A transformation of this magnitude requires significant adjustments to traditional business models, operations, processes, as well as product and service offerings. This is basically the process of rethinking the business, as well as realigning resources, physical assets, processes, and investments based on new customer value propositions—a process that can be complex and challenging, with dramatic results for the long term.

The global business landscape is unravelling, as new digitally enabled businesses stake a claim in the market and create competitive pressures for traditional organizations. These new entrants are focused on meeting the modern customer's needs and utilize disruptive technologies to enable improved customer experiences and business solutions. Traditional players struggle to keep up with digital businesses that are designed to be more fluid and responsive (i.e., lean, dynamic operations, optimized processes, flat organization structures, etc.).

In a typical business environment, daily operational challenges take precedence over new or innovative solutions. This is further reinforced by top-level communication and organizational metrics. Traditional approaches, such as creating an app or using social media to communicate with customers, only scratch the surface of digital transformation. Companies need to look deeper into their operations, review the evolving needs of their customers, and determine how to apply digital technologies to improve the business operations and offerings. In traditional organizations, the typical strategic planning process entails an annual cycle of defining business goals, identifying a list of key initiatives and projects to achieve those goals, followed by a lengthy budgeting process. These initiatives and projects are then tracked against traditional success metrics through the course of the next year(s) to determine return on investments.

Conversely, digital business transformation requires a more dynamic approach to manage the rapid development of disruptive factors such as emerging technologies, competitive landscape, and consumer behaviors. These factors notoriously have been known to shift within a narrow time frame, sometimes even within months or weeks. An annual strategic planning cycle will fall short of such demands and delay appropriate responses from organizations. A digital business transformation framework closely aligned with corporate strategy will require dynamic planning frequencies to evaluate potential trends and disruptors, as well as incremental funding to achieve intended business outcomes.

The Digital Business Transformation Strategy© framework helps businesses think about how such an organization-wide change will impact their business strategy and goals, providing an essential blueprint to identify and develop the right transformation initiatives. This framework is also flexible, allowing for customized solutions that meet the specific needs of each organization. As a result, strategic outcomes and priorities may vary depending on the objectives of the organization.

Digital business transformation may be triggered at any level or function in the organization (e.g., digital marketing, product digitization, business model innovation, etc.). However, in order to achieve sustained impact, transformation has to gradually occur across each level and function of the organization. Making the leap from vision to action can be challenging, especially when it involves a complete rethinking of how your business operates in an increasingly digital business landscape. I have applied the Digital Business Transformation Strategy© framework numerous times in organizations across various industries, and it has proven successful in providing a structured approach for delivering desired outputs. It also offers flexibility to meet the specific needs of organizations, while accelerating our work through a logical and proven structure.

This framework separates the strategic process into four high-level activities: Situational Analysis, Disruptive Vision, Strategic Roadmap, and Building & Implementing.

Situational Analysis   The first step is to conduct an organizational "health check" to assess your organization's strengths, shortcomings, pain points, and barriers. A review of the overall business ecosystem is necessary and this is accomplished by conducting a Digital Transformation Health Check© consisting of four assessments—the Outside-In and Inside-Out health checks focusing on assessing the trends, market, and organization, as well as its operations, and the Top-Down and Bottom-Up health checks focusing on assessing the leadership teams and employees for digital transformation readiness.

Disruptive Vision   Innovating your current business model is next; in other words disrupting your business from within before it is externally disrupted by the digital economy. This involves envisioning the future for your business, reimagining your company's value proposition in this changed landscape, redesigning your business model so that it thrives in the digital economy, and testing your assumptions for validity. The Vision Lab, a series of immersive workshop sessions designed for senior leadership teams, demonstrates the disruptive business model innovation process and helps create effective solutions to thrive in the digital economy. Based on the needs of the organization, solutions may include product or service digitization, process and operations automation, digital and physical customer experience design, as well as business model innovation.

Strategic Roadmap   Navigating your company from its current business model to the future business model your team has defined can be complex so developing a strategic roadmap is necessary to guide you through the transformation process. This strategic roadmap should include an analysis of the gaps between business models (Current vs. Future) and the identification of transformation initiatives required to address these gaps, prioritized accordingly. At this stage, an investment plan should be defined and a proof of concept developed to support the transformation process. The organization's key performance indicators (KPIs) and success measures should also be revised as it prepares to transition to the future business model.

Building & Implementing   The final step is to explore, test, or implement transformative initiatives necessary to actualize your future business model. Developing a business case would prove useful—it should include a detailed plan on commitment and sponsorship needed, the operationalization process, adapting the organization and its processes, planning resources and budget, identifying transition risks and pitfalls, and defining timing and milestones. Existing assets (e.g., people, processes, channels, operations, partners, organization, technology, architecture, etc.) should be leveraged for digital transformation.

The next sections describe the phases of the framework in detail.

Situational Analysis

In any transformation process with a potential organization-wide impact, the first step is a thorough and candid analysis of the existing environment. It is impossible to decide on and create a strategy for the future without first understanding the lay of the land or current business ecosystem of the organization.

The Situational Analysis (Figure 6.2) is the first phase of the Digital Business Transformation Strategy© framework. This is the diagnostic phase that focuses on understanding, analyzing, and reviewing the current internal and external business ecosystem. In addition, this phase also concentrates on identifying and prioritizing the impact of potential disruptive trends and change drivers that originate from various sources including consumer behavior, technology developments, competitive landscape, regulatory frameworks, and business models.

Gather Insights and Information

As a starting point, a review of existing research and information will provide an overview of the current business landscape. As an external expert brought in to support and guide organizations in their transformation process, I typically start by reviewing existing internal strategies, documents, research, or analysis that may have already been developed. For example, business strategy and objectives, vision and mission, market research, customer personas and journey maps,

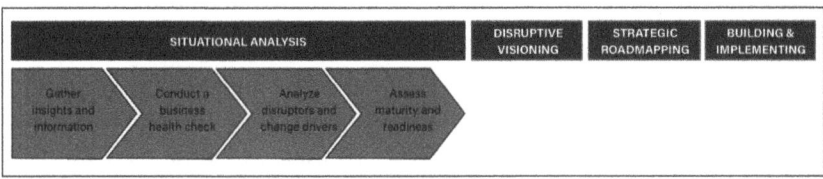

Figure 6.2   Digital Business Transformation Strategy© framework— Situational Analysis.
SOURCE: Kamales Lardi, 2015

customer or employee satisfaction studies, business functions over-view, product portfolio, financials and sales overview, ongoing or planned initiatives or projects, among others. Alternatively, if this process is being tackled by internal organizational teams, it is still a valuable exercise to review this information, and gain a refreshed view of the focus and priorities of the organization.

In addition, you should gather insights and perspectives from key stakeholders to gain a deeper understanding of the business ecosystem. Based on my experience in such engagements, it is important to keep in mind that the interview and information-gathering process across business functions and markets will need to be flexible. Several methods of information collection could be applied to accommodate this, including one-on-one meetings with key stakeholders, focus group meetings with teams or small groups where interview questions and data requirements are clearly prede-fined, as well as indirect formats such as surveys or questionnaires. The format and approach will vary depending on the size of the organization, geographic distribution of teams, as well as the avail-ability of key stakeholders.

In order to gather the input required, it is critical to review exist-ing information, as well as conducting diagnostic meetings with key people to gain a deep understanding of the business ecosys-tem. These sessions, conducted with selected key stakeholders or in groups, are aimed at gathering insight, experiences, and validation for the day-to-day business operations and culture in the organi-zation. In conducting group sessions, bear in mind that bias may affect the outcome. For example, in an attempt to maintain consen-sus, participants may agree with each other's opinions instead of providing frank responses, often leading to exaggerated responses and results that do not accurately reflect the actual current envi-ronment. Conversely, individual stakeholder sessions may contain personal perspectives or biases that do not reflect the experiences of all employees. As such, information gathered must be viewed in combination with structured content, such as processes, analy-sis, and reports, as well as observational research collected of the daily business.

Digital business transformation also aims to improve the value that the organization offers to customers. As such, it is critical to gain insights from customers, for example, customer surveys or, where possible, interviews with sample groups that describe the strengths and weaknesses of customer interactions and offerings. Conduct focus group sessions with external stakeholders from the business ecosystem, such as suppliers, service providers, partners and collaborators; this also brings value by identifying specific gaps, priorities, and opportunities.

In gathering insights and information, I would caution against falling into the "analysis paralysis" trap. Oftentimes, transformation teams struggle to move past the deep dive research and analysis stage. Stay practical and focus on gathering critical information that would guide the next phases and optimize the time required for the diagnostic exercise to deep dive into selected topic areas, as and when required.

Conduct a Business Health Check

The Situational Analysis phase offers an opportunity to conduct a diagnostic "health check" of the internal and external business environment. Just as you would do annual physical checkups with your healthcare provider to get an overview of your health and necessary preventative care, organizations can also benefit from a health check. I developed the Digital Transformation Health Check© to guide organizations in assessing the well-being of their business ecosystem.

The Digital Transformation Health Check© takes a structured approach to analyzing the internal and external elements of the current business environment. The holistic methodology also allows the identification of digital gaps and potential opportunities along the entire value chain that contributes to creating an implementation plan. The health check does not lock into any specific technology or solution, but requires an honest assessment of the organization, including its strengths, shortcomings, pain points, and gap areas. It is most effective when conducted as an audit or review by an objective external stakeholder or internal cross-functional team set up with this specific mandate. In my experience, this can be a particularly trying or emotional process that brings to the surface areas for improvement or issues in the existing business environment. This can trigger fears of losing control, position, or authority, as well as blame among teams that may have been bubbling under the surface of the hustle and bustle of daily business operations. However, it is a critical starting point to ensure sustainable success in the digital business transformation approach.

The health check consists of four dimensions offering a full review of the business ecosystem—The Outside-In and Inside-Out health checks that assess the organization and its operations, and the Top-Down and Bottom-Up health checks that assess the leadership teams and employees for digital transformation readiness (see Figure 6.3).

The four dimensions of the Digital Transformation Health Check© are described in more detail as follows:

Outside-In Health Check   Before embarking on a digital business transformation journey, organizations need to first understand the elements that are disrupting their business. A good

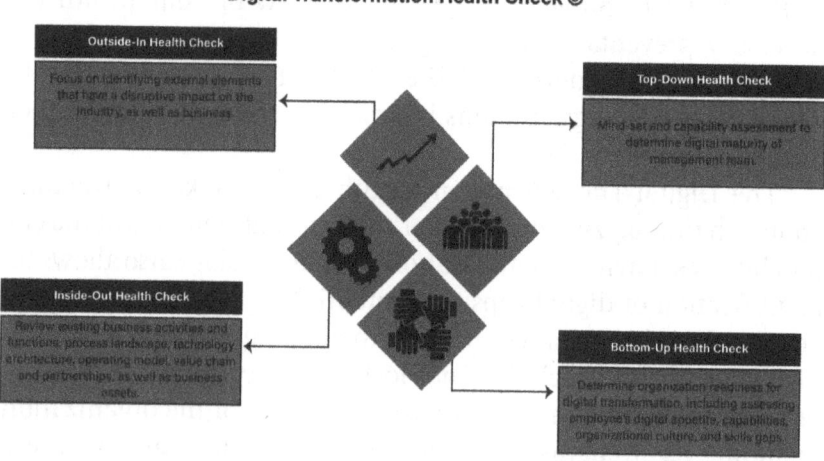

Figure 6.3   Digital Transformation Health Check©.
SOURCE: Kamales Lardi, 2015

place to start is to understand uncertainties in the business environment by conducting an external scan of rising trends impacting the company, business, and related ecosystem. These trends are prioritized according to the potential impact and time frame of occurrence, and high priority trends explored as a part of the digital visioning process.

There is often an assumption that technology is the key driving force of disruption. As a result, there is a high focus on investing in new technology solution implementations. However, there are several disruptive factors that impact the business ecosystem, which need to be assessed and prioritized. For example, evolving consumer behavior or a shifting competitive landscape could also be top drivers for disruption. Traditional approaches, such as creating new mobile apps or launching social media channels to communicate with customers, are insufficient and only manage to scratch the surface of digital transformation. Additionally, there are a myriad of new technology developments emerging on almost a daily basis. Leadership teams are constantly flooded with news of amazing technological breakthroughs, including artificial intelligence and machine learning, augmented and virtual reality, autonomous vehicles, 3D printing, wearables, blockchain, and many more (Chapter 8 provides an overview of these top disruptive technologies). Understanding and assessing the impacts of all these technologies could prove to be an impossible task, particularly considering the exponential rate of development.

The Outside-In Health Check focuses on identifying external elements that have a disruptive impact on the industry, as well as business. These groups of disruptors are then assessed against multiple scenarios to determine which are most likely to occur. By developing multiple scenarios that explore different perspectives and outcomes for disruptors, companies will be able to set the stage for an adaptive digital transformation strategy. An effective tool that I have often used for the Outside-In Health Check is the Trend Scan, described in the next sections.

Inside-Out Health Check   An Inside-Out Health Check is at times the most difficult to conduct as it requires a brutally honest view of the company's internal operations. This includes reviewing existing business activities or functions, process landscape, technology architecture, operating model, value chain and partnerships, as well as business assets. An assessment of the internal operations may bring to light hard truths about pain points and deficiencies that leadership teams may not be ready to address or may feel defensive about. However, this is a necessary step in transforming the organization, as well as in navigating disruptions. For example, a complex internal process landscape could create a barrier against establishing innovation management within the organization.

Reviewing and analyzing key pain points during the Inside-Out Health Check will help prioritize changes that are immediately required, and result in some initial quick wins for the organization. Effective tools that I have often used to conduct the Inside-Out Health Check are "Painstorming" and Gap Analysis. Painstorming is the process of uncovering pain points to create bigger and better ideas (Kaplan 2021), and unlike brainstorm sessions that jump to ideating solutions, the painstorming process reveals the fundamental drivers of new opportunities within employee or customer pain points. The ultimate goal is to get internal teams to think about who they serve, what their needs are, and how to solve the "pains" through meaningful innovation.

Top-Down Health Check   True digital business transformation strategy involves organization-wide transformation that could cover any area of the business, including customer interactions, employee engagement, product digitization, process improvements, new technology implementation, or even business model innovation. As such, it is imperative that transformation is driven, supported, and encouraged top-down by leadership teams.

A major barrier to digital transformation success is the lack of digital maturity or capabilities in the leadership team. This means that the senior management teams are unable to direct digital transformation initiatives, lack the entrepreneurial mindset to drive innovation, or are simply unsure who should own it. The Top-Down Health Check is a mindset and capability assessment that determines the digital maturity of the management team and plays an important role in identifying skillsets that are required to jumpstart the digital transformation journey. An effective tool that I often use to support the Top-Down Health Check is the Digital Maturity & Readiness assessment, as it identifies misaligned perspectives in leadership and management teams, and key gaps in understanding to focus on. Chapter 5 covers the maturity assessment in detail.

Bottom-Up Health Check Most companies tend to focus on external-facing elements of digital business transformation, for example, customer interaction or product sales. However, internal-facing elements are also a critical success factor of the transformation journey. This relates to the way the company develops products and services, employees work together or interact with customers, as well as their readiness for transformation and skillsets that are available in the organization.

Digital business transformation is a change journey that impacts the organization culture, that is, the company's core values and how it operates. As such, it is important to help employees understand the reasons for transformation, its impact, and the role they play to ensure its success. The Bottom-Up Health Check helps determine the organization's readiness for digital transformation, including assessing employees' digital appetite, capabilities, organizational culture, and skills gaps. The health check also identifies gaps and improvement opportunities to drive change, for example, highlighting potential candidates who could take on the role of change agents to drive transformation.

Analyze Disruptors and Change Drivers

As part of the health check, it is critical for organizations to set up a foresight process to gather the information that might inform the future of the business and industry. This information is usually gathered and presented in the form of trends of the future.

Organizations often establish an innovation team to conduct research on trends and market developments. Oftentimes, this information is gathered in a slick PowerPoint presentation that is disseminated across the organization as a "nice to have" research paper, read with interest by some and ignored by many. The major problems lie in relatability and urgency—how does this research relate to daily business, and how quickly will this trend disrupt the business, if at all? Organizations that have established robust trend analysis capabilities stand out as innovation rockstars across industries.

A Trend Scan is a tool that identifies a robust list of potential developing trends, change drivers, and disruptors that would impact the business environment over time. The Trend Scan assesses various categories of disruptors such as market and consumer behavior, emerging technologies and breakthrough solutions, competitive landscape, new business models, and political or regulatory changes. These trends and disruptors are prioritized based on the potential impact and risks to the organization and overall industry.

In the current dynamic business landscape, companies need to quickly assess and distinguish fads from trends that will have a lasting impact. Making sense of these emerging and ongoing changes helps transformation teams get an accurate picture of what is going on in the environment and what is coming up on the horizon. As part of the foresight process, trend research is conducted to identify developments and changes in the business, industry, and global market in general. There are several well-known business strategy frameworks that could be applied to support the research, including STEEP-V (Social, Technological, Economic, Ecological, Political, and Values); PESTLE (Political, Economic, Social, Technological, Legal, and Environmental), or STEEPLE (Social, Technological, Economic, Ecological, Political, Legal, and Ethical).

By setting up a structured approach to continuous information and insights collection, transformation teams will ensure that they do not miss any significant developments. Based on this research, you should create a trend map that illustrates the various topic areas and impact priorities (see Figure 6.4). In addition, several research organizations have published Trend Scans that could accelerate the foresight process, for example Gartner Trends Impact Radar and Board of Innovation Future Scan.

The table in Figure 6.5 illustrates an example of the trend categories, research sources, as well as prioritization and timeline considerations. As illustrated, an effective Trend Scan consists of a range of trends and disruptors from fringe to mature, estimating the time by which said trend will cause an impact on the business ecosystem.

In order to conduct the Trend Scan, a combination of primary and secondary research works well. Here are some suggested sources:

- national and global news;
- industry-specific news;
- business models ideas—e.g., Board of Innovation, Strategyzer, www.businessmodelideas.com;

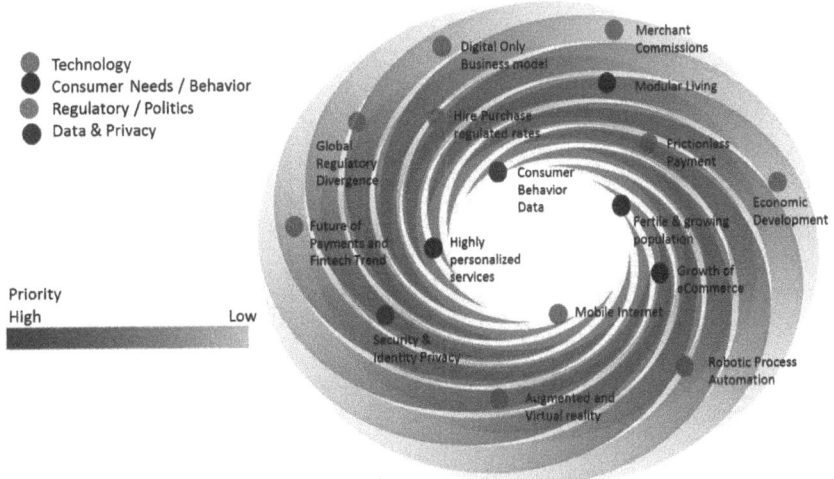

Figure 6.4   Trend Scan summary (example).
SOURCE: Kamales Lardi, 2019

Trend Category	Trend Topic	Description	Source (links, documents)	Impact on Company XX	Timeline Consideration (years)	Priority	Recommendations / Actions / Next Steps
Technology	Mobile Internet	By 2025, nearly 80 percent of all Internet connections could be through mobile devices, and a majority of new Internet users could be using mobile devices as their primary or sole means of connecting to the Internet.	McKinsey report - Disruptive technologies	2018 - 58% of population use internet, 69.7% have access from home, 82% individuals use mobile (1.9m subscribers) (ICT statistics, 2018)We can anticipate huge risk to business, if alternative channels aren't developed because competition has stepped up on using it, further these channels allow us to engage consumer suitably, which is critical for staying close to customer, obtain access to data etc.	3	Critical	Develop new channels across the business a) POS/Virtual POS/Proximity POS b) Online (web) c) Mobile d) Hybrid
Technology	Augmented, Virtual and Mixed Reality	The augmented reality and virtual reality revolution has reached a tipping point. Driven by a historic transformation in the way we interact with technology and data, market leaders are shifting their focus from proofs of concept and niche offerings to strategies anchored in innovative use cases and prototypes designed for industrialization. They are laying the groundwork for broader deployment by tackling issues such as integration experiences with the core, cloud deployment, connectivity, cognitive, analytics, and access. Some have even begun developing new design patterns and nurturing non-traditional skillsets, heralding a new era of engagement. These early adopters recognize a shift in the AR/VR winds: The time to embrace digital reality is now.	McKinsey report - Disruptive technologies	Stand out from competitors offeringsUtilize for onboarding, real time marketing, engagementDigital solutions and applications developed have a unique opportunity to incorporate AR / VR capabilities to create higher customer engagement and interactions.	3	High	Consider adopting technology that enables you to connect with customer in new ways but in a more closers, contextual, personalized way. Always, aim to deliver a wow moment.

Technology	Decline of Facebook (Social Media)	Criticisms over social media channels having too much control over what information the world has access to, as well as progressive sentiments of populism and political propaganda easily promoted through these channels result in its decline, and eventual demise.	https://www.businessinsider.com/sacha-baron-cohen-criticizes-silicon-six-billionaires-ad1-speech-video-2019-11?r=US&IR=T	5	Existing competitors and potentially future are all present or making their presence in social media, this will only mean more competitive landscape to grab attention of end consumer. One way to stay clear from the mad rush is enabling a unique channel.	Medium	Digital solutions and offerings would integrate / align closely with social media channels for customer reach, adoption and engagement. The most popular social media channel in Mauritius currently is Facebook. In-addition/Instead of utilizing social media, consider an in-app proprietary channel (e.g., similar to WeChat, WhatsApp) The advantage of in-app type channel would also help in differentiation.
Economy / Market	Circular economy	Circular economy models could add up to $1 trillion to the global economy by 2025. Global countries / industries make significant steps towards a greener economy, investing in renewable energy, clean waste management technologies and in public transport infrastructure.	https://www.un-page.org/files/public/mauritius_green_economy_assessment.pdf	5	Consumers look for sustainable solutions and greener living. Increase of sustainable investment trends	Medium	Consider applying these models in non-core areas of business to achieve easier cost effective solutions, an example would be to connect/collect customer information, add value such as extended services, collect requirements at their convenience instead having them to your POS, this can be extended to other areas.
Society & culture	High fertile & growing population	A pyramid with a wide base and narrow top suggests high fertility and a growing population, whereas a pyramid with a narrow base suggests an ageing population with low fertility rates.	https://www.worldometers.info/demographics/mauritius-demographics/	3	Consumers will be quick adopters of new technology and aspire to improve quality of life, budget conscious, goal oriented etc.	Critical	Given that 15-50 age group is growing, be aware this age group/demographics has wide training/enablement needs, ensure you engage them appropriately. Enable the various age group to achieve their goals, enable them embrace change, it will lead to brand loyalty and brand recognition.

Figure 6.5 Detailed Trend Scan (example).

SOURCE: Kamales Lardi, 2019

183

- podcasts—e.g., Future Squared, 10x Talk, Outside In, HBR Ideacast;
- websites, blogs, and newsletters—e.g., Futureloop, Next Nature Network, DigitalTrends.com, www.nowandnext.com, Imperial Tech Foresight;
- Social media, online forums, art and design, and other popular media.

These sources could also feed the Disruptive Visioning phase in sparking ideas and envisioning potential future scenarios that may develop.

Assess Maturity and Readiness

It is vital to assess the readiness level of both an organization and its workforce to transition into digitized workflows that are enabled by new technologies introduced during the digital business transformation. Rushing into change or transformation without sufficiently preparing the business and stakeholders is one of the most common reasons digital transformation initiatives fail.

Assessing the organization's current status in terms of digital capabilities is required before setting goals, creating roadmaps, or implementing any digital transformation initiatives. While the exact approaches are never the same, most available digital readiness self-assessment tools are making use of questionnaires and interviews that are built upon specific sets of criteria and indicators.

The Digital Maturity & Readiness assessment (described in Chapter 5) is a rapid online assessment tool that offers a quick way to determine the perceptions, understanding, and attitudes towards digital capabilities in the organization. In combination with the insights from qualitative information collection (e.g., interviews and focus group sessions), the quantitative output from the assessment offers a clearer picture of the current situation in the organization.

Disruptive Visioning

Once a clear assessment of the current business ecosystem has been determined, the next phase of the Digital Business Transformation

Strategy© framework, Disruptive Visioning, focuses on developing and setting a vision for the organization (see Figure 6.6). The output of the research and analysis conducted in the Situational Analysis phase contributes to defining the strategic direction for the organization. Here, the focus is to derive an overall vision and strategy for digital business transformation that will guide the development of a detailed roadmap of initiatives in the next phase. In my view, this is the most inspiring phase of the process, as it offers a chance to flex some creativity and push beyond the boundaries of traditional business rules and assumptions.

In the current dynamic business landscape, incremental change is no longer an option for any industry. To lead the organization towards sustainable digital business transformation, a clear vision of what the future would be and how the business will add value in that new ecosystem should be defined. Additionally, a clear vision that is effectively communicated will be crucial in leading key stakeholders, both internal and external, towards a shared outcome.

Step into the Future Together

The future is unpredictable. However, with the right level of information and insights, a little imagination, and an instinct for connecting the dots, it is possible to make a close "guesstimate" of what the future might look like in your business ecosystem. In the 1970 book, *Future Shock*, author Alvin Toffler painted a picture of what future societies will look like. Many of these "prophecies" were spot on and have become a reality today, such

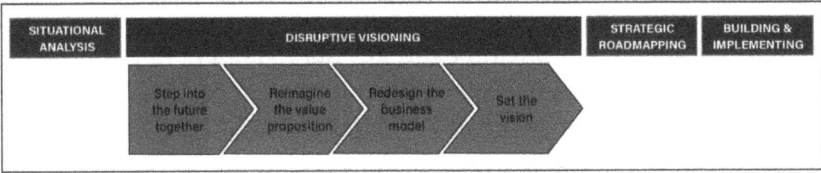

Figure 6.6   Digital Business Transformation Strategy© framework—Disruptive Visioning.
SOURCE: Kamales Lardi, 2015

as concepts that closely describe the free-flowing information via personal computers and the Internet, and the sharing economy. As Toffler explained, futurists do not address predictions, but are simply open to the question of what may be possible in the future. Similarly, organizations addressing the future of business must be open to the possibilities of the future, outside of current limitations of the business landscape.

Business leaders today face not only a myriad of possibilities for the future, triggered by rapidly developing technology, but also a high level of uncertainty due to global shifts such as the coronavirus pandemic. So how should leadership teams build digital business transformation strategies for the organization if there is little certainty about the future, particularly a future that is rapidly changing? In reality, every decision made in an organization is a choice developed under a degree of uncertainty. At the end, a strategic plan is developed based on possible outcomes and best case predictions about where the future is going to go.

Scenario planning, commonly used for corporate strategy development, is an effective tool to identify plausible future scenarios and make better strategic choices under uncertainty. Traditionally, the scenario planning process involves crafting a set of different "realities"—descriptions of what might happen in the future of the business. These "realities" or future scenarios are used to address long-term challenges of uncertainty and complexity in defining the vision for the company, as they help to explore different alternative paths in the future. The timeline for the future scenarios typically considers five to 10 years. However, some companies may consider a shorter time frame of up to three years due to extenuating factors (such as industry-wide disruption already taking place and rapid adoption of breakthrough technologies, among others). I have found that the most effective and engaging approach to this step is to involve leadership teams and key stakeholders in a workshop session, where the future scenarios are described in detail across various categories, as illustrated in Figure 6.7.

The key trends and disruptors identified in the Situational Analysis phase, that have been prioritized based on impact and time

Foundations for Vision

In 3 years, this will be our business landscape

TECHNOLOGY
- Digital products and services
- Increased leverage on technology to offer customized products & services
- Further increased use of digital cards/apps
- Wider application of emerging/disruptive technologies incl. chatbots, wearables, NFC/RFID, IoT, blockchain, AR, "Smart homes" (Example – biometric identification of refugees on blockchain)

ACCESS POINTS
- Omni-channel, seamless access to loyalty programs
- Close integration of digital and physical touch points
- Cross-channel communication
- User-generated content
- Word of Mouth recommendations
- Influence marketing
- On-demand expectation

CONSUMER
- Digitally savvy
- Loyalty shifts quickly
- Wants hyper-personalization, convenience, quick response/service
- "Hybrid" loyalty (shifting segmentation/behaviour)
- Increased adoption of sharing economy (access vs buy)
- Convenience, one-stop shop for products/services
- Mobility
- Cash mindset, conservative, pay on invoice

COMPETITIVE LANDSCAPE
- New players in the market (start-ups, digital businesses)
- Unbundling of services (offerings parts of the value chain)
- Gradual consolidation of traditional players and offerings
- Cross-border entrants
- Competitor from non-financial players (Amazon, Apple...)

REGULATORY ENVIRONMENT
- Increased regulatory focus on data protection & privacy
- Increased privacy requirements across data lifecycle management
- PSD2 (API integration), SEPA Instant Credit Payment, P2P
- Personalization vs. Data Privacy

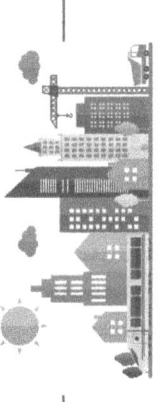

Figure 6.7 Future scenarios for Disruptive Visioning (example).

SOURCE: Kamales Lardi, 2018

187

frame of their occurrence, are used as key inputs to define these future scenarios. To begin the process, the big shifts in the trends, as well as the effect on the organization and industry, are described and discussed to ensure a common understanding of each. A subset of trends and disruptors is selected (those that have the most impact on the business) for deeper exploration. I have found "What if" discussions effective at this stage, where participants are asked to consider the outcome in the market or global business landscape if a specific trend were to become a reality. The "What if" scenarios are described in detail and relevance to the business defined by the group.

For example, "What If" additive manufacturing were to be commonly adopted in the fashion industry to design and produce 3D printed garments, ranging from clothes to accessories, jewelry and even shoes? With computer-aided design (CAD) software, designers will not spend as much time physically drawing and editing illustrations of prototypes during their ideation stage. They also will not need to assemble physical prototypes by hand in order to visualize their designs. The fashion industry supply chain would be transformed, enabling mass production of hyper-personalized garments closer to the consumer's touchpoints at low or near-zero costs (i.e., localized 3D printing centers). Additive manufacturing produces zero wastage and is more sustainable and environmentally friendly. This would allow brands and manufacturers to meet, and even exceed, corporate social responsibility and sustainability objectives. Organizations across multiple industries would be significantly impacted by this scenario, including textile and garment manufacturing, logistics, distribution and storage, as well as fashion retailers and resales.

The scenarios are assessed based on the implications for the business, and shortlisted to identify the most likely to occur with the highest business impact. The shortlisted scenarios are expressed in terms of how the organization will add value in the market and for consumers (value creation), business models that may develop (value capture), as well as how the organization could leverage existing capabilities to offer this (value delivery). The Disruptive

Visioning process of creating future scenarios helps reveal the myriad of ways the business and industry could change over time, allowing companies to better map out the steps to take for digital business transformation. The trends and disruptors, as well as future scenarios, should be periodically evaluated and updated to ensure new developments are being taken into consideration.

The next step is to develop a future vision or goal that the organization should strive to achieve, in alignment with the corporate strategic goals and the selected future scenarios identified. Several tools could be applied to develop the future vision or goal, however I like to utilize the Why/How/What approach to develop a massive transformative purpose (Ismail 2014) as described in Chapter 4. The ultimate objective is to define a vision that is ambitious enough to create competitive advantage in a digitally enabled future that is rapidly developing and uncertain, while still concrete enough to translate into pragmatic action. The Why/How/What approach meets this requirement by helping to turn the audacious vision into specific actions on how the company will address and deliver on opportunities created in the market.

Reimagine the Value Proposition

With a clear vision or goal developed, it is time to reimagine or redefine the value that the company promises to deliver to customers and the overall market. In advising leadership teams, I often emphasize that technology is not a "silver bullet" solution for an organization. A clear value proposition should drive any digital business transformation effort. Reimagining the value proposition within the context of the vision and future scenario allows the transformation team to think through reintroducing the brand to the consumer, including what the company stands for, how it will operate, and why it deserves their business.

A great value proposition may highlight what makes your company different from competitors in the new business landscape. However, it should prioritize how customers define the company's value. When developing a vision for the future of the business, you need a practical tool to help execute things faster and better. A great tool to utilize for this process is the Value Proposition Canvas, developed by Strategizer, a commonly used and fairly simple tool that quickly offers the clarity required to start turning a vision into practical action. The Value Proposition Canvas is often used by marketing experts, product owners, and value creators to help ensure that a product or service is positioned around what the customer values and needs. However, in the context of the Disruptive Visioning phase, it is used to explore the elements of the organization that contribute to a strong value proposition for the future.

In exploring the sections of the Value Proposition Canvas, focus on the perspectives of the future consumer groups. For example, define high-level consumer segments and imagine how your organization could play a role in increasing pleasure or reducing consumers' pain points in this future scenario. Also, explore the emotional drivers (wants), rational motivators (needs), and any undesired outcomes (fears). Keep in mind that even in a digitally immersive environment, consumer actions, interactions, and purchases can still be motivated by emotions.

The development of a value proposition is a vital part of a company's business strategy, as it provides a method to influence the decision-making of customers. While technology may lie at the heart of digital business transformation, it is critical to recognize that a relevant value proposition—and true digital business transformations—should be driven by what consumers want. Some of the most successful digital natives, such as Google, Amazon, and Apple, have created significant value by leveraging on the shifts brought about by their customers' requirements.

A great value proposition may highlight what makes you different from competitors, but it should always focus on how customers define your value. When developing a vision for the future of the business, you need a practical tool to help execute things faster and better. A value proposition sits at the pivot point of an entire business model. Mapping the business model of a new product or service is one of the most important parts of building an overall business strategy.

Redesign the Business Model

During this step, all the elements defined during the Disruptive Visioning phase are brought together to redesign the business model for the future. This involves conscious changes in how the company will create and deliver value to customers, while simultaneously capturing value for itself by transforming the underlying operating model. At the value proposition level, these transformative changes address target segments, product or service offerings, channels and touchpoints, as well as revenue models. Operating-level transformations focus on how to gain competitive advantage and drive profitability by addressing where to play along the value chain, cost models to gain attractive returns, and changes in the organizational structure and capabilities that will be required to achieve this.

The process of redesigning the business model raises common concerns for many business leaders, particularly in companies that are still performing well or excelling financially. This is the roadblock that I have frequently faced while advising companies in their transformation efforts. While often willing to initiate changes in customer engagement, channels, products and services, as well as the technology landscape, leadership teams resist deeper changes to the core business and revenue model. The old adage "if it ain't broke, don't fix it" comes to mind. However, organizations in the current global business landscape are only considered stable and successful when viewed through the traditional business lenses. Most dominant business models that exist today have stayed true to their original form established decades before, or experienced minimal iterations of change, and are ill-equipped to take organizations into the next decade of business in the digital ecosystem.

The global business landscape of today is a hybrid environment where technology solutions have triggered and reinforced new levels of engagement, scale, growth, and profitability. Technology implementation within existing business models will fall short of the true potential that can be achieved. Pouring new technologies into existing business models does not simply translate into customer acquisition or new revenue. Additionally, technology solutions, products and services, as well as channels and engagement strategies are easily replicated by industry peers, providing little competitive advantage in the long run. Sustainable competitive advantage comes from building innovative business models that are able to leverage and commercialize these solution implementations.

The coronavirus pandemic has also fundamentally changed the pace of business globally. According to a global survey by McKinsey (May 2021), many respondents recognized that their companies' business models are quickly becoming obsolete. Only 11% of survey respondents believe that their current business models will remain economically viable through to 2023, while approximately 64% indicated that companies need to build new digitally enabled models to thrive in the years to come. The survey also demonstrated that the pandemic has created new vulnerabilities and opportunities, resulting from customers, employees, and value-chain partners increasing their use of technology, lowering the barriers to digital disruption. This has paved the way for more rapid, technology-driven changes, and highlighted the need to transform existing profit structures, products, and operations.

Peter Drucker, described as the founder of modern management practices, defined innovation as changes that create a new dimension of performance in the business. Rapidly developing technologies drive innovations that create opportunities for these new dimensions like we have never seen before. To leverage these innovations, organizations will need to make informed, deliberate decisions to abandon outdated or traditional activities and implement new initiatives that target the future business landscape. This process of redesigning the business model will at times involve choosing the "right things to do" because it makes sense, and at other times making conscious decisions or tough choices on what the next phase of the business will be, and how it will grow and develop.

To illustrate this point, let's consider the example of IBM. Although today it is known as a successful multinational technology corporation, IBM was on the verge of bankruptcy in the early 1990s.

The company is over a hundred years old, and has had to implement transformation several times to keep up with the dynamic and disruptive global business environment. At that time, IBM made several difficult decisions as part of the process of redesigning its business model. The company not only repositioned its activities to leverage the skills and capabilities within the organization, but also refocused the value to the market and the customer by specializing upstream in the design and maintenance of software. In the early 2000s, when tablets and smartphones entered the market, IBM adapted its business model once more to deliver on customer expectations and stay at the forefront of technology.

For IBM, redesigning the business model meant implementing changes across several core dimensions, including redefining its value proposition in the market, new partnership requirements, different resources and capabilities, as well as redefining the revenue and cost structures. While it may seem like radical change, the company recognized that while the old business model could serve well up to a point, it is critical for survival, growth, and long-term success that the business model is consciously reviewed and updated on a regular and structured basis. This approach may provide tweaks to the elements of the business model or even full-scale business model innovation.

One of the most accessible frameworks to use in this process is the Business Model Canvas, developed by Alexander Osterwalder (2012). The canvas visualizes the elements that describe a company's value proposition, infrastructure, customers, and finances. The international popularity and simplicity of the framework makes it an ideal tool to map the existing business, redesign the business model, as well as visualize proposed transformations to key stakeholders, management teams, and board members.

Set the Vision

The final step in Disruptive Visioning is to define and communicate the vision for transformation. As a strategist, I fall back on application of a strategy map to develop a solid base for discussion

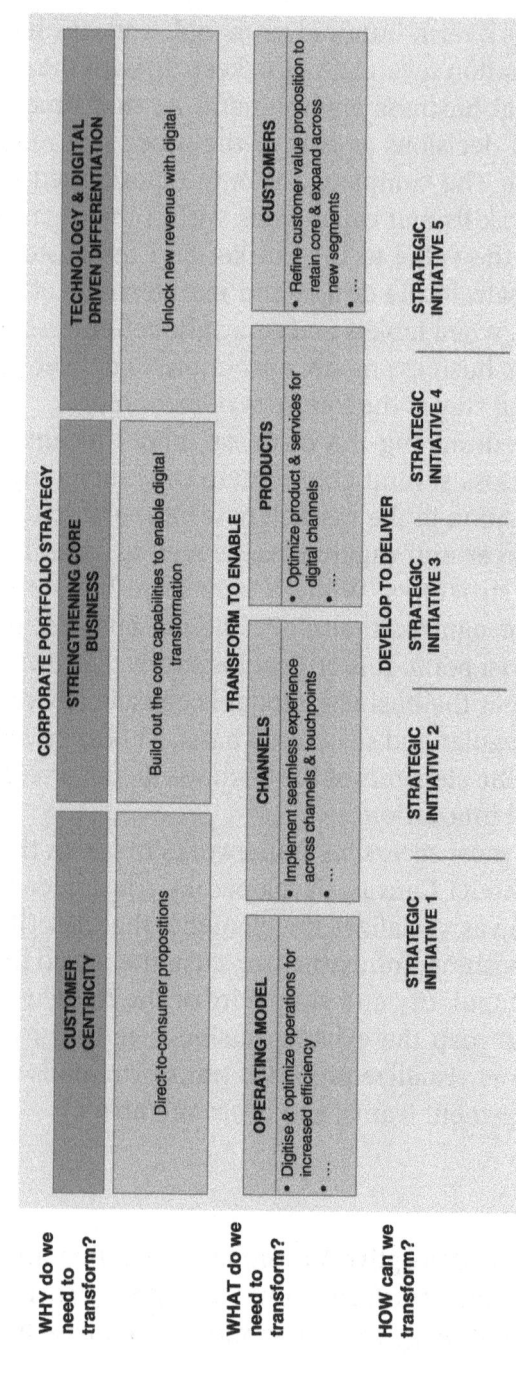

Figure 6.8 Strategy map (example).
SOURCE: Kamales Lardi, 2019

194

and execution of the digital business transformation strategy. The main purpose of the strategy map is to provide a visual blueprint or description for the organization to drive discussion and execution (see Figure 6.8). The strategy map aligns to the corporate strategy and should provide a cause-and-effect connection with a clear logic that goes from top to bottom. The elements in the lower section explain how the organization plans to achieve the vision in the higher section.

WHY do we need to transform? This is the Guiding Star for the digital business transformation strategy, taking key imperatives from the overall corporate mission and defining strategic themes to focus on as a priority.

WHAT do we need to transform? Specific themes or pillars are identified to help organize top-level choices for the organization, providing a clear starting point for prioritization, continuous monitoring of progress, and success measures. The Balance Scorecard offers a great tool to identify and define strategic themes for transformation.

HOW can we transform? This takes the strategy into a clear area of execution, where high-level initiatives describe how the vision and strategic themes will be executed, and links to specific performance metrics that can be continuously monitored.

The strategy map, once defined, can be reviewed, refined, and validated with various key stakeholders in the organization, as well as the broader business ecosystem. This map is a living concept, and should be revisited often as the organization progresses along the transformation journey to ensure alignment, strategic fit, and continued relevance.

Disruptive Visioning is a great starting point to generate a commitment to the organization's vision and transformation strategy. Leadership teams should communicate the vision in a way that matters to people and provide clear signals on the overall direction that will be taken. This early employee engagement and communication of the direction, as well as a clear indication of how the organization culture may change, instills commitment. The digital business transformation strategy must address both the initiatives and the people simultaneously, in order to realize the disruptive vision.

Storytelling is a highly effective strategy for communicating the vision for change. It helps the listener understand, and when stories help connect employees with the present state and the future vision, storytelling invokes the emotional attachment needed to engender employee engagement. In his book *Executive Presence*, *New York Times* bestselling author Harrison Monarth highlights how good stories help to develop trust, solicit feedback, and serve to reinforce the vision. In my conversation with Monarth, he points out that a good vision story should be told in five minutes or less, focusing on simplicity, clarity, and engaging attention. Authenticity in leadership is built in an environment of trust and transparency, in which leaders demonstrate accountability and responsibility. This encourages people to discuss their concerns and issues, enables the leadership team to address fears and take action to show that the organization values its people and the contributions they make toward achieving the vision.

Monarth agrees that no change initiative ever runs smoothly. However, authenticity of leadership, where leaders are honest when things go wrong, follow through on their promises, and act consistently in line with organization values and beliefs, builds the trust necessary to overcome hurdles through periods of change. It is not enough to communicate vision verbally, leaders and managers must model the behavior that they expect to see in their people. Without this consistency between words and action, credible leadership and the change project will dissipate rapidly, and resistance will grow. To communicate a vision for change effectively, business leaders must do so in a way that connects with a wide range of people with different preferred communication styles. Additionally, make the vision memorable by employing metaphors to explain organizational culture and guiding people to the discovery of the vision using visual aids to map a path from the current state to the future vision.

Strategic Roadmapping

The Strategic Roadmapping phase is the third phase of the Digital Business Transformation Strategy© framework (see Figure 6.9). The output from the Disruptive Visioning phase will be used to identify specific initiatives for digital business transformation in the organization, as well as shape the strategic roadmap and rollout plan.

In the previous phase, the focus was on identifying what the company and business landscape might look like in the future, as well as how significant a transformation would be required to create sustainable competitive advantage. The Strategic Roadmapping phase focuses on identifying specific initiatives and actions that will be required to take the company from the current state to the vision or desired end state. These initiatives will span across the entire business value chain, but prioritization will be required to focus efforts and investments on the actions that bring highest returns within the defined time frame.

The strategic recommendations defined in the previous phase will be assessed against the business model and value chain to determine the impact of implementation across the various operating model elements. This will provide a clear overview of the changes that may be required across the business to successfully deliver the digital transformation initiatives, including cost, resources, and infrastructure impacts. This is approached based on the Target Operating Model (TOM) framework, assessing each layer of the

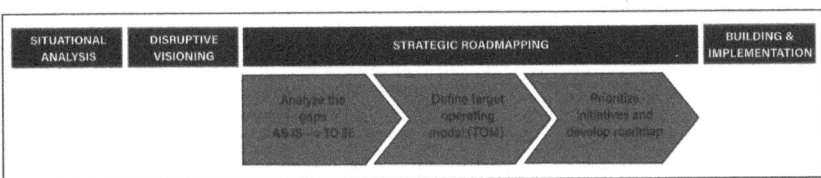

Figure 6.9   Digital Business Transformation Strategy© framework—Strategic Roadmapping.
SOURCE: Kamales Lardi, 2015

operating model—customers and markets, channel, products and services, processes, people capabilities and organization, as well as technology infrastructure.

Analyze the Gaps As-Is –> To-Be

The gap analysis aims to identify the specific actions that are required in the organization to turn the vision into reality. It identifies the gap between the status quo (As-Is) and the desired end vision (To-Be), to pinpoint specific areas for improvements required to achieve the digital business transformation strategic goals for the organization. By defining and analyzing these gaps, leadership teams will be able to create an action plan to move the organization forward and fill in the performance gaps.

Describing both the current (As-Is) and the desired future (To-Be) state in detail creates a visualization of the digital business transformation that is required—everything an organization needs to do in order to get from the current situation to the target situation. This description of the desired changes or actions is critical in providing focus and direction, as well as control on effort, investments, and the quality of change required.

The first step is to accurately outline and define the organizational goals or targets, all of which need to be specific, measurable, attainable, realistic, and timely. Based on the strategic goals identified in the Disruptive Visioning phase, analyze the current state and gaps that exist between the two areas. For example, consider an organization that aims to increase the revenue growth of digital channels by 25% a year, but currently it has been growing by only 8% a year. That puts the current state at 8% growth (As-Is) and target state at 25% growth (To-Be). To achieve the target state, consider actions that need to be taken within a reasonable time frame and potential scale. Typically, a gap analysis is conducted within the context of a business strategic plan; the targets may be three to five years out, which is ideal. In the current digital business ecosystem, technology solutions are able to significantly accelerate the time frames to achieve a certain scale of solution implementation.

To bridge the gaps in current and desired states, first identify why the gaps exist. Do this by asking questions—and questioning the answers to those questions—until the root causes of the gap become clear. An effective tool for this is the "5 Whys Technique"—a simple problem-solving method that highlights when a problem occurs and drills down to its root cause by asking "Why?" five times. When a counter-measure becomes apparent, follow it through to prevent the issue from recurring. If required, consider also using more in-depth problem-solving techniques like Cause and Effect Analysis, Root Cause Analysis, or even Failure Mode and Effects Analysis (FMEA).

In addition to the gap analysis, potential areas for improvement and initiatives are also derived from the following areas covered in previous phases of the Digital Business Transformation Strategy© framework:

Digital Maturity & Readiness Assessment Identifying the largest gap areas in the assessment results based on target states across the maturity dimensions.

Trend Scan Identifying specific trends and breakthrough technologies that could be addressed to gain competitive advantage. For example, growth in consumer adoption of voice technology may indicate application of an AI-based virtual assistant on the website to increase customer engagement.

Research and initiatives Ideas generated within the organization based on research or existing issues faced in daily business may already suggest effective solutions to bridge gaps.

Another great tool to utilize at this point is the ExO Canvas (Palao, Lapierre, and Ismail 2019), part of the Exponential Transformation sprint process. The ExO model comprises of 11 components or attributes, which are building blocks that allow organizations to achieve exponential growth, scale, and impact. The attributes leverage existing and emerging technologies that enable an organization to access and manage abundance in the form of available resources, potential clients, or useful information. In practice, these set industry leaders and digitally enabled organizations apart from the rest.

Each attribute offers the opportunity to shift from a traditional mindset of managing the business within traditional limitations to one of abundance or unlimited potential in growth and scale. There are five externally focused ExO attributes that allow the organization to access global abundance, and five internally focused attributes that enable organizations to manage abundance and drive culture, enabling them to grow exponentially. The ExO attributes and related examples as described in the *Exponential Transformation* book are provided in the table below. In order to ensure the organization will become exponential by tapping into and managing alternative ways of doing business, the ExO canvas drives a new mindset on how to leverage each of the SCALE and IDEAS attributes (see Figure 6.10). The solutions should always be considered in alignment with the vision defined in the Disruptive Visioning

SCALE (Tap Into Abundance)	IDEAS (Manage Abundance)
STAFF ON DEMAND Leverage external workers rather than "owning" employees in order to increase speed, functionality, and flexibility while decreasing fixed costs.	**INTERFACES** Customized filtering and matching to process the output of external attributes (SCALE) into the internal organization.
COMMUNITY AND CROWD Attract, engage, and leverage a community whose like-mindedness inspires support, adding creativity, innovation, validation, and even funding.	**DASHBOARDS** Make real-time information with essential company and employee metrics accessible to everyone internally with short feedback loops.
ALGORITHMS Leverage automated functions, including machine learning and deep learning, to get new insights about customers, products, and processes.	**EXPERIMENTS** Lean start-up methodology in all departments to experiment with new ideas and processes, culturally enabling rapid, validated learning.
LEVERAGED ASSETS Access, rent, share, or otherwise outsource assets to stay nimble and reduce capital expenditure.	**AUTONOMY** Flat structure allowing individual employees and/or self-organizing, multidisciplinary teams to operate effectively.
ENGAGEMENT Leverage outside interest through gamification, digital reputation systems, and incentive prizes to create network effects and positive feedback loops.	**SOCIAL TECHNOLOGIES** Leverage collaborative tools to have real-time conversations with transparency and connection across the organization.

Figure 6.10   ExO attributes—SCALE and IDEAS.
SOURCE: *Exponential Organizations*, Ismail, S. 2014

phase and the areas for improvement identified in current state and desired state gap analysis.

The outcome at this stage is a list of initiatives and action items aimed at bridging the gap between the current state and vision set for the organization. These initiatives may still be high-level descriptions or ideas, but should not be left ambiguous. Formulate the initiatives and actions based on what each will address or the gap it will fill, how it will fill this gap, when a possible outcome could be achieved, as well as what elements of the organization may need to change to achieve this outcome. Only with the appropriate level of description will the leadership team, as well as other relevant key stakeholders, be able to prioritize the initiatives in a reliable manner.

Develop Target Operating Model

The organization's target operating model (TOM) is a blueprint of the core business capabilities of a company. While the business model defines the value proposition (value creation for customers and product offerings to the market), the operating model details the elements of the physical implementation and execution of the business model for value delivery.

A TOM is a blueprint of how the company should operate or run at a future point in time based on the new vision and strategy developed. In the context of digital business transformation, it is essential to reassess the existing operating model and identify changes or transformations that will be required to deliver the vision and strategic objectives defined in the Disruptive Visioning phase. Organizations should develop a TOM when there is a substantive transformation in how the company intends to function in the future—product/service portfolio, customer segments, price points, channels, and the value proposition. Considering that digital business transformation requires organization-wide change over a span of time, most incumbent organizations will need to reassess their current operating model and develop a TOM to deliver the digital vision.

The initial stages of the digital business transformation journey can have a profound impact on the ultimate outcome that is achieved. It is in the stage of Strategic Roadmapping that the big decisions are made and the end state for the organization is determined. The quality of the outcome is in direct relation to how clearly you understand where you are trying to go. As such, developing the TOM can help empower the digital vision and translate it to reality.

The TOM methodology that is typically applied addresses a comprehensive scope that includes six "layers"—Customer/Market Demand Generation, Channels, Products & Services, Process, People/Organization, and Technology & Infrastructure (see Figure 6.11). Addressing the target operating model across these six layers ensures that an integrated and highly functional solution is defined and developed.

My time at Deloitte Consulting offered numerous opportunities to sharpen my skills in operating model design and implementation. The methodology typically used involves deconstructing the organization into its constituent parts (i.e., layers) and analyzing the impact of the proposed transformation or change. This analysis can then be clearly mapped and visualized to gain a full understanding of how the value delivery model of the organization will need to change in order to successfully deliver the digital business transformation strategy.

Figure 6.11   Target Operating Model applied for digital business transformation.
SOURCE: Deloitte Consulting, 2016

Layering of the proposed changes in this way may require effort, but it offers distinct advantages:

- The gaps between current operating model and proposed target state operating model are clearly understood.
- The transformation or changes can be visually communicated in a clear and concise way to achieve stakeholder and sponsor buy-in and support.
- The leadership will have a real opportunity to optimize all change opportunities, specifically in terms of the scope or consistency across the business.
- The business can effectively communicate this new model to all relevant members of the organization.

The TOM exercise will result in additional areas of improvement and initiatives being identified. These should be included in the list of initiatives already identified in the previous phase.

Prioritize Initiatives & Develop Roadmap

Most organizations operate with limitations of investment, resources, and time, and it is crucial to allocate these to the right portfolio of initiatives that bring the best outcome for the company. There are multiple methods for organizations to prioritize initiative and action items. The key to prioritization is to utilize a model that works best for the specific organization and capabilities. Based on my experience, an effective approach to prioritization focuses on aligning initiatives with the company's strategic priorities and filters across two axes: value and complexity. Value is assessed in terms of the initiative's value to both the organization and its customers, while complexity is assessed in terms of the level of complexity to develop and execute the initiative in the context of the existing business environment.

Prioritize the areas of improvement and initiatives across these two primary dimensions—value vs. complexity—by addressing several critical questions:

Value

- How valuable is this initiative for the company and its related business?
- What value does this initiative bring to customers?
- Does the value only relate to existing business, or future opportunities as well?

Complexity

- How feasible is this initiative to operationalize within our company?
- How complicated is this to build?

It may be tempting to delve into detailed analysis and assessments to determine the value and complexity of these initiatives. For example, detailed calculations on the potential value of the initiatives in terms of financial returns, or complexity in terms of detailed cost assessments to build. However, the prioritization stage serves only to shortlist and identify where to focus, after which detailed business cases will be developed (see Figure 6.12).

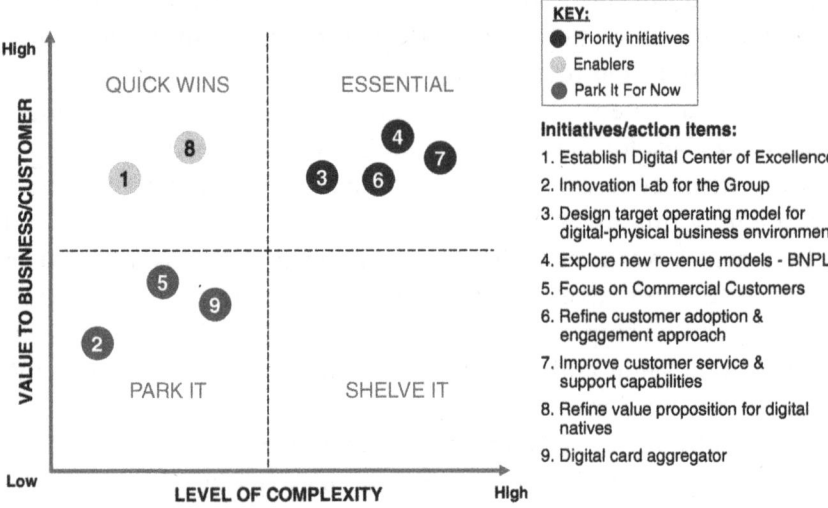

Figure 6.12   Value/complexity prioritization matrix (example).
SOURCE: Kamales Lardi, 2018

The areas of improvement and initiatives may be grouped into four categories based on the prioritization matrix:

Quick wins These are the low hanging fruit—initiatives that are not difficult to execute and have high value for the company and/or customers. These initiatives may be tackled right away for more immediate or shorter-term benefits.

Essential These initiatives are assessed as high value for the company and/or customers, but require significant amounts of effort, cost, and capabilities to complete. However, these initiatives are deemed critical to the company's overall success and future competitive advantage. A selection of the essential initiatives should be started right away, along with a mixture of quick wins for balance.

Park it Overall, these initiatives are not difficult to execute but bring low value for the company and/or customers. As such, these initiatives will be pushed to the backburner and may be addressed if certain conditions change, resulting in a reprioritization.

Shelve it These initiatives are difficult to execute and offer low value to the company and/or customers. These should be shelved, or cut completely, until they make more sense for the company to focus on.

In order to successfully achieve the digital business transformation vision, group the areas of improvement and initiatives into workstreams (see the example in Figure 6.13). Categorize the initiatives and action items according to the Digital Transformation Building Blocks© (described in Chapter 5) to create a link to measurable strategic objectives and outcomes. By identifying multiple workstreams, you will be able to distribute resources across the initiatives, as well as prioritize programs and projects within each workstream.

The Strategic Roadmap is prepared for the prioritized projects against the implementation timeline. The prioritized projects are grouped into workstreams or sub-categories for execution (see Figure 6.14). A high-level plan is drafted including estimated start and end dates, responsible teams, and key milestones.

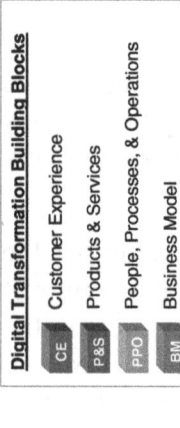

Digital Transformation Building Blocks

- **CE** Customer Experience
- **P&S** Products & Services
- **PPO** People, Processes, & Operations
- **BM** Business Model

The following are classified as **priority initiatives**:

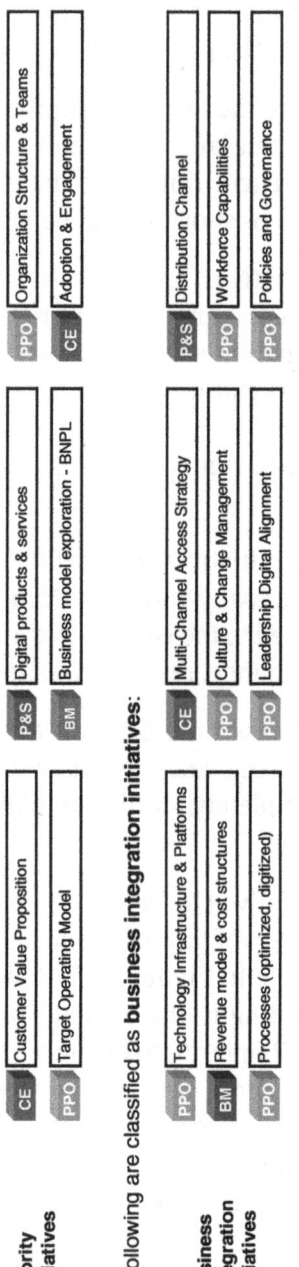

Priority Initiatives

- **CE** Customer Value Proposition
- **PPO** Target Operating Model
- **P&S** Digital products & services
- **BM** Business model exploration - BNPL

The following are classified as **business integration initiatives**:

Business Integration Initiatives

- **PPO** Technology Infrastructure & Platforms
- **BM** Revenue model & cost structures
- **PPO** Processes (optimized, digitized)
- **CE** Multi-Channel Access Strategy
- **PPO** Culture & Change Management
- **PPO** Leadership Digital Alignment
- **P&S** Distribution Channel
- **PPO** Workforce Capabilities
- **PPO** Policies and Governance

The following are classified as **continuous improvement initiatives**:

Continuous Improvement Initiatives

- **PPO** Data analytics & insights
- **PPO** Performance Measures
- **BM** Innovation Management
- **PPO** Organization Structure & Teams
- **CE** Adoption & Engagement

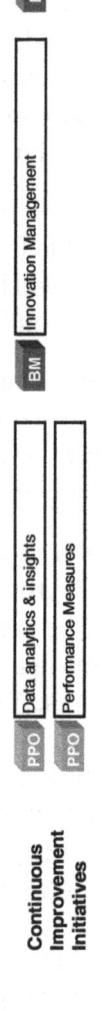

- **BM** Ecosystem Partnerships

Figure 6.13 Portfolio of initiatives for execution (example).

SOURCE: Kamales Lardi, 2018

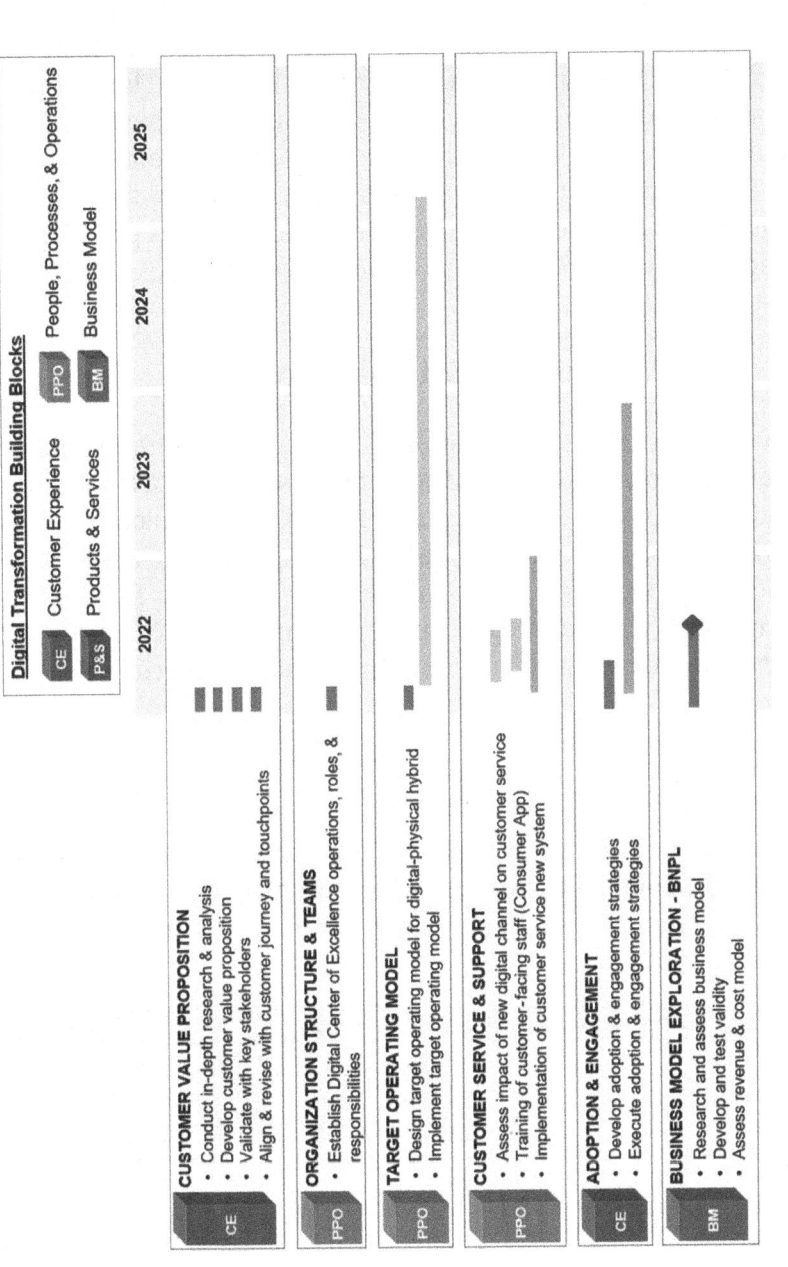

Figure 6.14 Roadmap of initiatives (example).
SOURCE: Kamales Lardi, 2018

207

I would advise organizations to start their digital business transformation journey with quick wins—projects that are less complex, easy to deploy, but still valuable and financially viable. This provides a strong footing to gain return on investments early, as well as buy-in and support from key stakeholders to the overall transformation journey that will span a longer time frame. Plan the transformation journey in phases, ensuring that results are seen periodically through measurable actions that increment over time.

Building & Implementing

The next phase, Building & Implementing, moves into the actual implementation of prioritized and shortlisted initiatives defined in the previous phases. This phase may include exploration and experimentation, in-house development, engaging external service providers, as well as piloting and scaling initiatives for sustainable returns. The Building & Implementing phase (Figure 6.15) depends heavily on the elements defined and developed in the first three phases.

Develop Business Case & Investment Plan

In advising a large financial services company, I worked closely with the CEO and executive team to develop a digital business transformation strategy investment plan that spanned over three years.

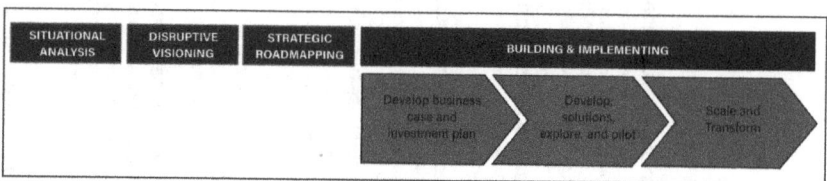

Figure 6.15   Digital Business Transformation Strategy© framework—Building & Implementing.
SOURCE: Kamales Lardi, 2015

We had prepared the investment plan for board review, describing in detail the rationale for the transformation journey, priorities, and focus areas. The board challenged the proposal to evaluate if the plan was too costly, aggressive enough for the shifting market, and had the right focused priorities. Often, boards and top leadership teams accept or reject transformation plans and investments based on the volume that is delivered in terms of business returns. To support this process and guide decisions in the right direction, a robust business case and investment plan need to be developed to recommend the best way to act in order to create business value.

Taking the time and effort to create a solid business case will ensure that key stakeholders are not only well informed, but also buy in to the transformation journey and support potential continued investment throughout the journey. A well-documented business case will include the rationale for transformation, key priorities, as well as recommendations that align with the strategic priorities of the organization and promote confidence for the journey ahead. The depth of analysis carried out in the previous three phases—Situational Analysis, Disruptive Visioning, and Strategic Roadmapping—provides sufficient details that justify the proposed direction, size, and complexity of the investment decisions.

The true value of investing in digital business transformation is to generate long-term revenue growth, and the business case must demonstrate value through the eyes of the customer in order to maximize the impact of these investments. In addition, traditional return on investment (ROI) calculations may work for technology implementations, but are less effective for shifts in the core business model.

The business case and investment plan should be developed in a phased approach, with small amounts of the total budget allocated on delivering preliminary proofs of concept or pilot implementations. This approach provides a low barrier for budget approvals and gives the transformation team opportunities for exploration and testing hypotheses, a necessary step with utilizing emerging technology solutions. When applying the phased approach, it is critical to move into full-scale implementation and avoid getting stuck in the test environment.

The business case should also describe clear governance structures that provide key stakeholders and board members with trackable checkpoints and milestones. For the transformation team, this spells the difference between success and failure, as management of issues, conflicts, priorities, and decision points can be carried out quickly and in a structured way. Along with governance structures, provide details on scope, roles and responsibilities, cross-team involvements, risks, and hidden costs that may arise from the transformation journey. Also, ensure that the price of "doing nothing" is clearly stated to indicate what may be lost in the coming months or years if the organization continues along the current course.

Develop Solutions & Implement

Successful digital business transformation is not simply a matter of strictly implementing plans. The development and implementation of solutions may vary, depending on the type of initiative and impact it has for the organization. For example, optimization of a functional area through robotics process automation (RPA) requires review and redesign of the process landscape to identify bottlenecks, gaps, and improvement areas. Once this is done, RPA solutions may be deployed to streamline workflows and automate repetitive tasks with the aim to increase productivity and efficiency. This project will require specialized skills to quickly understand where RPA could be applied and effectively implement automation across the business landscape.

Conversely, implementing a new digital customer channel or touchpoint will require more focus on the evaluation of customer behaviors, journey, and needs, as well as building experiences that are interactive and engaging. There are a range of technology solutions to be explored that can offer digitized experiences, ranging from social media and mobile apps to augmented reality. Capabilities, readiness, and technology compatibility are several areas that will need to be assessed in the selection of technology solutions. The approach to developing and implementing these initiatives can vary and requires leadership strategic guidance, cross-functional teams to coordinate their efforts, as well as solution providers that are able to deliver the intended outcome.

Exploration may require a different approach. A few years ago, I supported a client in the financial services industry who was keen to explore blockchain as a solution the trade commodity unit. As a traditional and highly regulated business, my first step was to establish a cross-functional team tasked to build capabilities and experience on the technology, and develop a feasibility study on blockchain application. Over a span of six months, the team developed the required knowledge and training that created a solid foundation for the next phase—development of a pilot solution for application within a limited scope of the business. During this time, the team provided frequent and consistent progress reports to the digital transformation steering committee, a cross-functional governance structure established to guide decisions, monitor and track progress, as well as resolve issues and conflicts that were escalated. Clear objectives and success measures were defined for the pilot implementation, in order to assess the feasibility and viability of blockchain application for the business. This approach offered the legal team time to explore the regulatory frameworks around blockchain application, which was developing at a national and industry level in parallel. At the end of the pilot phase, the results proved valuable, not only for the organization's leadership team in assessing whether to continue scaling the solution, but also used as an essential input to regulators and industry experts.

Scale & Transform

A mistake that I have frequently observed in many organizations is to stay at the small-scale pilot implementation. The true benefits and sustainable returns of initiatives are often only visible once it is scaled across the entire business.

The main purpose of proofs of concept or pilot projects is to identify and test new solutions to particular problems, as well as the feasibility and application within the organization's unique environment. Pilot implementations typically include a narrow scope of technical, process, or business function. While this is a logical approach, based on many years of advisory and implementation experience, I can attest that successful pilot projects do not always lead to successful scaled implementations. Although pilot projects try to simulate the actual business scenarios, often teams and stakeholders involved have already bought into the potential benefits of the solution. Large-scale implementations will face a wider range of resistance and real-world challenges that have not been addressed in the pilot. As part of scaling the solution, you need to create the conditions that allow people and teams to adapt the solution to their unique circumstances and make it their own (Ashkenas and Matta 2021).

Additionally, it is worth considering that implementing meaningful large-scale change almost always calls for the creation of new organizational structures or for major changes to existing ones. Even when this is not the case, there is an enhanced need for sharing information and resources and for more concerted coordination, particularly during the transition period.

Based on extensive experience in implementing digital business transformation strategies, I have detailed several key learnings and best practices for sustainable success in Chapter 7.

Chapter 7
Best Practices for Successful Transformation

For organizations around the world, digital transformation has become a matter of survival. A large number of digital transformation initiatives continue to fail, and organizations seeking to implement a successful organization-wide transformation should take the following best practices into consideration. The selection of best practices provided in this chapter are based on my personal experiences and collective insights that will help business leaders accelerate digital business transformation outcomes, and avoid typical pitfalls that arise in the process.

The People Side of Value Driven Digital Business Transformation

In a typical business environment, concerns over daily operational challenges take precedence over new or innovative solutions. This is further reinforced by top-level communication and organizational metrics. Traditional strategic planning approaches lead leadership teams to view disruption in a binary way—to assume that the world is either certain, and therefore open to precise predictions about the future, or uncertain, and therefore completely unpredictable. Many companies are still locked into strategy-development processes that churn along on annual cycles. Typically, the traditional strategic planning process identifies a list of key programs and projects; an estimate of each is then fed into a tedious budgeting process. These traditional strategic planning processes that align to annual business cycles fall short of addressing the high levels of uncertainty in the current business landscape. Conversely, knee-jerk reactions based current trends may result in companies investing in transformation solutions that are the latest hype. We saw numerous examples of this situation during the coronavirus pandemic, as investments in technology solutions increased sharply. However, these organizations now face the challenge of assessing and realigning these investments to a longer term, sustainable business strategy.

In a value-centered business environment, upfront program budgets are replaced with incremental investments in business outcomes that will be achieved through transformation initiatives. These business outcomes can be articulated as Measures of Success (MoS) describing the value that an organization is willing to pay for them. The budget is refined continuously as value is demonstrated and costs outlined through the implementation of the initiatives. This approach also forces business leaders to think about what market problem they are solving through the initiatives, instead of what business they are in or what product they are trying to sell.

According to a McKinsey Global Survey (Bucy, Schaninger, and VanAkin 2021), organization transformation research spanning over 15 years confirms that the more transformation actions a company takes, the greater the chances for success. However, success in reality is an exception, not the rule. Less than one-third of the respondents, all of whom had been part of a transformation in the past five years, indicated that their companies' transformations have been successful at both improving organization performance and sustaining those improvements over time. The potential for value loss in a transformation begins as early as day one, and the largest share of value is lost during implementation (see Figure 7.1). However, on average, nearly one-quarter of value loss occurs during the target-setting phase, indicating that the full potential of transformation value may be compromised even before organizations get started on their journey.

Specific core actions demonstrated by companies with successful transformations provide guidance on how to drive more value capture throughout the transformation process. The best results are demonstrated by companies that focused on embedding transformation disciplines into business-as-usual structures, processes, and systems. This reflects aligning digital business transformation goals to the overall company strategic objectives, and subsequently embedding these goals into "business-as-usual" processes. For example, defining ambitious value capture goals, i.e., maximum financial benefit that can be achieved by the transformation efforts, and embedding these into annual business planning processes and review cycles top-down throughout the organization, from executive-level weekly briefings and monthly or quarterly reviews to individual performance appraisals. According to the research, one of the most important steps that successful organizations took was to set an ambitious yet realistic overall financial target that reflects the full potential of transformation efforts. This set the tone for the entire journey, and more likely than not, people tended to meet the expected outcomes set by the targets.

When maximun financial benefit was lost, by transformation phase*, %

22	23	35	20
TARGET SETTING	PLANNING	IMPLEMENTATION	AFTER IMPLEMENTATION

*Financial benefit is defined as the potiential increase in earnings before interest, taxes, depreciation, and amortization (EBITDA) that the transformation could achieve.

Figure 7.1 Transformation value loss.
SOURCE: McKinsey Global Publishing, December 2021

Another core action relates to adapting these digital business transformation goals for employees at all levels across the organization. Similar to business goals that are broken down by units and align to each employee's performance appraisals and rewards structure, transformation goals must also be translated to what it means for their day-to-day jobs and what they will be expected to do differently to achieve it. Leadership teams need to make digital business transformation goals more tangible for all employees by engaging in continuous, in-person communication and ensure that critical information cascades throughout the organization. Many organizations that have proven successful in digital business transformation utilize change ambassadors or influencers selected from across the organization to create authentic, personal touchpoints that support the transformation process. These change ambassadors, people with influence rather than authority in the organization, whom other employees look to for advice, input, or ideas, are given ownership of initiatives or activities that make them an invested part of the transformation.

Value creation through digital business transformation can also be significantly impacted by assigning high performers to high-value initiatives. According to the research, organizations that were able to realize their full financial benefit from digital business transformation efforts matched their best talents to the most important initiatives. This approach emphasizes the importance of linking transformation goals and talent priorities by having a clear view of where value is generated in the company, and who in the organization has the experience and skills to deliver that value. It is crucial, however, to avoid overburdening high performers with too many initiatives. I have personally observed selected high-talent individuals being spread too thinly across initiatives as they are called to be involved in numerous critical initiatives. Apart from risking burnout, these individuals face high levels of frustration, and poor performance or even blame for not achieving any one specific outcome. Alternatively, keep high-performing talent focused on high-profile and high-value impact initiatives, and spread allocation of smaller initiatives to a wider group of managers and employees.

Balancing Digital Business Transformation with Business as Usual

A core challenge of successful digital business transformation is preserving and sustaining the existing business, while in parallel preparing for a future shaped by disruptive change. Digital business transformation is often perceived as a singular journey, shifting from one state to another. We often see this reference to transformation illustrated as a caterpillar turning into a butterfly, one of the most common images used in digital business transformation. This reference can be misleading for organizations going through the transformation journey, as it implies that there is one change happening and omits the complexities of an existing business environment. In reality, most incumbent organizations will face the struggle of finding the right balance between maximizing the resilience of its existing core business while at the same time creating a new growth engine for sustainable success in tomorrow's market.

This balance is well described in the book *Dual Transformation* (Anthony, Gilbert, and Johnson 2017). In it, the authors describe a practical and sustainable approach to transforming an organization in the wake of disruption, while at the same time repositioning the core business to maximize resilience. Disruption in the business environment is almost always viewed from the perspective of potentially replacing the existing core business. The history of Kodak offers a great illustrative example of this.

For almost the entire twentieth century, Kodak was a dominant company in the photography and videography industries. Kodak had adopted the "razor and blades" business model—first sell the cameras (i.e., the razors) with a small margin of profit, and once customers are bought in, they will have to purchase the film, printing sheets, and other accessories (i.e., the razor blades) repeatedly at high-profit margin. Rapid technology development resulted in the invention of digital cameras in 1975. However, Kodak dismissed the potential impact of the digital camera, which incidentally was invented by Steven Sasson, an electrical engineer working in Kodak at the time. Kodak ignored digital cameras because the core business of films and paper was very profitable at that time, and if these items were no longer required for photography, it would result in shutdown of factories manufacturing these products and subsequently huge losses for the company. The idea was then implemented on a large scale by a Japanese company by the name of "Fuji Films," as well as many other companies, leaving Kodak behind in the race for the future of photography. The Kodak company leadership team chose to focus on their existing core business, rather than face the existential challenges brought on by disruptive innovation in the industry.

The disturbing reality for many organizations is that daily business operations can consume full focus and energy to the point of being blindsided by disruption in the market. On the flip side, companies that approach innovation and transformation as a separate journey or pathway will inevitably face challenges in trying to realign, or even cannibalize the existing business. This very question was the source of great fear when I began advising a consumer finance company in the African region. The large established organization had a strong presence in the market, offering products and services via a network of physical branches and counters at major merchants across the country. With the sole aim to further strengthen their position with the emerging hybrid customer base, the next generation of customers with high digital affinity, the leadership team favored setting up a separate digital business unit focused on offering existing products and services via digital channels to market. Although on the surface this appeared to be a good direction, further assessments during the digital business transformation strategy Situational Assessment phase demonstrated that the existing customer base (users of the physical channels) were increasingly adopting digital solutions, and this would result in cannibalizing the existing core business. This would be expected for any organization as new digital offerings pick up pace with customers. However, putting in place a multichannel strategy to help plan for the transition of physical to digital business would be critical to managing the impact on the business profit and loss structure over time.

Additionally, the existing operations environment was heavily dependent on manual processes, outdated core systems, and complex physical resources. Over a 20-year period, as the business rapidly grew, the traditional operations structure was patched and extended to meet market demands. Any increase in customer requests or acquisition would result in over-burdening the operations delivery of products and services, crashing a delicate structure that had been held together by a large body of employees. It was expected that a digital business unit would enable quicker and easier products and service acquisition, resulting in a rapid influx of demand that the organization would not be able to deliver on. The outcome of the digital business transformation strategy was a clear roadmap and plan to modernize the existing business environment, while at the same time, developing a digitally enabled growth engine to meet shifting market demands.

These examples demonstrate the complexities that incumbent organizations face in trying to balance the demands of digital business transformation with business as usual. A dual-focused approach is required to achieve sustainable results in transformation. This approach raises additional complexities in the transformation journey that could throw off any business leader. Undoubtedly, the challenges posed by disruption alone can be daunting for an organization, forcing its leadership team to face existential change in order to survive. Add to this the critical need to reposition existing core business and capabilities to increase resilience, and we have a recipe for failure.

Incumbent organizations and market leaders can capitalize on their established positions and existing business ecosystem, that bring advantages in capabilities, infrastructure, customer relationships, channels to market, data, and brand awareness, to take on new markets and opportunities intelligently. *The Dual Transformation Equation* (Anthony, Gilbert, and Johnson 2017) illustrates how efforts to manage disruption and generate new business engines overlap with transformation of the existing core business. These efforts are further linked by the capabilities that give existing organizations an upper hand in the business landscape (see Figure 7.2).

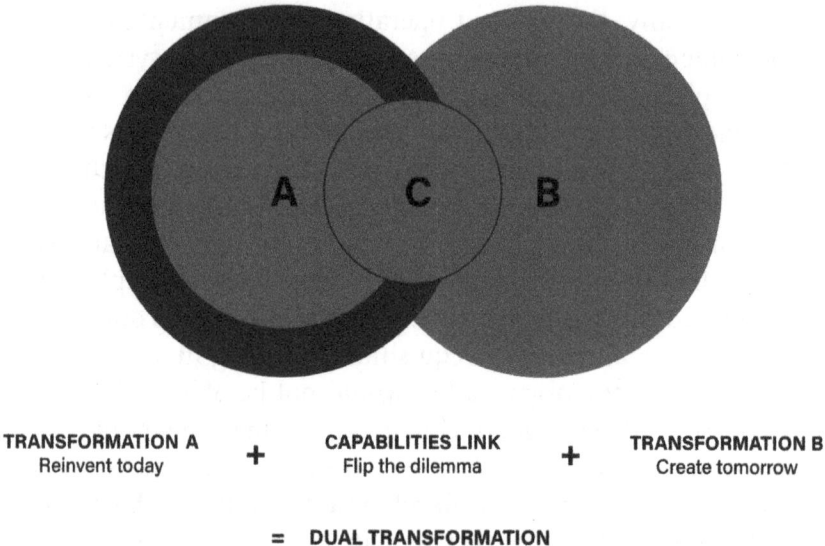

TRANSFORMATION A   +   CAPABILITIES LINK   +   TRANSFORMATION B
Reinvent today   Flip the dilemma   Create tomorrow

=   DUAL TRANSFORMATION

Figure 7.2   Dual transformation equation.
SOURCE: Dual Transformation, Anthony, S.D., Gilbert, C.G., and Johnson, M.W., 2017

The equation looks simple enough. However, based on my extensive field experience in the trenches advising companies on tackling the challenges of transformation, parallel change can be a daunting effort to take on. At one level, the transformation of the existing core business (Transformation A) focuses on determining the customer problem around which to reposition and innovate the business to deliver against the problem. This includes redefinition of the products and services portfolio, value delivery mechanisms, skills and capabilities, as well as tracking and measuring new metrics that reflect this transformation. Here, rapid and agile execution is key, in order to avoid loss of business, disruptions in offers and service, as well as missing the mark in delivering what customers do not need. In parallel, exploring the creation of new growth and revenue opportunities (Transformation B) focuses on identifying new markets triggered by disruption, iterative development of new business models, and acquiring the right capabilities to deliver on it.

Successful parallel transformation is achieved by leveraging existing capabilities to gain an advantage over peers and emerging digitally enabled competitors in the market. This is where many companies struggle, as existing capabilities typically represent constraints that limit innovation. For example, often when I advise companies in highly regulated industries such as financial services or pharmaceuticals, a common barrier to exploration of new growth opportunities is the holy trinity of control functions, that is, risk, compliance, and legal. Similarly, I hear this reasoning to prevent existing core business transformation initiatives such as process optimization or digitization. The trick is to be able to leverage these existing capabilities link just enough to enable innovation and core transformation, without being stifled.

Rapid and iterative exploration of new business opportunities may push the boundaries of the regulatory framework just enough to meet the evolving demands of hybrid customers, but still remain within regulatory boundaries to be trustworthy. In addition, corporate control functions should aim to work closely with regulators to explore these growth opportunities. In terms of existing core business, leverage the deep experiences of control functions to optimize processes and operations for increased turnaround time, while still ensuring reliable compliance for customers and the company. Startups or new digitally enabled businesses will find it hard to compete on this level without existing capabilities link to depend on.

Assembling the Right Team for Digital Business Transformation

We can find the best lessons and deepest inspirations from the most unlikely sources. As a fan of Marvel, a media franchise centered on a series of superhero films, I draw reflections for digital business transformation from the Avengers movies. A core premise and success factor for the Avengers' success is the team, as the movies repeatedly demonstrate. It is not easy to bring together a team of talented individuals with differing motivations to collaborate. Firstly, getting the right combination of abilities, personalities, and incentives, and then getting them to work together in a cohesive and productive way. The Avengers offer a masterclass on bringing the right people to the team, each with something valuable to offer the collective, and close collaboration and communication.

We can draw similarities in the digital business transformation journey for an organization. The challenges and subsequent changes required are too great to handle for one individual. Many organizations install a chief digital officer or transformation lead role to manage the digital transformation journey. However, organizations that have successfully moved forward on this path have demonstrated that bringing in the right group of people is a critical element.

Digital business transformation starts with good leaders driving change. In the reality of the business world, I have observed organizations appoint leading roles based on how digital transformation is viewed and what it entails. A common approach is to appoint an executive to take the lead in digital transformation as their only role, such as a chief digital officer or chief strategy officer, focused on developing and leading the end-to-end transformation efforts. Alternatively, existing leadership roles, such as chief information officers (CIO), chief technology officers (CTO), or chief operating officers (COO), are appointed to take charge of transformation, alongside other existing responsibilities in the organization. Whichever approach is taken, I have seen success in digital business transformation in organizations where top leadership teams, including the chief executive officer (CEO), take responsibility and have continuous involvement in the development and implementation of change. Here, involvement refers to demonstrating commitment, communicating change and impact, as well as leading strategic direction and governance.

Selecting the right team of people with the required capabilities and skills is the next crucial step for digital business transformation success. This is a big challenge for many organizations, as the required skills may not be available in the existing workforce, not only in relation to professional qualifications and experience, but also in terms of the personalities and attitudes required to build the right change culture. Many organizations turn to external support to drive digital business transformation, relying on consultancies and service providers to fill critical skill gaps in the organization. External advisors must work closely with internal teams, ensuring knowledge transfer, and mutual learning is a key part of the journey.

There are several core capabilities required for successful development of digital business transformation. However, this does not indicate the size or construction of the team, which will depend on the scope of change being tackled, and the size and type of organization.

Executive sponsors   The executive sponsor includes an individual (or several) from the top leadership team appointed to lead and support the digital business transformation journey. Executive sponsors play a critical role in ensuring the initiatives stay the course, continuously ensuring that initiatives are meeting the defined goals, and assessing what adjustments are required as the journey develops.

Organizations going through a major change need to have confidence that the end goal can be achieved. The executive sponsor will contribute to building confidence by communicating a clear business case for change, laying out the journey and overall plan, acknowledging the challenges and risks that will be faced along the way, and providing a positive outlook and confidence that the end goal will be achieved.

The transformation journey will be a challenging one and, in many cases, teams involved in this process may be exposed to failure, blame, or other risks. The executive sponsors will need to take the transformation team under their wing, at times shielding them from the internal politics, and often providing a Guiding Star or reference point for the direction and goals to be achieved.

Business-technology liaisons   It is the work of business-technology liaisons that sets the tone for successful digital transformation programs. These are people who are familiar with the business concepts and have a deep understanding of customer needs and evolving behaviors. In addition, they have a good grasp of the digital strategy and capabilities of the technology solutions proposed. The business-technology liaison role will have close and regular contact with business and functional departments, including sales, marketing, product development, and customer-facing teams, ensuring they are in tune with the market developments, and business challenges or possibilities. They must be adept in gathering insights and connecting the dots to ensure that the digital business transformation initiatives will address issues or capitalize on opportunities. In my experience, the business-technology liaison does not have to be someone in a formal leadership role within the organization, but should carry influence with the teams as they represent the core interests of the business in digital business transformation.

Technology experts   The technology experts bring a deep understanding of the technology capabilities and proposed solutions, as well as an overview of the rapidly developing technology landscape. These are the experts in the cutting-edge emerging technologies, applications, and tools available in the market, as well as having a deep understanding of the existing technology and security infrastructure in the organization. The technology experts must be able to guide the development of the digital strategy and define potential investments required for the transformation. This may include ensuring new solutions are interoperable with the existing technology architecture and infrastructure, any updates or overhaul required for legacy systems, as well as informing decisions on whether to buy or build in-house. The technology experts also play a critical role in providing input and guidance in the process of identifying, evaluating, and selecting the most appropriate technology solutions and service providers required to deliver the digital business transformation strategy.

Change ambassadors or evangelists   An essential part of the digital business transformation execution includes identifying and appointing change ambassadors from within the employee base. These ambassadors play the critical role of supporting the transformation process by helping to drive it forward and positively influencing their peers throughout the journey. Ambassadors understand the need for the change journey and how it impacts the people in the organization. They act as the liaison between the transformation team and employees in general, working to generate excitement about the change and raise support for it across departments. The ambassador role wields considerable power and appointees must possess excellent communication skills and influence with people in the organization.

Although it is often understood that these individuals must be "digital natives," I have seen successful ambassador programs consist of people with a range of digital maturity, position or seniority, interests, and age. The ambassador roles could also be segmented according to the transformation plan, depending on the type of initiatives, scope, focus, and needs. For example, one strategy could be allocating selected digital-savvy ambassadors as pilot users and trainers to support the deployment and adoption of an internal collaboration platform.

Implementation team and project managers   The implementation team is responsible for carrying out the digital transformation plan and roadmap. The team will consist of experienced individuals with capabilities and skills ranging from strategy execution, customer value proposition development, process design, data analytics, user experience design, financial modeling, and agile development, among others. The capabilities required will truly depend on the scope and focus of the digital business transformation initiatives and stage of the change journey. Additionally, the implementation team may evolve over time, with capabilities required at the start shifting over time as the team goes deeper into execution work. The project or program managers will also be crucial to develop and manage the detailed project plans. Project managers will work with transformation leads and executive sponsors to ensure that the teams are adequately staffed, on schedule, and within budget.

Communications and marketing leads   Often, digital business transformation implementations focus on the development and delivery of solutions for the organization. As the teams face challenges and issues, a negative perception for the change process may grow, resulting in a loss of support and buy-in. The communications or marketing role will focus on ensuring that the vision and strategy for the digital business transformation journey is continuously communicated within the organization, working closely with the leadership team to craft the key messaging. The progress and achievements through the change journey will be shared to build ongoing support in the organization. In addition, the communication and marketing lead will play a crucial role in connecting business and customer insights to the transformation project, ensuring evolving market needs are catered for.

Assembling a team of "superheroes" with the right capabilities and skills will increase the success of digital business transformation in the organizations.

Think Big, Start Small, Scale Fast

As an organizational leader, when you are preoccupied with concerns of keeping the lights on and ensuring business continuity, the long-term vision of the business starts to lose focus. Contradictorily, this is the critical moment when the idea of a higher, aspirational purpose is needed to survive and thrive. Devising a massive transformative purpose (MTP), a way to think big, is pivotal to ensuring sustainable digital business transformation. In Chapter 4, we delved into the details of developing an MTP as the starting point for transformation. It acts as a Guiding Star for the reason for the organization to exist, its future direction, as well as the beacon that drives the people in the organization.

However, to turn this vision into action, transformative initiatives need to be implemented with proven results. A blended approach that aligns the "think big" vision with the execution of small, phased initiatives that are quickly scaled across the business.

"Think big" Realize that the way value and competitive advantage are created in the digital age is very different. Define goals that aim to capture this new value.

"Start small" Identify smaller explorative initiatives or experiments that are easier to start, fund, learn from, tweak, and "kill" if they do not produce the intended value or outcome. The smaller size and scope also mean that more of such initiatives can be conducted, in parallel or sequentially.

"Scale fast" Once smaller initiatives demonstrate value or financial benefit, move to scale the initiative in order to monetize it, as well as create robust capabilities and momentum.

In order to effectively build an adaptive and responsive organization, digital business transformation strategies must be broken down into a portfolio of small pieces of value that can be prioritized. Big things take a long time, while smaller things require a shorter time to develop, rapidly implement, learn quickly from feedback, and refine for further scaling. Digital business transformation is a journey, and identifying small proof-of-concepts or pilot initiatives to set a path for larger implementations will achieve organization-wide buy-in and support. Proving its value within a shorter, limited time frame will create momentum for the overall digital business transformation effort. In devising transformation plans, I advise companies to identify "quick wins" that can be swiftly implemented and demonstrate results within six months or less.

A few years ago, as I worked with a consumer finance company to develop the digital business transformation strategy, I realized that the leadership team and board were still skeptical about a multi-million-dollar investment into initiatives that span across several years. In order to gain buy-in and support, I helped the project team to identify several quick wins that would address some critical business challenges and could be implemented within a short time frame. For example, one key issue faced in daily operations was the physical exchange of documents and contracts that required customer signatures. This manual process was heavily people-dependent, and received complaints from customers due to the long turnaround times required. I proposed the use of a digital signature solution, DocuSign, which could be quickly implemented in the existing sales and operations processes, cutting down turnaround times from days to less than two hours. Such quick wins demonstrated impact on the value creation process and gained the trust of the top management and board members for broader transformation initiatives.

Smaller, targeted initiatives also provide an opportunity to learn and take quick corrective action. Going into any new transformation or change process, it is important to be aware that it is not a perfect process—many explorations or experimentation projects face hurdles or even failure. The most important factor is to evaluate the failure in order to understand how it came about. A few years ago, I was asked to support an IT transformation project for a pharmaceutical industry giant. When I met with the project leads, it quickly became clear that the project had been launched, stalled, and relaunched multiple times, without success. Despite this, the team had neglected to analyze the root cause for this, preferring to fire and rehire technology partners each time. I turned the project down at the time, as I felt that readiness for the change initiative in the organization was low.

Companies need a system in place to successfully de-risk the development of new initiatives and business models. This system should allow them to strategically identify which areas they want to test, what mechanisms they want to test them with, and include a framework to measure the impact. They require regular milestone metrics that identify whether a project is something that should be pursued further with additional funding or whether it should be abandoned altogether. Furthermore, employees who are involved in these initiatives must be compensated in a different way—performance-based compensation does not work when failures outnumber successes. Many organizations make mistakes when it comes to identifying areas to test, and this is one area in particular. Although digitization is frequently referred to as the "holy grail," automating parts of a business will not prevent a start-up or digitally enabled business from gaining market share because they typically identify market value by addressing unmet customer needs, according to Gartner, the well-known technological research institution. The most important elements will be systematic frameworks for scaling processes quickly, as well as a cultural shift—enabled by C-suite buy-in—in which transformation is treated on an equal footing with business as usual, with its own distinct measurement criteria and reward mechanisms.

Scaling transformation is a common struggle that most organizations face, according to Tony Saldanha, President of Transformant and former Procter & Gamble Vice President for IT and Shared Services. In his bestselling book *Why Digital Transformations Fail: The Surprising Disciplines of How to Take Off and Stay Ahead*, Tony shares insights on how digital transformation can be made routinely successful and leveraged as an opportunity in the Fourth Industrial Revolution. In our conversation, Tony explains that in his experience, companies typically view digital business transformation as a project, particularly as a technology implementation. This creates a poor understanding of how transformation should be managed, and a disconnect in the language used for change. In reality, Tony considers digital disruption equal to the impacts of the Fourth Industrial Revolution. However, the companies that have been successful in changing to meet the needs of previous industrial revolutions will not necessarily be successful in the future. In order to successfully implement and scale digital business transformation, leadership teams need to understand that strategy in business will now need to include a significant focus on people and motivating them towards the change.

Harnessing the Power of the Ecosystem

An organization does not operate independently, it exists in a larger ecosystem of stakeholders and players. However, less than 30% of an organization's suppliers and service providers are active partners in the digital business transformation initiatives (Newman 2017). Organizations have core competencies—things that they excel at and should focus on. Identifying and fully leveraging on a network of key partners and providers outside of these core competencies will not only accelerate transformation, but also create new opportunities and foster collaboration internally and externally.

For example, the adoption of application programming interfaces (APIs) allows organizations to modularize their systems to facilitate replacements and upgrades. In addition, APIs serve as a way for external stakeholders and partners to gain permissioned access to internal resources. These functions allow companies to rapidly develop technology-based solutions in response to targeted issues or opportunities, as well as enabling external partners to utilize and build on top of the internal digital assets. Research demonstrates that close collaboration with external partners for API application grew an average of 38% over a 16-year period, compared to organizations that focused mainly on developing internal solutions (Benzell et al. 2021).

Sustainable success in digital business transformation relies heavily on engagement with external contributors. However, this looks very different from a traditional outsourcing or vendor agreement that organizations are accustomed to. Real value is derived from openness to collaborating with partners and exploring ideas that are outside of the organization's scope of expertise and capabilities. Greater value is created when external stakeholders are invited to join an active ecosystem where resources are made available to foster open collaboration. This shift in mindset—from controlling to enabling, from protectionism to trusting—creates a thriving ecosystem that shares ideas, invests knowledge and capabilities, and secures commitment to a greater shared value and outcome.

The network effects that result from leveraging the power of an ecosystem can be a major source of unprecedented scale and growth for an organization on the digital business transformation journey. There are numerous examples of accelerator programs that offer start-ups the opportunities to drive scale through strategic partnerships with larger corporates. I have personally observed the benefits of such partnerships as a start-up mentor for over three years at the F10 Fintech Incubator & Accelerator, a global innovation ecosystem that was founded by SIX, a global financial infrastructure provider and operator of the Swiss and Spanish stock exchanges.

The F10-enabled tech start-ups collaborate and engage with corporates to shape the future of banking and insurance by providing access to experienced coaches and business experts, access to investments, as well as real industry data to test and prove new concepts and business models. In return, corporate sponsors experience a relief from the constraints of traditional corporate culture and access to explore new technology in a risk-free entrepreneurial environment. Such partnerships can be complex, as I have coached start-ups through the frustrations of collaborating with mammoths of the banking and financial services industry looking to modernize their business offerings. However, when these noncompetitive collaborations are successful, it can be an effective vehicle to scale and grow.

Think Like an Agile Start-up

In the current global business landscape, most start-ups consider technology as part of their core DNA. Regardless of the industry they are in, companies founded in recent years exist in a digital-first ecosystem and cater to an increasingly digitally savvy global consumer base. Conversely, incumbent organizations typically consider technology as a support function or enabler within the existing business infrastructure. For example, an apparel manufacturer may consider itself in the consumer retail industry. However, the consumer retail value chain has been completely disrupted by emerging technologies, from sourcing and production to channels to market and post-sales engagement.

Although it is not practical to consider rebuilding from the ground up like a start-up, incumbents are still able to adopt a start-up mindset that is agile and adaptive, while leveraging the advantages of their existing business environment. In the context of digital business transformation, understanding, collaborating, learning, and remaining flexible are all aspects of the agile mindset that are necessary for achieving high-performing results. Combining an agile mindset with the change processes can help internal organizations better adapt to transformation and realize incremental value for customers.

Making good decisions is a critical part of business and strategic management. However, in large organizations, the decision-making process has become clouded by bureaucracy, stringent policies, and internal politics. Oftentimes, this delays the ability for an organization to respond quickly to a critical change, growing trend, or opportunity. Quick decision-making does not have to translate to risky decision-making, however, and can involve calculated, insightful choices. This is based on establishing processes that quickly bring together key stakeholders, due diligence and governance procedures, and data to facilitate rapid decisions. The agile mindset recognizes the importance of the human element, driven by creativity, out-of-the-box thinking, and core problem-solving capabilities of the team members. These elements contribute to a fluid and adaptive environment where digital business transformation initiatives can thrive.

Another factor that enables start-ups to move quickly is their ability to focus. Start-ups typically exist in an environment that is starved of resources, investments, and capabilities. By focusing and prioritizing where these limited resources are allocated, they are able to accelerate progress within a specific time frame, which is usually a crucial requirement for founders or investors. In contrast, large organizations tend to overburden implementation teams and project managers with multiple initiatives at the same time, in addition to team management, and they are in turn also responsible for multiple simultaneous project executions. Such fragmentation of resources and focus results in slower progress, higher costs, slower decision-making, as well as increased potential for friction along the way. Incumbents may not have the luxury of focusing on a singular implementation, as with start-ups. Alternatively, the digital business transformation roadmap should be carefully prioritized according to value and complexity. This approach is described in further detail in Chapter 6.

The value of thinking like an agile start-up for a large corporate was clearly demonstrated in Bayer. In 2013, a strategic review of the business triggered an exploration of what the future of the business and industry could look like, as well as potential opportunities in business model innovation. At the time, availability and access to more granular customer data, an increase in transparency across the business value chain, as well as rapid development of digital solutions offered a new perspective to market needs, business challenges, and emerging trends. Based on this new understanding of the market, Erik Dam, Head of Global Procurement at Bayer Environmental Science, spearheaded an initiative to explore the application of emerging technology solutions to transform essential weed control maintenance on railways. The solution would transform the capability to eliminate potentially dangerous weed infestations with advanced precision.

Erik shared the story of how the idea was initiated through chance conversations with customers, and the solution was built in close collaboration with technology start-ups that were focused and committed to delivering the solution. Initially, the initiative received little strategic priority as it was outside of the organization's core business. However, Erik saw the exponential potential of the solution and was able to engage an executive sponsor within the business to support the development of a minimum viable product (MVP). Fast forward two years, the MVP was developed in the form of a train equipped with 18 cameras and an innovative GPS tracking system that automatically shuts off the pesticide spray nozzles when the train approaches a "Non-Treatment Zone," such as a watercourse or bridge. The solution essentially is able to identify weeds along the railway tracks at a speed of 200 km per hour. The spray application is conducted at a far lower speed to ensure a targeted application and to avoid drift. The outcome is a successful reduction of 50% in the quantity of pesticides utilized on railroad tracks. Today, this solution is a profitable business area for Bayer and continues to generate higher revenue. The value of the solution was even recognized by industry peers and competitors. For example, a leading German railway company liked the solution so much that they decided to support the implementation, rather than compete. By thinking like an agile start-up, Erik was able to lead Bayer towards creating an edge organization outside of the core business, building a market leader in weed management on railroad tracks.

My full conversation with Erik Dam is available in Chapter 9.

In 2019, Amazon was named best-managed company in the United States by the Drucker Institute, a leadership-focused think tank based at Claremont Graduate University in California (Drucker Institute 2019). A key factor contributing to this was the company's intense emphasis on innovation. According to the findings of Drucker researchers, Amazon outperformed its competitors in terms of patent applications, trademark registrations, and spending on research and development. Due to this, the company abandons patent applications at a higher rate than its competitors, demonstrating its commitment to moving beyond obsolete technology.

According to Amazon founder Jeff Bezos, failure and innovation are inextricably linked. However, the key difference between good failure and bad failure lies in testing the viability of ideas and solutions iteratively, and learning quickly from the outcomes. While the desired outcome may not be achieved, the feedback and insights from the process will indicate how to improve and drive decisions in the right direction. On the other hand, failures that result from rash decisions or poor execution would be considered bad failures.

Fail fast is a term that is often associated with digital business transformation and seen as a necessity to foster an innovation culture. However, the problem with this approach is the acceptance of failure and forced quick action before thoroughly thinking it through. This can be counterproductive, as a failed explorative solution could be perceived as a failure of the entire digital business transformation initiative and lose top leadership support and investment. Additionally, an organization with a highly risk-averse culture will resist embracing failure and create significant hurdles for transformation initiatives. Conversely, I would advise transformation teams to position failure within the scope of a measured hypothesis that would require careful analysis and time to prove effective.

Bezos is well-known for insisting that meetings must be conducted in a productive way in order for them to be successful. Presenters are required to write a memo of no more than six pages in length, which is circulated and silently read at the beginning of each meeting by everyone in attendance. The memo process was lauded by Bezos in an investor letter (Bezos 1997): "Some have the clarity of angels singing. They are brilliant and thoughtful, and they set the stage for a high-quality discussion to take place in the meeting." According to employees who have adopted the approach, the process sharpens ideas and improves decision-making and discussion, but it can take several weeks to perfect the memos before presentation.

Often, in advising corporate leadership teams, I have had good experience in bringing in alternative thinking exercises. For example, when facing decisions or exploring possible solutions to a challenge, several tools could be applied:

Opposites thinking By using opposites thinking, teams will be able to challenge their assumptions about the problem and possible solutions, and come up with innovative solutions that were previously unthinkable. It's important to remember that opposites thinking is more than just an ideation technique; it's also a mindset that you should strive to maintain throughout your innovation journey.

The "How might we" method An example of this method is a (proven) design thinking activity that instructs participants to simply rephrase known challenges as a question beginning with the phrase "How Might We?" The "How Might We" method creates an environment for innovative solutions by reframing known challenges that surround your product, service, or initiative. The "How Might We" method helps you identify and capitalize on these hidden opportunities.

What would "x Company" do?   Borrowing from the Christian bracelet craze of the 1990s, "What Would Jesus Do?" (WWJD), I often ask leadership teams to consider: "What Would Amazon Do?" (WWAD). What would Amazon do to help you with your business problem? If you prefer, you could ask Google how they would solve the problem. Or how about Apple? Or how about Netflix? Any company could be applied to this exercise, depending on industry relevance, allowing leadership teams to learn from what is happening around us, and take action before they do.

These tools, when incorporated in traditional meetings, workshops, or leadership strategy sessions, free the mind from the traditional, limiting operational environment and offer an opportunity for people to flex their creative muscles. The results can be inspiring and lead to new ways of doing things.

Managing Change in the Organization

Culture is at the heart of digital business transformation. Shifting existing cultures to create a business environment that will embrace change and enable different groups within the organization to work together in a more coherent and effective way is critical to sustainable successful transformation. A key component to bringing about successful culture shift is the implementation of an effective change management program. Culture represents the "being" of an organization—why it exists, the purpose, and how it brings value to the market and customers. Change management is the "doing"—methods and approaches designed to prepare and support the people in an organization during critical change to mitigate disruption. This includes establishing the necessary steps for change, as well as monitoring pre- and post-change activities to ensure successful transformation.

Digital business transformation usually fails for human reasons and managing change effectively could spell the success (or failure) for transformation in any organization. Based on my experience, companies that are successful start by addressing change management early, and demonstrate commitment to change through clear communication of new strategic direction, the pathway to execute transformation, and new ways of working. The ability to respond and adapt to change within an organization has become a critical element for the survival of many modern societies in today's digital transformation environment.

We are describing this element separately from the phases described above because we view change management as more than just a deliverable—it is a proactive and ongoing process that needs to be lived in the organization. Unlike project management—where it is easy to assign schedules, visible goals, and concrete results—change management follows a more reactive and uncertain path. Failure in delivering digital business transformation strategies almost always comes down to a lack of preparation and strategy in managing the change for people in the organization. The organization's highest priority in adopting and implementing transformation initiative should be a watertight change management strategy.

Change management should be at the center of your digital business transformation strategy. However, in order to gain the required support for their plans, leadership teams often focus on the tangible elements of strategic development to secure commitment, funding, and resources. Managing change for the people in the organization by laying the right foundation from the start is frequently missed, left on the backburner or prioritized as "nice to have." Any transformation or change that affects the fundamental operation and structure of an organization should be led top-down. The role and impact of leadership teams during periods of change has been well documented in business management research.

Leadership teams frequently underestimate the amount of effort required to run change management programs, particularly when change teams are required to manage these initiatives while still carrying out their daily business responsibilities in parallel.

I have often observed leadership teams set change programs in motion, for example, video messages or emails that remind people of the strategic important of change, and then become distracted by other digital transformation initiatives or daily operational issues. These inauthentic approaches result in the rapid demise of change programs. Transformational change starts with an honest acknowledgement of the efforts required and leadership commitment to sponsoring these changes (Carucci 2021).

Additionally, what I have found in a practical way is that senior leadership teams have the most impact during strategic development and initiation of the transformation process. However, as the digital business transformation gradually shifts into building and implementing phases, it is middle management that has the most influence and impact. They are the key to any change, particularly as their support, commitment, and attitude toward the transformation initiatives has significant influence on the teams and wider employee base. As change leaders in the organization, middle management need to support their teams and individual employees through the transformation process. More importantly, middle managers support the leadership by building ownership and accountability for adoption of change and realizing the benefits of transformation. Collaboration and close alignment between senior leadership and middle management is a critical driver for successful change.

Leadership presence, guidance, and support signal to the employees a deep level of commitment and confidence in the future direction that the organization will take. It also depicts a unified leadership, which dispels fears, reduces anxiety, and helps employees feel more confident about the decisions that are being made to drive transformation. This is the only way to elicit and promote the culture needed to encourage the rest of the organization to embrace transformation.

In addition, transformation or change initiatives designed to make management and operations of the business more efficient may trigger anxiety or fear in employees. For example, leadership teams may see the introduction of automation into the core business function as a way to increase productivity and reduce turnaround times and costs. However, employees who work in these functional roles on the ground may face fears of being replaced, threatened with obsolescence, or a lack of direction. Organization restructuring as a result of digital transformation may result in employees who are moved to another position feeling indignant or confused about what was wrong with existing structures. It is not hard to imagine that the result in both these scenarios is lower morale, decrease in performance effectiveness, and potentially even loss of talent as employees may decide to leave.

Harvard Business Review (Musselwhite and Plouffe 2010) defines change readiness as the ability to continuously initiate and respond to change in ways that create advantage, minimize risk, and sustain performance. Such a continuous and integrated approach to change requires the coordinated participation of every person and level in the company, not just a few ambassadors, change agents, or leaders.

In practice, I have often relied on a holistic approach to change management during the digital business transformation execution as illustrated in Figure 7.3, where clearly defined change elements will drive the specific actions that need to be taken in the organization.

There are four closely related attributes of business culture that have a strong impact on enterprise maturity, collaboration, direction, and business value:

How we make decisions   This refers to the general leadership style in a business unit, department, or organization, as well as its impact on the company's ability to react quickly to incoming signals.

How we engage   This refers to the methods that groups and teams employ to collaborate internally and externally in order to achieve their objectives.

What we measure   These are the metrics for measuring organizational performance, as well as their impact on the focus and direction of a group or team's efforts.

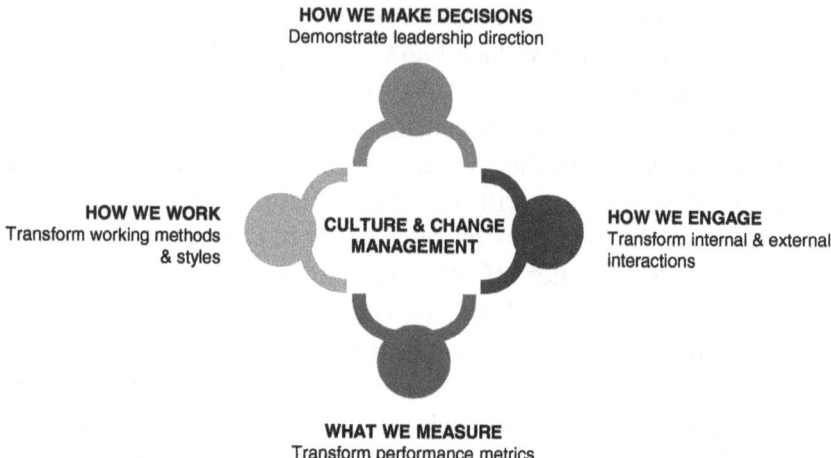

Figure 7.3 Change and culture management for complex transformation.
SOURCE: Kamales Lardi, 2019

How we work This is the working style of a group, which includes how solutions are developed and how problems are solved, has an impact on the group or team's perception of the business value it creates.

Every organization is unique, in terms of culture, behavior patterns, and values, so the transformation process will have different effects. The change management strategies that will be effective will also differ. At its core, successful change requires bold leadership that promotes proactive communication, a culture of learning, and a clear vision for what is needed. Transformation is an indispensable and fundamental element of business in today's world. However, by being willing to accept change, companies can turn change into opportunity instead of challenge. All of these changes bring some disruption to the organization, but its impact can be reduced significantly through managing the change for people.

Using the Culture Design Canvas, organizations can map their culture in order to make it clearer and understand the differences between the current and future states of the organization.

The workplace culture is the heart and soul of any organization, large or small. Despite the fact that it is intangible and soft, it can have a significant impact on the way people and businesses are moved. When you map out your workplace culture, it will be easier for people to understand what your organization is all about. It also aids in the identification of the difference between current and future conditions. Organizational culture is not static, but rather dynamic. The Culture Design Canvas is a flexible tool that allows you to capture the "soul" of an organization (see https://www.fearlessculture.design/blog-posts/the-culture-design-canvas).

Effective implementation of organizational change requires actions to change or adjust the internal components of the company, including internal processes, underlying technology or infrastructure, organization culture, structures, and capabilities, as well as key measures for success (refer to Figure 7.4). All of these elements, driven by the strategic direction for change, need to work in cohesion to support the transformation process.

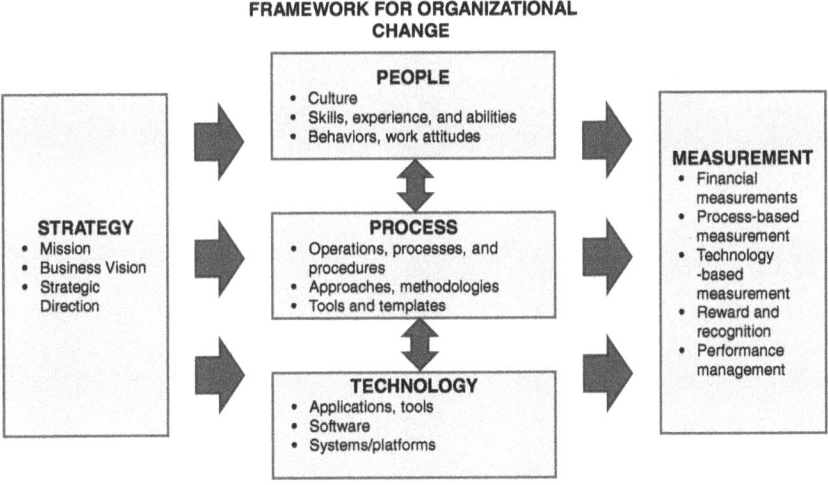

Figure 7.4   Elements of organizational change.
SOURCE: Kamales Lardi, 2019

Additionally, the nature of organizational change can be either adaptive or transformational (Miller 2020). Adaptive changes are small, gradual, and iterative shifts in the products, processes, workflows, and strategies implemented over time in order to improve and stay relevant. On the other hand, transformational changes have a larger scope and scale, and are often characterized by the unexpected shift from the status quo. Digital business transformation may involve either adaptive or transformation change, both of which need to be managed effectively for success. However, the approach to managing these changes varies, transformational change requiring more in-depth effort and bigger investment to drive the change.

The types of technology solution being implemented also impact the transformation or change journey. In Chapter 8, we address several top disruptive technologies, and its value to the digital business transformation journey.

Chapter 8
Emerging Technologies and Human-Centered Transformation

The world we live in today is digital, connected, and mobile. Digital technologies have invaded every aspect of our lives and the business world. Today, over 62% of the world's population have internet connection,

According to Peter Diamandis, cofounder and Executive Chairman of Singularity University, technology is now democratized. When something is digitized it begins to behave like an information technology. In the past, powerful technologies were mainly available to large organizations or governments. Now, technology has become more accessible and affordable to a broader range of people. This has also created a higher potential for entrepreneurs to disrupt industries and challenge the stronghold of large corporates. Globally, there are about 1.35 million tech start-ups trying to achieve exactly this.

Diamandis explains this disruption in terms of the 6D framework on how exponential technologies go from being deceptive, where few people see them coming, to disruptive, where they became the main way of doing things in the world, as shown in Table 8.1. (Diamandis and Kotler 2016).

Reflecting on this framework, we can take a lesson from the well-documented demise of Kodak. Once a market leader in the

Table 8.1   Six Ds of Exponentials

Digitized	Anything that becomes digitized enters the same exponential growth we see in computing. Digital information is easy to access, share, and distribute. It can spread at the same speed as the Internet. Once something can be presented in ones and zeros, it becomes an information-based technology and enters exponential growth.
Deceptive	When something starts to be digitized, its initial period of growth is deceptive because exponential trends don't seem to grow very fast at first. Exponential growth really takes off after it breaks the whole number barriers: 2 quickly becomes 32, which becomes 32,000 before you know it.
Disruptive	The existing market for a product or service is disrupted by the new market the exponential technology creates because digital technologies outperform in effectiveness and cost. Once you can stream music on your phone, why buy CDs? If you can also snap, store, and share photographs, why buy a camera and film?
Demonetized	Money is increasingly removed from the equation as the technology becomes cheaper, often to the point of becoming free. Software is less expensive to produce than hardware and copies are virtually free. You can now download any number of apps on your phone to access terabytes of information and enjoy a multitude of services at costs approaching zero.
Dematerialized	Separate physical products are removed from the equation. Technologies that were once bulky or expensive are now all contained in a smartphone that fits in your pocket.
Democratized	Once something is digitized, more people can have access to it. Powerful technologies are no longer only for governments, large organizations, or the wealthy.

SOURCE: Diamandis, P., and Kotler, S., "The Six Ds Of Exponential Organizations," 2016, Singularity Education Group

photography industry, Kodak was the first to invent the digital camera in 1975. However, the conservative leadership team decided to forgo it in favor of maintaining the traditional camera and film industry, which existed in a scarcity environment. Analog cameras have a significant dependency on the physical device, as well as film—both of which place a limitation on the number of pictures taken, related costs, and the need to have them developed by a specialized provider. The business model for this was heavily dependent on post-sales continuous investment, requiring consumers to buy and develop the film at a high margin. In 1996, Kodak had a $28 billion market capitalization with 95,000 employees. The company avoided risking their existing position, but did not recognize that their core business was shifting.

When digital cameras hit the market, consumers did not want to take pictures in the traditional way anymore. They were able to take an unlimited number of pictures, without having to be concerned about cost of film or developing pictures (see Figure 8.1). Unfortunately, Kodak went bankrupt in 2012 after a downward spiral. During that time, smartphones became increasingly popular, incorporating sophisticated digital cameras that were able to produce relatively high-quality images. Adoption of digital photography skyrocketed, and once digital photo-sharing apps hit the

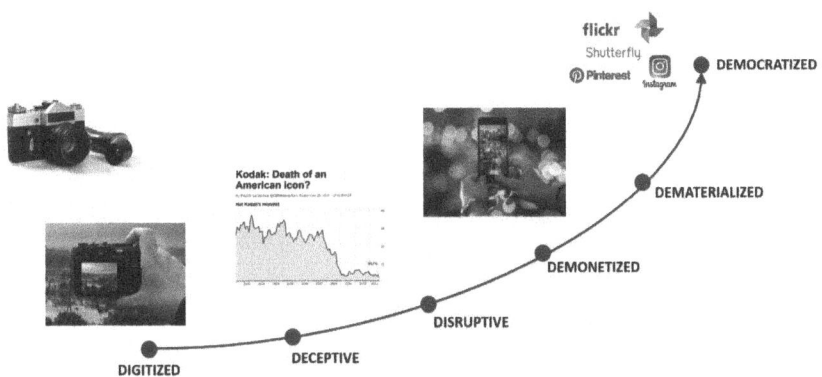

Figure 8.1   Application of Six Ds of Exponentials for photography industry.
SOURCE: Peter H. Diamandis LLC

market, consumers were able not only to take as many images as they liked, whenever, wherever, they were also able to share them online with millions of people. Now the photography industry that had been limited by physical scarcity shifted completely into an exponential environment.

In the same way that technology became democratized and disrupted industries, people are also increasingly heading towards the convergence of the physical and the digital (see Figure 8.2). At first, we developed technology to help solve problems, which in turn created new problems, so we developed more technology to solve those problems as well. Human-operated machines supported our daily activities and work, for example, in agriculture and industry. As we progressed, we started to outsource our physical and mental capabilities, with devices such as the mobile phone taking over the need to remember phone numbers and addresses. Once we gained more access to technology capabilities, we moved beyond human external devices and became more open to converging with technology to enhance our capabilities. Consider solutions such as prosthetics, bioprinting, or even the exoskeleton. As we venture deeper into convergence, where machines are gaining the ability to learn and develop themselves, we are seeing new innovations in human–machine interfaces. For example, two such innovations are developments at Neuralink, a brain–computer interface venture founded to allow humans to keep up with the advancements of technology,

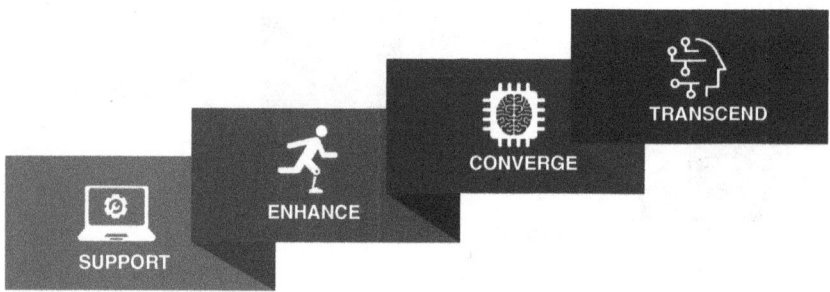

Figure 8.2   The convergence of humans and technology.
SOURCE: Singularity University

and Myndplay, an interactive mind-controlled media player and platform that will eventually gain the ability to read our brainwaves to execute commands. Many researchers believe that we will reach a point in the future where technology intelligence will surpass our ability to control and understand it. Personally I believe mankind will remain at the forefront, simply due to our humanity—empathy, creativity, and consciousness.

In any case, with each step forward, we have relinquished a small portion of ourselves in exchange for predictable, preprogrammed outcomes. Our tools could begin to perform larger and larger tasks on our behalf, allowing us to devote our time and energy to other, more desirable tasks.

A strong understanding of emerging technologies becomes increasingly critical as we move further into the hybrid world of digital and physical. This offers many organizations the opportunity to upgrade their business processes in such a way that their potential customers can connect with them very easily, as well as better assess how technology could be applied in business. Although there are a wide range of emerging technologies that impact the business world, this chapter will explore five top disruptive technologies that I assess as most relevant for digital business transformation implementation at the moment.

Artificial Intelligence

The story of "Clever Hans" stands out in my mind every time a discussion on Artificial Intelligence (AI) comes up (and it does come up quite often in my line of work). I often find myself in discussions with people—experts, industry leaders, or even friends and family—on AI and its potential impact in our lives. Almost everyone has an opinion on the topic, sometimes very strong and polarizing opinions, perhaps due to the popularity of referencing AI in mainstream media. Since the 1920s, Hollywood movies have been using AI as a protagonist, and often even antagonist, solidifying a mass perception of the technology, its capabilities, and potential impact on mankind. Movies such as *Her, Ex Machina, A.I. Artificial*

Intelligence, and more recently *Mother/Android*, tell stories of a powerful AI that has the potential to experience consciousness and overpower humans.

In the early 1900s, retired math teacher and horse trainer Wilhelm von Osten presented Europe with a fascinating discovery—a horse that was claimed to have performed arithmetic and other intellectual tasks (Craw 2021). Hans the horse would tap out answers with his hoof and reliably arrive at the correct answer to complex problems, including solving math problems, telling time, identifying days on the calendar, differentiating musical notes, and spelling out words. The discovery became the "viral" sensation of its time, as people gathered to see the intelligent animal perform these feats. However, there were also those who doubted the intelligence of Hans, and a commission was set up to assess if this was an elaborate hoax by von Osten. Although the Hans Commission conducted a thorough evaluation, they could not find evidence to support their suspicions. Eventually, what they discovered was far more intriguing—the horse provided correct responses by responding directly to involuntary cues in the body language of the human trainer, who was entirely unaware that he was providing such cues. This came to light when the commission discovered that Hans was not able to provide the correct response when the trainer was unsure of the answer.

Von Osten had attempted to reproduce human intelligence in a non-human entity, in this case the horse, working under the assumption that intelligence is uniquely embodied by humans, and that it could be created through training. It also excludes critical elements of intelligences that are developed through social, cultural, and experiential contributions. In my view, Hans the horse displayed emotional intelligence while reading the trainer's subtle reactions, a critical element in the realm of intelligence that cannot be excluded. Although there have been a multitude of developments in the field of AI, there is still a rather narrow view of what constitutes intelligence and how it could potentially be reproduced.

Artificial intelligence can be defined as the automation of cognitive processes—the science and engineering of making intelligent machines and using computers to understand human intelligence

(McCarthy 2004). It is a field that combines computer science with large, reliable datasets in order to facilitate problem-solving. Machine learning and deep learning are two sub-fields that are frequently mentioned in the context of AI. These disciplines are made up of AI algorithms that aim to develop expert systems that can make predictions or classifications based on the data they are fed.

It is important to understand the differences between AI (automation of cognitive processes); machine learning (an approach to achieve AI that teaches computers the ability to do tasks with data, without explicit programming); and deep learning (a specialized technique to implement machine learning). These terms are often used interchangeably in the business environment but carry distinct meanings and implications (see Figure 8.3).

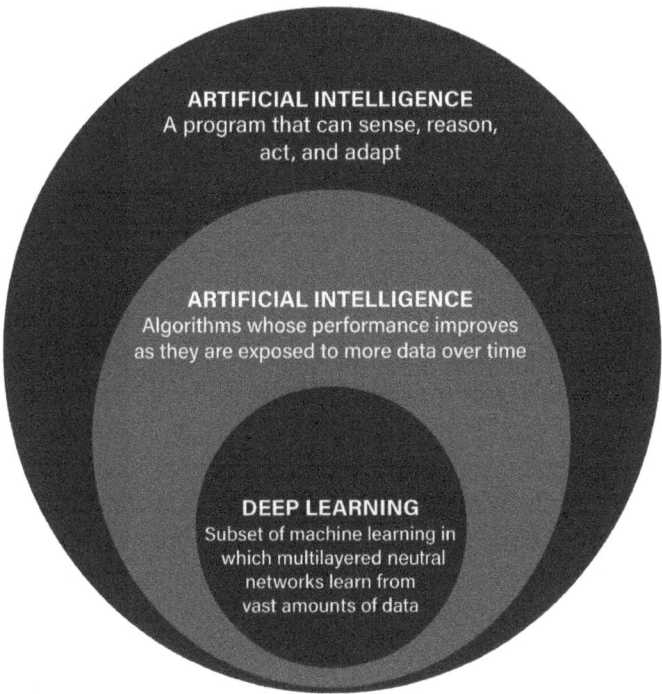

Figure 8.3 Distinction between AI, machine learning, and deep learning.
SOURCE: Stack Exchange community, 2019

Artificial Intelligence   Artificial intelligence, also known as machine intelligence, is intelligence that can be understood by another intelligence, as opposed to natural intelligence, which is demonstrated by humans and animals. Designing intelligent devices and systems that can creatively address problems that are often treated as human prerogatives. As a result, artificial intelligence refers to the ability of a machine to mimic human behavior in some way.

Machine Learning   Machine learning is a subset of AI that includes techniques that allow computers to recognize data and provide AI applications. In machine learning, a variety of algorithms (e.g., neural networks) are used to solve problems.

Deep Learning   This is also known as deep neural learning or deep neural network. Deep learning is a subset of machine learning that makes use of neural networks to evaluate various factors in a manner akin to that of a human neural system. It has networks that are capable of learning from unstructured or unlabeled data without the need for external supervision.

Research and development in AI has existed since the early 1950s. Although John Von Neumann and Alan Turing did not coin the term "artificial intelligence," they were the founding fathers of the technology that underpinned it, making the first transition from computers to nineteenth-century decimal logic. Since then, AI has developed in several waves (see Figure 8.4), as AI capabilities have increased over time.

It is only in the past decade that AI development has truly accelerated and its application exploded in the business world across industries. This is because we now have the right foundational elements in place to support this rapid acceleration—unparalleled processing power, unlimited storage capacity, global connectivity, low cost of technology production, as well as mass acceptance and adoption of emerging technology.

In more recent years, AI has made its way into the mainstream business landscape as a necessary component of the digital

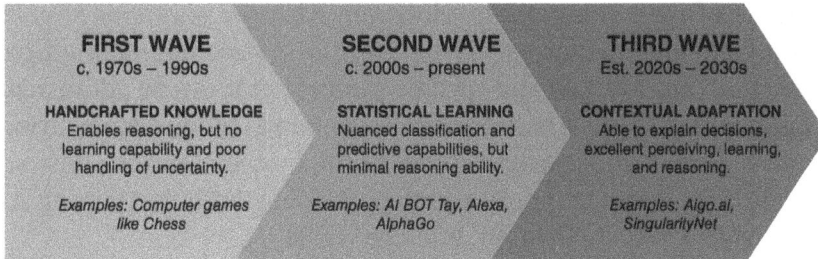

Figure 8.4   The three waves of AI.
SOURCE: Adapted from John Launchbury, 2016

business transformation roadmap. However, there is still a great deal of misunderstanding in the business world about what AI is and how it contributes to the digital transformation of an organization. Often, while advising leadership teams on their organization's digital transformation strategy, I encounter strategic goals that are too vague to realize, for example "implement AI-based solutions to realize xx% revenue gains" or "implement AI to increase productivity and efficiency." These broad, high-level strategic objectives reveal a lack of understanding of the capabilities of AI-based solutions and how they can truly add value to businesses (Lardi 2021).

Artificial intelligence solutions assist organizations in a variety of ways, including the automation of redundant activities, the digitization of processes, and the fast analytics of data, particularly large datasets. Organizations can also combine different datasets to gain rapid insights and knowledge that can be used to help them make more informed business decisions. Furthermore, AI-based solutions provide scalability in a traditional business environment that is otherwise relatively inflexible. For example, increasing the number of digital access points, such as chatbots and virtual assistants, to provide more hyper-personalized customer interactions and support.

Artificial intelligence is a critical emerging technology that could help organizations reimagine consumer experiences and business processes, as well as unlock revenue growth and cost savings at the expense of their competitors. However, AI-based solutions should not be implemented as part of the transformation roadmap unless there is an appropriate and specific problem that can be addressed. This means initiatives based on their value and viability by ensuring there is a clear, concise description of the problem and the desired outcomes before starting. In addition, the data, both for training AI systems and real application, must be viable.

Data is at the heart of AI systems, and it has become a prerequisite for the deployment of AI solutions, particularly for any type of data analytics application. Organizations need to determine whether the data is balanced (free of bias), exhaustive (captures all relevant variables), diverse (captures rare situations), and of sufficient volume, among other things. I usually advise companies to develop an effective data strategy at the outset of AI implementation, which includes the definition of data requirements; gathering or acquisition of high quality, contextual data; as well as storage, management, and security requirements.

In order to maximize AI-based solution applications in the organization, it is important to build a deep understanding of AI, as well as a culture of widespread acceptance of experimentation and uncertainty (Moioli 2022). The foundation of AI implementation is rapid learning, which means trying new things, learning, and adapting to create a "virtuous cycle of AI"—learning from data, experiences, successes, and failures. People are the foundation of AI-driven culture in the context of digital business transformation, which requires individuals with varying competencies in research, engineering, production, and strategy. You need to create a culture where diverse ideas are shared and adaptable problem solving is prioritized, in order to build AI-based solutions that deliver on the required business outcomes. Strong talent in AI is in short supply, and effective management of both internal and external resources will be required.

Leadership teams must ensure that the appropriate people and skills are available to define, implement, and maintain the AI systems that are being implemented. The roles and capabilities that will be required will be defined in accordance with the solution strategy that you wish to implement. If your organization wishes to implement an AI system for internal data analysis, it will be necessary to hire personnel with the necessary skills to ensure data privacy and confidentiality. As an alternative, if your company decides to develop Application Programming Interface (API) links for the necessary AI solutions, you may only require people with technical knowledge of APIs and connectivity to existing systems, which may be either internal or external resources. As an additional benefit to using external platforms, AI skills and capabilities can be acquired much more quickly than they would otherwise be.

Currently, AI solutions are primarily focused on business process problems and range from human augmentation to process improvement to planning and forecasting, allowing for superior decision-making and results. However, a key issue related to AI applications is bias, an anomaly in the output of machine learning algorithms, due to the prejudiced assumptions made during the algorithm development process or prejudices in the training data (Dilmegani 2022). This occurs due to cognitive biases that seep into the algorithms via designers unknowingly introducing them, as well as incomplete or nondiverse datasets. In developing AI-based solutions during the digital business transformation process, organizations can identify potential biases through human-related processes or technical solutions. However, a far more effective and critical approach would be to ensure diversity in the teams developing AI-based solutions. People, particularly diverse teams of people, are usually the first to notice bias issues; maintaining a diverse AI team can help you mitigate unwanted AI biases.

The worldwide revenues for the AI market, including software, hardware, and services, are growing fast and expected to break the $500 billion mark in 2023 (IDC 2022). Artificial intelligence should be viewed as a component of your organization's digital transformation journey, and it should only be implemented when it makes sense for the business goals that you are attempting to achieve.

Key Takeaways for the Human Side of AI:

• Build a culture of AI in the organization, ensuring key stake-holders and employees understand the value of AI application in business.
• Ensure underlying data strategy is developed in preparation for implementation of the AI-based solutions.
• Continuously communicate the role of AI in the organization's digital business transformation strategy and roadmap.
• Build internal capabilities and skills in the application of AI for business.
• Ensure a diverse group of people and skills are involved in the AI solution development.

Blockchain and Decentralized Technologies

I started to deep dive into the concept of blockchain in 2014, when clients began asking questions about its application in business. The hype around blockchain and cryptocurrencies was increasing, and companies, particularly in financial services, were becoming ever more curious about its impact. I started to deep dive into the topic and discovered a significant potential to disrupt businesses and industries.

Distributed ledger technology (DLT), more popularly known as blockchain, is a digital ledger system that stores information electronically in digital format. There is a slight difference between DLT and blockchain, in that blockchain is a type of DLT (in the same way not all sticky notes are "Post-it," not all DLTs are blockchain). However, blockchain has become the successful namesake that has overtaken the category of technology that it belongs to. Blockchain became popular for its critical role as the ledger system behind cryptocurrency systems, namely Bitcoin. However, the potential value and application of this technology has far surpassed its ties to cryptocurrencies. In the case of blockchain technology, the innovation is that it guarantees the fidelity and security of a record of data while also generating trust without the need for a third party to be trusted.

Historically, ledgers have existed since the beginning of modern times. Humanity has built a global economy based on these traditional ledger systems. We have been using ledgers to record the exchange of money or goods, as a way to secure trust and validity of these transactions. And TRUST is the fundamental currency of commerce—without it, we cannot continue to do business. Over time, as distances grew, environments and transactions became more complex, and we started to rely on multiple ledgers and eventually intermediaries and third-party validation to secure trust in the transaction, for example, the financial institutions, banks, notaries, and legal firms that we have today. These systems have several fundamental issues, which became apparent over time:

Lag time   We can instantaneously send an email to another person anywhere in the world, but it takes two to three days to transfer funds.

High costs   Our dependency on intermediaries has given them the ability to charge high fees for these transactions and exchanges.

Inefficient processes   Many of these interactions contain frictions that slow the process down, for example, physical documents to prove credibility, or physical signature.

Accessibility   There are over 1.7 billion people globally without access to traditional financial services, for example, people without proper identification documentation, from war-torn regions, from remote locations without access to physical banks, or below the poverty line.

Corruption   The more we started to depend on intermediaries to help us secure trust, interact with one another, and develop economically, the more powerful these central groups became, resulting in the risk of corruption. "Power corrupts, absolute power corrupts absolutely."

In 2008, someone decided to address these issues by developing a new financial ecosystem, one that would be fairer for all and more inclusive. Known only as Satoshi Nakamoto, the true identity of this person (or group) is unclear. This proposed new design for the global economic system did not rely on intermediaries to secure trust; instead it designed a ledger that was digital, open, and shared. By completely eliminating the middleman in transactions, the economic system saves time, reduces costs and risks, and increases peer-to-peer trust across a business network. This marked the launch of distributed ledger technology or blockchain.

Blockchain is basically a decentralized network of computers that records and stores data as a chronological series of events on a transparent and immutable ledger system. It can store anything of value, where the data stored acts as a single source of truth to the network. A key difference between a traditional database and a blockchain is in the way the data is organized. A blockchain is a collection of information that is organized into groups of information known as blocks, with each block holding a set of information. Blocks have specific storage capacities, and when a block is completely filled, it is closed and linked to the block that was previously filled, resulting in a chain of data known as the blockchain. All new information that occurs after that newly added block is compiled into a newly formed block, which will then be added to the chain once it has been completely completed.

By design, this structure creates an irreversible time line of data. When a block is filled, it is set in stone and becomes a permanent part of the time line being constructed. When a new block is added to the chain, it is given an exact time stamp to identify it as having been added to the chain. Additionally, when a block is created, the records are time-stamped and each block is given a "hash"—a unique mathematically generated identifier made up of numbers and letters. If the data is changed in any way, the hash will also be generated again, creating an auditable trail of records (see Figure 8.5). In addition, smart contracts, digital programmable contracts stored inside a blockchain, can be used to automate the execution of an agreement so that all participants can be immediately certain of the outcome, without any intermediary's involvement or time loss.

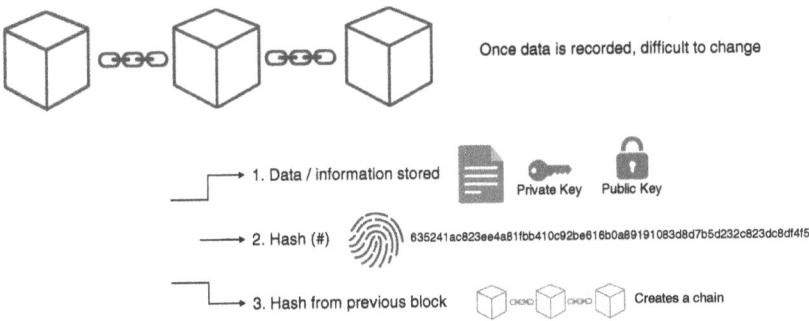

Figure 8.5   What makes blockchain unique?
SOURCE: Kamales Lardi, 2017

The blockchain is quite different from traditional databases that have been used for decades. Imagine that a traditional database is like a whiteboard located in a meeting room of an office. Anyone with access to that meeting room (i.e., admin users of the database) will be able to write on the whiteboard, modify, or erase its content. The blockchain can be likened to a book. Data stored is like the printed pages of the book. Once printed, it cannot be changed without damaging the book in some way. The pages are numbered and bound together, information is stored in a chronological order with page numbering. We cannot change the content or page order once the book has been bound and published. Just as a published book cannot be altered, a single node in the blockchain network cannot alter the information held within it.

Since its development, blockchain application has exploded across finance, business, government, and other industries. For example, peer-to-peer payment services such as Venmo are convenient, but have their limitations. Some services restrict transactions based on the location of the customer, while others charge a fee for the use of their services. Many of them are also vulnerable to hacking, which is not appealing to customers who are putting their personal financial information on the line in this manner. Blockchain technology has the potential to remove these roadblocks. In health care, there are many opportunities for blockchain-based solutions as well. For example, storing medical records on a shared blockchain in a secure way, allowing for it to be accessed by numerous individuals without undue privacy concerns or specifically identifying any particular patient.

The immutable nature of blockchain makes it an appropriate solution for provenance and real-time tracking of goods as they move and change hands throughout the supply chain. This became a personal passion for me, particularly the blockchain application in agriculture. In 2017, I was engaged by the Malaysian Palm Oil Council (MPOC) to conduct a feasibility study on the application of blockchain in the palm oil industry. The emergence of blockchain technology has had a transformative impact on the palm oil industry by creating an end-to-end traceable and verifiable supply chain. Over the next two years, I worked with the agency to develop a proof of concept, and to design and develop a pilot blockchain-based solution implementation (see Figure 8.6).

Establishing and maintaining the traceability of palm oil across the value chain was complex because of a multitude of factors—complex value chains with multiple middlemen, regulatory challenges, and lack of consumer awareness, among others. Without a transparent and robust system of traceability, it is almost impossible to establish if the palm oil was produced sustainably (following the "NDPE"—No Deforestation, no Peatlands clearing and no labor Exploitation practices). In the Malaysian palm oil industry, blockchain alleviated any doubts by creating greater transparency and auditability across the entire supply chain. Instead of having to trust the elements of a certification process where doubt may be cast due to manual processes or human error, blockchain technology offered an infallible validation system that secured trust.

During the design and development of these solutions, I came to truly appreciate the impact of the people side of technology implementation. Even at a national level, the palm oil industry includes a range of digital maturity—from plantations that utilized digital tracking, drone technology, and modern harvest management, to

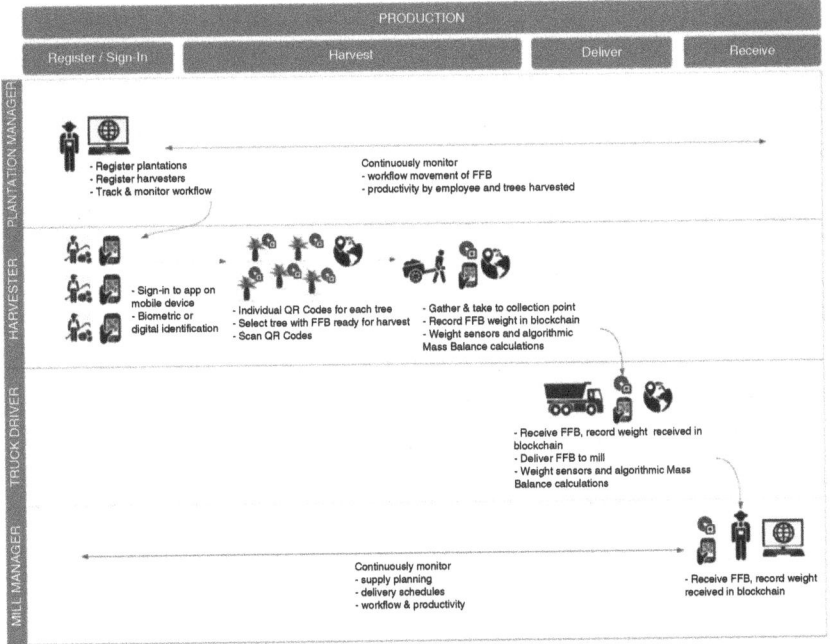

Figure 8.6   Provenance process overview on blockchain.
SOURCE: Kamales Lardi, 2019

smallholder plantations with zero connectivity (without 2G or 3G). Processes, from harvest to plantation management, as well as sustainability certification, included manual and human-dependent activities, and were subject to related weaknesses. The design principles of the blockchain-based traceability solution needed to take into account the poor connectivity, low-tech environment and users, as well as ensuring interoperability with various technologies utilized by each plantation. As an outcome, an interoperable solution was developed with a blockchain back end, and web-based and mobile app front end that was easy to use and built to fit into the existing daily processes of the plantations (refer to Figure 8.7).

In digital business, blockchain holds the promise of transactional transparency for businesses, as well as the ability to create secure, real-time communication networks with partners around

Figure 8.7   Blockchain-based traceability solution for palm oil industry.
SOURCE: Lardi & Partner Consulting

the world to support everything from supply chains and payment networks to secure mobile communications and health-care data sharing. More than 70% of all companies across industries consider blockchain to be part of their digital transformation strategy now or in the near future. The global spending on blockchain solutions will continue to grow in the coming years, projected to reach almost $19 billion by 2024 (IDC 2022).

Key Takeaways for the Human Side of Blockchain:
- Blockchain is not a silver bullet solution for all industry challenges. A good application of blockchain technology must solve real problems for the entire business or industry. As with any technology deployment, the unique properties of blockchain needs to be assessed against the business requirements for viability and strategic fit.
- Before development, ensure the blockchain technology is interoperable with the underlying technology infrastructure, as well as existing platforms and systems in the business ecosystem.

- The blockchain solution design should be intuitive and user-friendly, and specifically ensure that it fits with the existing human activities and daily operations in the business. This is particularly important with implementation in traditional industries such as agriculture, shipping, and logistics.

Extended Reality and the Metaverse

In 2007, I discovered a new world in online multimedia platforms. Second Life, a platform that allows people to create an avatar for themselves and have a second life in an online virtual world, was my favorite at the time. At the time, virtual worlds were still in their nascent stages and I was part of an internal corporate strategy team and presented the prospects of virtual worlds to the leadership team. There was more skepticism than curiosity, understandably for the time, when the hype-and-backlash cycle of emerging technologies cast a shadow of doubt over the potential business value of online and virtual platforms. In addition, the foundation technology at that time—computing power, internet bandwidth and speed, and headsets—was still rudimentary and did not offer the "wow" experience of the extended reality environments of today.

Extended reality (XR) really refers to three distinct sets of technologies—Augmented reality, virtual reality, and mixed reality. Augmented reality (AR) is the addition of digital elements to a live view, which is frequently accomplished through the use of a mobile device or smartphone camera. Snapchat lenses and the video game Pokemon Go are two examples of AR experiences. Virtual reality (VR), on the other hand, refers to a fully immersive experience in which the physical world is completely shut out. Users can be transported into a variety of real-world and imagined environments by using VR headsets or devices, such as the HTC Vive, Oculus 2, or the Microsoft HoloLens. In addition to AR and VR, there are other experiences that are growing in popularity. Mixed reality (MR) experiences combine real-world and digital objects, and have recently begun to gain traction. Extended reality incorporates a range of these technologies to enhance the senses, providing additional information about the actual world or creating completely unreal, simulated worlds to experience. Figure 8.8 describes the three forms of XR, which differ mainly in terms of the levels of immersion and interaction with the physical world.

Unlike VR, which is entirely digital, AR derives its strength from the combination of the virtual and real worlds. When used in conjunction with the physical world, AR aids in bringing things to life in new and exciting ways by superimposing digital information, objects, and tools over people's field of vision. This makes it appealing not only for gaming, but also for employee training and collaboration, which can be transformed into an extremely robust and immersive experience thanks to the use of AR. A more efficient and cost-effective method of facilitating teamwork and instruction than meeting in person can be found in AR for business applications. This has been particularly apparent during the global pandemic, which has accelerated AR's growth by necessitating remote working.

The use of AR can help businesses save time while also decreasing their environmental impact, which is a significant benefit to employees and customers who are becoming increasingly concerned about sustainability. The wow factor captures more of

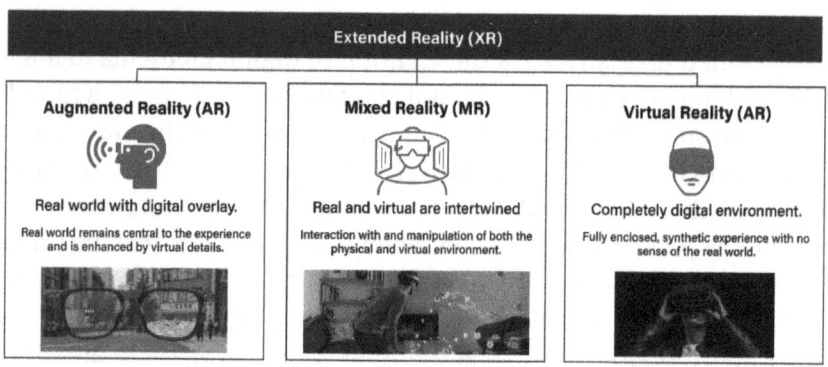

Figure 8.8 The forms of extended reality differ mainly in terms of their levels of immersion and interaction with the physical world.
SOURCE: Lardi

your attention, and there is a greater sense of immersion. Providing complex information in a way that is easy for the learner to understand is much easier than the reverse. It improves the effectiveness of training in terms of engagement, retention, and overall enjoyment. The genius of AR lies in the fact that it allows employees to "learn by doing" in these and countless other organizations. While AR can connect workers to real-time support from remote colleagues, it can also allow them to work alone without feeling like they are actually alone. Through the use of their webcam, remote trainers can assist learners in the use of technical equipment, while the trainer uses AR to overlay specific information on the learner's screen.

In the near future, I would envision a world where handheld and other devices will fully integrate AR, offering an impactful medium for forward-thinking companies interested in collaboration and training solutions that affect their bottom line. Mercedes Benz uses the Microsoft HoloLens to give technicians specialized training, reports CNET. Doing so improves collaboration and employee performance while decreasing turnaround time. Aerospace giant Boeing deployed AR to help airplane technicians reduce errors, while the US Marine Corps uses it to train for hostile, real-life scenarios without placing marines in actual danger. The National Aeronautics and Space Administration (NASA) teaches astronauts to repair the International Space Station (ISS) using the Microsoft HoloLens, perhaps the most ubiquitous AR device.

Virtual reality technology is also not new, although global adoption has increased significantly in recent years. This is due to more affordable VR devices, as well as increased application across various industries beyond video and online games. Health care provides great use cases for VR applications, for example, in treating phobias and lowering anxiety, as well as more advanced applications for medical practitioner training and even remote surgeries. These solutions go a long way to making high-quality medical treatments available at lower cost and in remote areas.

Virtual reality is a rapidly growing industry that currently accounts for a significant portion of all content produced around the world. Shipments of VR headsets have also increased significantly over the last two years. Virtual reality provides enterprise users and consumers with immersive experiences for collaboration and remote productivity. By 2024, VR revenues will have surpassed $12 billion on a global scale. Despite the fact that VR revenues were expected to decline slightly in 2020 as a result of Covid-19, demand has increased and is expected to continue to grow steadily. In addition, those engaging in social VR experiences spend over three hours a day in virtual reality (Social VR Lifestyle 2021).

The biggest hype word of 2021 was the term "metaverse," which ignited a lively global debate about what it represents, whether it is already here, and who will own it in the future. As XR devices, software, and platforms improve in terms of features, user interface, accessibility, and usability, the metaverse environments will keep developing beyond the hype and generate significant business value. The term metaverse does not really refer to one specific type of technology, but rather a broader shift in terms of how consumers interact with technologies. Extended reality devices, as well as other devices such as PCs, game consoles, and phones, offer these interaction capabilities to virtual worlds that are expanding rapidly, and integrating with one another. The rapid acceleration of the metaverse was also triggered by a functioning digital economy, enabled by blockchain technology and digital currencies.

However, despite the fact that it may appear to be a world of science fiction, in the metaverse it will be possible to carry out activities that include everything from attending virtual concerts to traveling and shopping to going to the movies and even trying on clothes. It has the potential to alter the way we work, as video calls will move away from the 2D of a screen and into a virtual call-in format. There are a range of big brands joining the metaverse, including Gucci, Sotheby's, Disney, Nike, and Zara, among others, to explore new ways of engaging with consumers. For example, Gucci launched two initiatives: Garden Archetypes, an immersive multimedia experience, and Gucci Garden, a unique and interactive virtual exhibition. Visitors' avatars become mannequins as they enter the "gardens," and they wander through the different rooms to absorb elements of the exhibition, retaining fragments of the spaces and ending a journey as unique creations.

As part of the digital business transformation roadmap, XR solutions offer the potential to increase digital capabilities of traditional processes and tasks by increasing efficiency, and reducing costs and time. For example, during the coronavirus pandemic, companies increased the use of augmented reality devices and applications to support front-line workers, reducing the need for physical contact and the number of people required. Extended reality solutions have the potential to change the way companies operate, for example (Vigros et al. 2021):

Manufacturing processes   They increase efficiency, reduce mistakes and need for on-site personnel in assembly and maintenance through real-time visualization of instructions, particularly critical in high-risk industries.

Product development   They significantly reduce costs and accelerate turnaround time for creative designing and prototyping process, as well as facilitating more intuitive and simpler interaction between the manufacturer and clients.

Collaborative working   Virtual meetings allow for deeper interaction and immersive collaboration between participants. Also, remote guidance and supervision allows for real-time support to on-site staff, reducing the need for travel, saving money and time, and reducing carbon impact.

Customer engagement   They engage and interact with customers on a deeper level through virtual try-ons, product visualization, virtual tours, post-sale training, and support.

According to a report by Bloomberg Intelligence, this digital environment has such excellent economic prospects that it is expected to reach $800 billion by the middle of this decade, and by 2030 that figure is expected to multiply to $2.5 trillion (Bloomberg 2021).

Key Takeaways for the Human Side of Extended Reality and the Metaverse:

- Sophisticated AR tools do require a high degree of integration to perform these specific functions. Extended reality tools perform best when connected with the broader upstream and downstream processes across the entire manufacturing value chain.
- Start with small scope applications to familiarize the employee base with these new ways of learning, interacting, and collaborating.
- Utilize education potential of XR capabilities to enable faster learning and education, particularly in upskilling workforce digital capabilities.
- Follow the developments of consumers on XR and metaverse environments to understand how to add value as a business.
- Engage with experts to understand the impact and capabilities of XR and metaverse environments, to properly leverage for business value.

3D Printing and Additive Manufacturing

In the simplest terms, 3D printing is the process of making three-dimensional solid objects from a digital file. The production of 3D printed objects is accomplished through the use of additive processes, where an object is created by adding successive layers of material on top of one another until the object is fully developed. With the use of 3D printing technology, complex shapes can be created with less material than would be required with traditional manufacturing methods. The concept of 3D printing can be traced back to the 1980s, and has since been developing as researchers and organizations have explored the technology for rapid prototyping and manufacturing.

In recent years, 3D printing methods and technologies, as well as materials that printers use have evolved significantly. The technology has improved, becoming more accessible and cost-effective for application across various industries, for example:

Prototyping and manufacturing The concept of "agile tooling" was created by 3D printing where modular processes enable quick prototyping and responses to tooling and fixture needs. There are numerous companies that offer mass customization services enabling consumers to directly customize objects through a simple web-based interface and order the resulting 3D printed objects.

Bioprinting This technology has created countless opportunities in the medical field, including versatile production of tissue-like structures for prosthetics, orthopedic implants, and more recently even printing artificial organs, helping to solve organ failure issues in patients faster. 3D printed tissues have also been developed for pharmaceutical testing as a cost-effective and ethical way of identifying side-effects and validating safe dosages.

Construction 3D printing technology is an increasingly popular method to produce architectural scale models for faster turnaround and reduced complexity. Beyond this, 3D printer houses and buildings are also being explored as cheaper and quicker alternatives to traditional construction, with completed constructions in Germany, Netherlands, the US, Africa, and other countries.

Digital fashion 3D fashion and virtual models have improved design workflows, setting new standards for the fashion industry. As the demand for more sustainable production increases, 3D digital fashion development eliminates unnecessary physical sampling and wasted materials, shortening production and lead times. Additionally, the digital and 3D printed fashion industry is set to skyrocket due to the increasing popularity of XR and metaverse environments.

Food   3D printed food is still in its infancy and has a long way to go before seeing a broader adoption from professionals and consumers. However, it is a growing industry, with Fused Deposition Modeling (FDM) printing that requires paste-like inputs extending possibilities for doughs, mashes, cheeses, frostings, and even raw meats.

Additive manufacturing is 3D printing at an industrial scale that brings significant flexibility and efficiency to design, production, and manufacturing operations. Apart from quicker turnaround and cheaper prototyping processes, additive manufacturing enables companies to produce lighter parts and provides increased opportunities for mass customization. Additive manufacturing is opening up new possibilities in business models, particularly in the areas of production and customization, as well as in a variety of other areas that have an impact on people's daily activities. 3D printing and additive manufacturing capabilities are now accessible to virtually anyone, as an increasing number of "fabshops" (fabrication shops) open up worldwide. From designers, entrepreneurs, and small businesses to large organizations, rapid prototyping, cheaper production, and customized manufacturing are now easily available. In combination with secure transactions offered by blockchain technology for exchange of proprietary designs and instantaneous payments, this becomes a powerful environment for global supply chain management.

Key Takeaways for the Human Side of 3D Printing and Additive Manufacturing:
- Close engagement with people involved in the processes that would utilize 3D printing and where additive manufacturing would be critical in order to truly understand how it could be applied.
- It is also essential to map the interaction of stakeholders to address the challenges of 3D printing adoption in practice.
- Beyond application in a specific part of the business, explore the potential for new or alternative business models enabled by transformed supply chain management.

Robotics and Automation

Debates on the impact of robotics and automation on the workplace have been perpetual since the Industrial Revolution. Fears regarding the rise of automation and intelligent machines replacing people in the workplace has only increased in recent years as companies adopt technology to improve productivity and efficiency while reducing costs. The use of industrial robots in factories around the world is accelerating at a high rate, with 126 robots per 10,000 employees (Edwards 2022). This is a new high average of global robot density in manufacturing industries, nearly doubling the number from five years ago (66 units in 2015).

Frequently, the impact of technology is seen as either a positive or a negative impact for the human workforce, particularly in the space of robotics and automation (Nunes 2021). The singular view that workers are either displaced by technology solutions, or technology allows for the creation (or reinstatement) of work, is limiting and falls short of the exponential potential of the digital economy. Alternatively, one should consider redesigning organization structures and roles, reskilling employees, and reviewing incentives to work in collaboration with robotics and automation solutions. By shifting people towards focusing on high-value and complex tasks, organizations have the opportunity to increase employee satisfaction and define a clearer, more meaningful purpose-driven environment.

Robotics and automation are often referenced together, but there is a clear distinction between the terms:

Automation   This involves the use of self-operating physical machines, computer software, or other technologies to perform tasks that would normally be performed by people. This process is designed to automatically perform a predetermined sequence of actions or operations, or to respond to encoded instructions without the need for human intervention.

Robotics   This is the study of the design, development, and application of robots to perform tasks. These are physical robots that perform actions in place of (or in imitation of) humans.

From an industrial perspective, robotics and automation are applied to automate physical processes, utilizing physical robots and control systems. A good example of this is the vehicle assembly line in a factory that utilizes automation with robotics. In recent years, the city of Dongguan, China, made new headlines for its "unmanned" factories. In 2019, the city announced that it had replaced 280,000 manufacturing workers with 91,000 robots, resulting in savings of $1 billion. During the global pandemic, as factory doors reopened and manufacturing capacity was restored, the demands for industrial robots further increased, with sales of industrial robots increasing by 19% from the previous year, reaching $1.2 billion in 2020. In addition, a growing number of service robots for low-touch environments, such as contactless service robots, disinfection robots, and temperature-taking robots, are becoming increasingly popular because they provide a safer environment for people.

More popularly applied across various industries are software automation solutions such as robotics process automation (RPA) and intelligent automation. The application of RPA solutions as a transformational tool is becoming increasingly simple, as service providers and vendors in this field are quickly growing. In addition, there are many low or no code platforms that offer user programmable solutions to accomplish automation of business tasks. The RPA software bots can copy routine and repetitive actions performed by employees, allowing them to focus on higher value tasks. The RPA approach is effective for automating rule-based tasks that use structured digital data, and offers cost and effort savings over time. The successful application of RPA depends on having a clear scope for it and being able to identify processes in the business value chain that would truly benefit. Last year, I was engaged with a financial service company in the process of implementing the digital business transformation strategy that we had defined. The transformation roadmap included a redesign of the business operating model and process landscape. The internal IT team had decided to engage an RPA vendor to implement automation of the operations processes, which would have resulted in a particularly high-cost solution with limited benefits. Alternatively, we initiated an operations centralization initiative, where processes were standardized, and optimization and specific areas for automation identified. This resulted in an overall improvement in turnaround time and cost savings, as well as operational services that could be leveraged by the overall business. Following this, the RPA solution could be applied to the future state optimized process landscape to enable the true promise of robotic automation.

The global RPA market value is expected to exceed $2.7 billion by 2023, propelled by its ability to provide higher efficiency, improved customer experience, and greater ease in managing business operations. Additionally, the Covid-19 pandemic positively impacted the RPA market as the virtual workforce and consumer demands in financial service, health care, and the public sector demanded efficient digital services.

Intelligent automation (IA), often referred to as hyperautomation, creates end-to-end business processes that think, learn, and adapt on their own. Intelligent automation applies advanced technologies such as artificial intelligence (AI), analytics, optical character recognition (OCR), intelligent character recognition (ICR), and process mining to achieve accelerated business outcomes with minimal human intervention. Ultimately, customer experience improvements and employee satisfaction are achieved through increased process speed and resilience, reduced costs, enhanced compliance and quality, as well as optimized decision-making (Bornet, Barkin, and Wirtz 2021). Solutions provided by IA effectively create a software-based digital workforce that, by collaborating with the human workforce, creates synergies and increased efficiency. The true value of IA can be seen in areas of the business where it augments human capabilities, for example, in rapidly processing large, hard-to-manage volumes of structured and unstructured data to derive critical insights for business operations.

Intelligent automation is a term that is often used in combination with other emerging technology concepts such as AI technologies. However, it is important to have clarity on how the concepts interact and overlap, in order to best apply to solutions (see Figure 8.9).

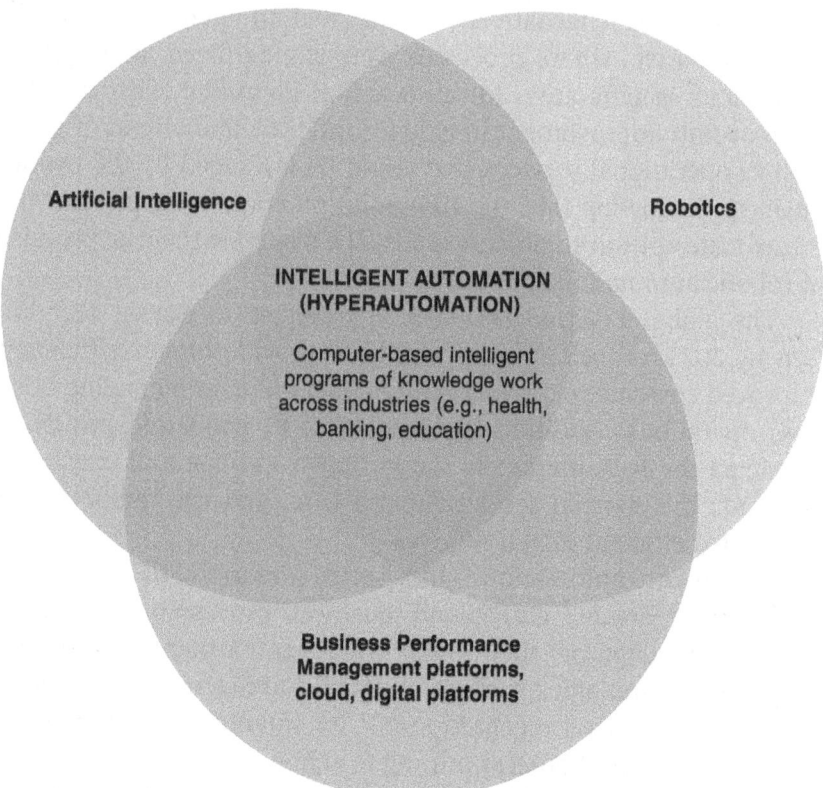

Figure 8.9   Positioning IA with other recent technology concepts.
SOURCE: Bornet, Barkin & Wirtz, Intelligent Automation, 2021.

Gartner has listed hyper-automation as a top strategic trend for 2022 (Gartner 2022). As part of the digital business transformation roadmap, hyper-automation and RPA offer powerful tools that deliver the efficiency, speed, and agility required to support the needs of digital business environment.

Key Takeaways for the Human Side of Robotics and Automation:

- Find the more appropriate or best use cases for robotics and automation that will provide a substantial return on investment within a reasonable time frame, typically 18 months or less.

- Ensure that there is a dedicated internal team that has a deep understanding for the business environment and capabilities of robotics automation solutions.
- Executive or leadership team support and sponsorship in delivering robotics and automation as part of the digital transformation roadmap is critical.
- Working in close collaboration with trained experts in this field (either external or internal) will be critical to ensure the solutions are implemented for sustainable success.
- In order to alleviate fears or misconceptions, develop clear communication for the internal workforce to explain the advantages of automation, its impact and role in the transformation journey, as well as any possible impact on jobs and skill requirements.

Convergence of Emerging Technologies

Although the development of each technology drives transformation, I believe the convergence and combination of these technologies have far greater potential for change across industries and businesses. Combining emerging technologies creates new solutions that not only leverage the advantages of each technology, but also accelerate solutions to achieve new levels of efficiency, performance, human ability, societal outcomes, and business results.

For example, the capabilities of blockchain technology, AI, and the Internet of Things (IoT) complement each other to create new solutions, products, and services. Connected devices and sensors enable real-time tracking and monitoring, as well as in-depth data gathering for a range of activities. However, enabling continuous communication, monitoring, and transaction between millions of heterogeneous devices creates challenges in data security and effectively analyzing large quantities of data. Blockchain technology offers a secure, decentralized environment to efficiently share data between peer-to-peer connected devices and sensors. This creates a more scalable, Cloud-based environment, providing secure audit trails of information coming from a sensor and making it easier to monitor connected devices. Blockchain technology also supports interoperability of various devices by providing a trusted, common communications layer, and smart contracts enable autonomous machine-to-machine transactions.

Similarly, AI-based systems do not have an accepted standard for data sharing. Today, data is produced at an exponential rate, by people, channels, platforms, and devices. In addition to the large amounts of data that could be analyzed, there still exist silos that make it hard to combine data points to derive insights. Additionally, AI models used for decision-making provide little transparency, where large datasets are pumped into systems and results are produced in the form of analysis, reports, or recommendations. This creates the issue of trust and questions the credibility of the system, particularly considering the existing challenges with datasets that may be incomplete, poorly sourced, inaccurate, or contain biases.

Combining these elements with the capabilities of blockchain technology offers clear data provenance and audit trails, transparency, and traceability of data, as well as interoperability across various platforms, and results in more trustworthy AI-based systems for analysis and decision-making. The combination of blockchain, IoT, and AI could be applied across various industries, such as in health care for patient data management, real-time care, and monitoring, as well as traceability of medicine and vaccine supply chains.

Chapter 9

Case Studies

Bayer Environmental Science

Erik Dam, Head of Global Procurement

Erik Dam is CPO, Head of Global Procurement at Bayer Environmental Science. He joined Bayer 10 years ago and worked first as Director Global Supply Strategies. He is an ExO Certified Coach, Consultant, Disruptor, and Speaker at OpenExO. Erik Dam has been leading the initiative to develop a high-tech approach for a focused vegetation and weed mitigation program along rail tracks with a significant reduction of chemicals necessary.

Bayer is a global enterprise with core competencies in the Life Science fields of health care and agriculture. Bayer aims to benefit people and improve their quality of life with its products and services, while creating value through innovation, growth, and high earning power. The products help address some of today's biggest challenges, including global population growth, an aging society, and the need to make efficient—and, wherever possible, sustainable—use of natural resources.

With its mission statement "Bayer: Science For A Better Life," Bayer aims to improve people's quality of life by preventing, alleviating, or curing diseases. This includes the provision of an adequate supply of high-quality food, feed, and renewable plant-based raw materials. For these endeavors, Bayer focuses on

275

developing and successfully commercializing innovative products and solutions based on scientific knowledge.

According to Erik Dam, any innovation needs vision and purpose. Starting in 2013, Bayer started an innovation cycle called vision 2020. Bayer regularly undertakes such revisions of their strategy and business operations. One central conclusion from vision 2020 was the fact that the revenue was much more tied to services and not just the sale of products. Previously, Bayer saw its strength in the development and sales of products. With vision 2020, Bayer realized that the revenue streams for services were far more significant. For instance, Bayer can sell chemicals for the weed control on golf courses. Compared to irrigation the costs for the chemical products are small. On the other hand, offering a service to maintain weed control allowed Bayer to increase the revenue per golf course significantly. At the same time, weed control management as a service aims to reduce the products used.

At the same time—starting 2013—Bayer looked at ways to make use of digitalization for the development of the business. As a third pillar, the development of personal resources was identified as a focus. In his role as Global Supply Strategist, Erik Dam became involved in the rethinking of weed and pest control management along rail tracks. Originally, specialized trains would spray chemicals evenly along all train tracks to control pests and weed. This would lead to a situation where chemicals were used in places where there was no unwanted growth. At the same time, chemicals would enter into unwanted spaces, for instance, when a train would cross a river over a bridge. The project started as an Edge Initiative and was executed by the respective business unit. Instead, Erik Dam teamed up with another internal resource who could see the benefits of the new idea. At the same time, a start-up of three new graduates began to work on setting up a company. The funding was taken from an internal project where the budget existed to build a conventional train composition.

This team developed the vision to create a service that would allow for deploying the chemicals only where the need has been identified, whereas on other surfaces no chemicals would get sprayed, leading to a reduction in use of such chemicals by 50–80%. The benefit of the initiative is evident since such chemicals impact the environment. The example illustrates how vision and purpose are the drivers for innovation. This new solution set a new global standard for pest and weed management along train tracks. It turned out to create one of the most profitable business solutions that Bayer had developed in recent years and is an example of a service offering, instead of a product, that is sold to Bayer's customers.

To develop the algorithms that determine where to spray, photographs of each weed under every possible condition such as daylight, darkness, or rain are taken. In other words, a plethora of images are collected to make sure that the system recognizes which type of weed is growing in order to choose the right chemical product to apply. This allows for establishing along the rail track system where and when maintenance is needed. In other words, additional value is created that was not originally intended or planned.

Developing this initiative as an Edge project allowed for a flexible and focused approach. Difficulties arose when the business unit realized that the new system was economically promising. On the one hand, there is resistance from those who might lose revenue in their own existing business solution even though overall the company will do better with an innovative new solution. On the other hand, once success is imminent, others want to appropriate the opportunity. This slowed the development down. Cooperation between big corporate players and start-ups turns out to be difficult when start-ups feel impeded in their drive to innovate and when the corporate player tries to impose too much control. These are the reasons why collaboration often fails or the corporate player ultimately takes control over start-ups.

Erik Dam points out that the change of the services offered and the development of the information technology has a fundamental impact on the requirements for employees working in the different branches of a company. They must be able to work with data and algorithms, to understand and use a completely different terminology. Therefore, the employees have to be ready to develop new skills and the company might need to hire new employees with other skillsets. This does not only apply to those employees who develop or sell new products and services. Human Resources, Marketing, or Legal need to understand and work with the changes as well. For instance, the Legal department needs to understand the implications of a new set of IP-related challenges. Human Resources has to understand what skillsets are required. These changes can only happen if the employees display a high level of flexibility. If the vision and purpose are understood and shared employees are ready to put in the extra effort needed.

If innovation is only sought in the existing organization, you can't expect that the teams will develop completely new solutions, but they will rather tend to stick to their core competencies. Whoever is developing new chemical products will endeavor to target more efficiently a particular problem presented to them. That is where Edge Initiatives can provide new insights and groundbreaking innovation. External parties are not bound by corporate guidelines and bring new perspectives. Erik Dam sees the incentive culture in the corporate environment as a potential impediment to innovation. Most targets relate directly to revenue streams of the existing business. Innovation on the other hand will only lead to future revenue that can't be measured immediately. On top of that, businesses might resist innovation if they think that the business solution that is impacting their current bonuses with the revenue stream should not be made obsolete or be impaired by new, innovative solutions. Erik Dam is arguing that innovation should be more financially rewarded than it is today since it impacts the future chances of the company in the long run.

data42 at Novartis

Nazim Ünlü, Head of People & Organization

Nazim Ünlü is Global HR Head of the data42 program at Novartis. He has worked for the last 13 years for Novartis in different roles relating to HR. The data42 program shows Novartis' intent to go big on data and digital. Novartis is betting on both human inquisitiveness and computer expertise to harness the wealth of its digital research and development platform, data42. As Global HR Head for data42, Nazim Ünlü is responsible for the setup of the team working in the program.

Novartis aims to reimagine medicine to improve and extend people's lives. As a leading global medicines company, Novartis wants innovative science and digital technologies to create transformative treatments in areas of great medical need. In Novartis' quest to find new medicines, they consistently rank among the world's top companies investing in research and development. Novartis products reach nearly 1 billion people globally while finding innovative ways to expand access to the latest treatments. About 125 000 people of more than 140 nationalities work at Novartis around the world. With data42, Novartis is leveraging data science to reimagine research and development.

The development of new drugs and treatments is very costly and takes a lot of time. Novartis aims to improve on reducing costs and developing new drugs and treatments in a shorter time frame by making use of data. With the initiative data42 Novartis—and in the future even its competitors—will aggregate as much data as possible in a data lake which facilitates the development of new drugs and treatments.

According to Nazim, the issue in Big Pharma companies is the mindset of its employees that is strongly driven by regulatory requirements. On top of that, employees are used to working with fixed roadmaps and predefined goals. Within a very highly regulated internal corporate framework, to follow all guidelines and respect the form often takes priority over innovation and flexibility.

Novartis was looking for a different mindset for their digital initiative in connection with building the data lake for data42. Therefore, Novartis was not looking to hire employees with a track record within Big Pharma companies who are used to working within a corporate framework, but rather talents that would not have this type of background. The goal was that the team of data42 would resemble the mindset of a start-up environment instead of a corporate department. When setting up the team, diversity and inclusion were an important consideration. This included not only both sexes, but also roles and capabilities. This meant that Novartis hired talent for data42 that they normally would not hire. The start-up mindset entails a more flexible approach with a less predefined outcome compared to an initiative-driven approach within the corporate framework that is based on clearly predefined milestones.

At the same time, Nazim pointed out that the company culture of Novartis—in particular under the influence of the CEO Vasant Narasimhan—has changed significantly overall. Novartis encourages its employees to take risks and they are allowed to fail. Success is not required at all costs, but instead people are allowed to make mistakes and learn from them.

Regarding the transformation from a HR and leadership perspective, Nazim pointed out the following changes. Leadership accepts that it doesn't know everything and admits its own shortcomings by asking for support from specialists. This is expressed in the goal to hire the experience people have to offer instead of just filling predefined boxes within which the employees have to perform. It is accepted that younger employees who join might display more skills and capabilities than older employees. At the same time, it is important not to forget the present when planning for the future, since the employees live in the present—with their families, friends, and work colleagues. And the present has an impact on their capabilities to plan for the future.

The pandemic led to a situation with many more unknowns. While productivity and use of remote exchange increased, leadership became more challenging when direct interaction with the team in the office was reduced or excluded. More than ever, leaders needed to demonstrate vulnerability and empathy to effectively engage with their teams. Nazim suggests that every leader and every organization should develop his or her own type of authentic leadership. Copying other organizations is not advisable.

Haier

Vincent Rotger, President Haier France, Chief Strategy Officer
Haier Europe

Vincent Rotger has been the General Manager of Haier Europe since September 2015. He is a French national and the first European to hold this position at Haier Europe. His appointment reinforces the commitment of Haier to becoming a major player in the European market through a localization strategy. Before that, he served in an American corporation for almost 20 years, serving last as Business Unit Director for France.

Haier Europe is part of Haier Smart Home, the number one group globally in home appliances and among the Fortune Global 500 Companies. Haier Smart Home is present in all five continents with 25 industrial parks, 10 research and development centers, and approximately 100,000 employees. With an operating revenue worth €26.5 billion in 2020, the company's global sales network covers more than 160 countries.

Haier's vision is to become the global leader in IoT for smart home appliances. Haier Smart Home was the first Chinese company to enter the D-Share Market of the China Europe International Exchange (CEINEX D-Share Market) in Frankfurt in October 2018, with the aim of promoting the brand and supporting its business growth internationally and in Europe, where the company counts on successful brands such as Candy, Hoover, Haier, Rosières, GE Appliances, and Fisher&Paykel.

Having worked in the US for a big corporation for over 20 years, Rotger did not want to set up a start-up himself. Instead, he joined Haier because he felt that the company culture and the mindset within Haier would be very appealing to him.

Haier is a market leader in the development and production of electronic goods in China and is entering the European market. The approach and structure within Haier differ significantly from the traditional corporate model that entails a hierarchical structure. Haier is based on individual microenterprises (MEs). MEs consist typically of 5–15 employees. Each ME is developing a solution that is focused on customer needs. Haier aims to include such solutions in the ecosystems of their electronic products. Each ME has internally all relevant functions that you would find in a corporation, such as R&D, Marketing, HR, CFO, etc. Haier provides the funds and coaches the MEs. Unlike traditional corporate structures, the responsibility lies with the MEs while the management only advises the teams. There are centralized services within Haier which support MEs such as logistics, financial planning, etc. However, even these internal services are in competition with outside providers and the MEs are free to choose other providers if they are not happy with what Haier has to offer. The internal functions benefit from a feedback loop and understand what the needs of the MEs are. Therefore, they will tailor and adapt to the needs and requirements of the MEs.

This decentralized structure leads to an agile and innovative culture. There is no need to apply internally for approval at every step and turn, but the MEs can—supported by the advice of the management—decide quickly how to move forward. This system relies on three pillars:

- Self-motivating: The MEs set their own goals and are motivated themselves to reach them.
- Self-evolving: The MEs themselves develop their solution within the framework defined with the management.
- Self-funding: Each ME is a profit center and the team member will share in the financial success of their solution or product.

For Vincent Rotger, the role that he has to fill is much more demanding than in a traditional organization where he has three or four direct reports. Instead, he has multiple direct reports, one for each ME. With five MEs in Europe he therefore has more than 15 direct reports that he advises and supports. He has to address all relevant functions within the MEs.

Unlike traditional corporations, Haier does not have a top-down organization. Each ME is an entity with full responsibility for their enterprise. The teams have to present their product or service and their plan to the management. They have full responsibility over their budget. The management only approves while checking that the planned activity is aligned with the overall strategy of Haier. Furthermore, MEs have to respect the guidelines regarding the use, development, and positioning of multiple brands and they cannot change them. Finally, the management does assess whether the planned financial targets are feasible to start with and whether the ME's performance is living up to the expectations of Haier.

For Haier, the collaboration with start-ups is essential for their success. Haier could try to find out itself what the new consumer trends are. Some research is done internally. But Haier is relying strongly on start-ups to identify new customer needs, requirements, and emerging trends. There is a very high number of start-ups who try to seek and find such trends. Those start-ups which have found an innovative solution will display traction that Haier can pick up. Once such an opportunity is identified, Haier can tailor a solution, preferably making use of one of its ecosystems such as their IoT solutions for electronic goods like fridges or ovens. Vincent Rotger pointed out the example of JOW: A start-up developed an app that combined the idea of menu options for the week and planning for the purchasing of the food items to avoid food waste. The app proposes what has to be ordered online, based on the needs and preferences of each customer. Since the fridge is connected and the content of the fridge is known to the system, only the missing items are ordered. Based on the menus, the stove or oven is automatically programmed since these appliances are connected via IoT as well.

Vincent Rotger also explored aspects of successful leadership. As a basis, a leader has to know themselves to start with. To be successful requires being open-minded. This is also necessary to build diversity in teams. Diversity within your team ensures that you are getting richer in perspective and experience. Most importantly, you need freedom to thrive as a leader. This is only possible if your values align with the values of the company that you work for. To be authentic and avoid conflicts it is important that a leader is doing what they are passionate about. Then they do not have to worry about how to move forward but instead there is an immediate alignment.

References

Introduction

Montini, L. (2014). Then and now: how long it takes to get to a $1 billion valuation (infographic). *Inc. Magazine* (October). https://www.inc.com/laura-montini/infographic/how-long-it-takes-to-get-to-a-1-billion-valuation.html#:~:text=Many%20of%20today's%20startups%20just,he%20started%20the%20company%201913 (accessed 19 March 2022).

Vincent, J. (2021). Amazon is opening a hair salon in London to trial new technology. *The Verve* (April). https://www.theverge.com/2021/4/20/22393476/amazon-salon-london-concept-store (accessed 19 March 2022).

Chapter 1

Artificial Intelligence Index Report 2021 (2021). https://aiindex.stanford.edu/report/. https://aiindex.stanford.edu/wp-content/uploads/2022/03/2022-AI-Index-Report_Master.pdf.

Digital 2022 Global Overview Report (2022). We are social and hootsuite (January). https://wearesocial.com/uk/blog/2022/01/digital-2022-another-year-of-bumper-growth-2/ (accessed 19 March 2022).

Dormehl, L. (2022). Inside the U.K. lab that connects brains to quantum computers. digitaltrends.com (February). https://www.digitaltrends.com/computing/quantum-brain-network/ (accessed 19 March 2022).

Galindo, L., Perset, K., and Sheeka, F. (2021). An overview of national AI strategies and policies. Committee on Digital Economy Policy (CDEP), OEDC Publications.

Hajro, N., Hjartar, K., Jenkins, P., and Vieira, B. (2021). What's next for digital consumers? McKinsey Digital (May). https://www.mckinsey.com/business-functions/mckinsey-digital/our-insights/whats-next-for-digital-consumers (accessed 26 March 2022).

Jennifer (2020). What is the low touch economy? Board of Innovation (April). https://www.boardofinnovation.com/blog/what-is-the-low-touch-economy/ (accessed 20 March 2022).

Kantar BrandZ™ (2021). Top 100 Most Valuable Global Brands Report 2021. https://www.kantar.com/en-cn/campaigns/20.

McKinsey Global Survey of Executives (2020). How Covid-19 has pushed companies over the technology tipping point - and transformed business forever (October). https://www.mckinsey.com/business-functions/strategy-and-corporate-finance/our-insights/how-covid-19-has-pushed-companies-over-the-technology-tipping-point-and-transformed-business-forever#:~:text=their%20companies%20have%20accelerated%20the,by%20a%20shocking%20seven%20years (accessed 26 March 2022).

Montini, L. (2014) Then and now: how long it takes to get to a $1 billion valuation (infographic). *Inc. Magazine* (October). https://www.inc.com/laura-montini/infographic/how-long-it-takes-to-get-to-a-1-billion-valuation.html#:~:text=Many%20of%20today's%20startups%20just,he%20started%20the%20company%201913 (accessed 19 March 2022).

Vailshery, L. S. (2022). Voice recognition market size worldwide in 2020 and 2026 (in billion U.S. dollars). Statista.com. https://www.statista.com/statistics/1133875/global-voice-recognition-market-size/ (accessed 19 March 2022).

Vincent, J. (2021). Amazon is opening a hair salon in London to trial new technology. *The Verve* (April). https://www.theverge.com/2021/4/20/22393476/amazon-salon-london-concept-store (accessed 19 March 2022).

Chapter 2

Bray, P. (2020). The importance of people in executing digital transformation. *Technology Magazine* (17 May). https://technologymagazine.com/cloud-and-cybersecurity/importance-people-executing-digital-transformation (accessed 26 October 2021).

CNBC (2022). Roughly 47 million people quit their jobs last year: "All of this is uncharted territory." https://www.cnbc.com/2022/02/01/roughly-47-million-people-quit-their-job-last-year.html.

Cook, I. (2021). Who is driving the great resignation? *Harvard Business Review* (15 September).

Deloitte Global Human Capital Trends (2017). *Rewriting the Rules for the Digital Age*. Deloitte University Press.

Gartner (2022). Worried about employee turnover? Ask these 6 questions to size your risk. https://www.gartner.com/en/articles/worried-about-employee-turnover-ask-these-6-questions-to-size-your-risk.

Gomez, K. (2018). *Welcome to Generation Z*. Deloitte.

Hancock, B. and Schaninger, B. (2022). Back and forth: Covid-19's impact on business in 2021 - and today. https://www.mckinsey.com/business-functions/people-and-organizational-performance/our-insights/back-and-forth-covid-19s-impact-on-business-in-2021-and-today (accessed 23 February 2022).

International Data Corporation (IDC) (2021). New IDC spending guide shows continued growth for digital transformation as organizations focus on strategic priorities (November).

Ismail, S. (2014). *Exponential Organizations*. Singularity University.

McGowan, H. and Shipley, C. (2020). *The Adaptation Advantage*. Wiley.

McGrath, R.G. (2019). The pace of technology adoption is speeding up. https://hbr.org/2013/11/the-pace-of-technology-adoption-is-speeding-up (accessed 9 November 2021).

McKinsey & Company (2020). How Covid-19 has pushed companies over the technology tipping point - and transformed business forever (October). https://www.mckinsey.com/business-functions/strategy-and-corporate-finance/our-insights/how-covid-19-has-pushed-companies-over-the-technology-tipping-point-and-transformed-business-forever (accessed 26 October 2021).

McKinsey Global Institute (2016). Independent work: choice, necessity, and the gig economy. Gig Economy Data Hub (October).

Mastercard Thought Leadership (2020). Fueling the global gig economy: how real-time, card-based disbursements can support a changing workforce (August).

MIT News (2021). MIT Professor Claude Shannon dies; was founder of digital communications. https://news.mit.edu/2001/shannon#:~:text=CAMBRIDGE%2C%20Mass.,He%20was%2084%20years%20old.

Moussa, M., Newberry, D., and Urban, G. (2021). *The Culture Puzzle*. Berrett-Koehler Publishers.

Saldanha, T. (2019). *Why Digital Transformations Fail*. Berrett-Koehler Publishers.

SalesForce (2020). *State of the Connected Customer* (4th edition). https://www.salesforce.com/resources/research-reports/state-of-the-connected-customer/ (accessed 1 February 2022).

Shannon, C. E. (1948). A mathematical theory of communication. *The Bell System Technical Journal* 27(3): 379–423.

Smet, A.D. and Schaninger, B. (2021). From the great attrition to the great adaptation. https://www.mckinsey.com/business-functions/people-and-organizational-performance/our-insights/from-the-great-attrition-to-the-great-adaptation (accessed 23 February 2022).

Tappe, A. (2022). A record number of Americans quit their jobs in 2021. *CNN Business* (February).

Unitonomy (2022). How to start to change organizational culture. https://unitonomy.com/how-to-start-to-change-your-organizational-culture/ (accessed 26 October 2021).

Upwork (2013). Millennials and the future of work. http://workplaceintelligence.com/millennials-future-work-study/ (accessed 9 November 2021).

Warr, A., What makes a good digital transformation? (2021). https://www.bcs.org/articles-opinion-and-research/what-makes-a-good-digital-transformation/ (accessed 30 October 2021).

Westerman, G., Bonnet, D., and McAfee, A. (2014). *Leading Digital. Turning Technology into Business Transformation*. Harvard Business Review Press.

Wiles, J. (2021). Great resignation or not, money won't fix all your talent problems (9 December). https://www.gartner.com/en/articles/great-resignation-or-not-money-won-t-fix-all-your-talent-problems (accessed 25 June 2022).

Chapter 3

Adobe Team Life (2021). Adobe named a world's best workplace for sixth year in a row (October). https://blog.adobe.com/en/publish/2021/10/19/fortune-worlds-best-workplace-sixth-year (accessed 26 February 2022).

Clarke, L. (2017). Insights into Adobe's award winning company culture. https://inside.6q.io/adobes-award-winning-company-culture/#:~:text=Since%20Adobe's%20establishment%2C%20their%20worldwide,offering%20staff%20huge%20company%20perks (accessed 18 November 2021).

Conley, C. (2017). *PEAK: How Great Companies Get Their Mojo from Maslow*. Wiley.

ERT Editor (2021). Haier – the number 1 global major appliance brand for 12 years running. www.ertonline.co.uk.

Fischer, W. (2022). Zhang Ruimin's vision of leadership for the future. IMD (9 February).

Forrester Consulting Thought Leadership (Commissioned by Adobe) (2018). The business impact of investing in experience. https://business.adobe.com/content/dam/dx/us/en/solutions/industries/manufacturing/pdfs/adobe-impact-of-cx-spotlight-manufacturing.pdf (accessed 25 June 2022).

Forbes (2021). How Adobe is leading with compassion and reimagining marketing for the post-pandemic future. https://www.forbes.com/sites/adobe/2021/11/01/how-adobe-is-leading-with-compassion-and-reimagining-marketing-for-the-post-pandemic-future/?sh=3233056d2c9e (accessed 18 November 2021).

Haier.com (2021). Haier originates new mechanism for ecosystem enterprise succession. Haier.com (5 November). https://www.linkedin.com/company/haier/.

Hamel, G. and Zanini, M. (2018). The end of bureaucracy. *Harvard Business Review* (1 November).

Hemerling, J., Kilmann, J., Danoesastro, M. et al. (2018). *It's Not a Digital Transformation Without a Digital Culture*. Boston Consulting Group.

Ismail, S., Malone, M.S., and Van Geest, Y. (2014). *Exponential Organizations*. Diversion Publishing Corp.

Ismail, S., Palao, F., and Lapierre, M. (2019). *Exponential Transformation: Evolve Your Organization (and Change the World) With a 10-Week ExO Sprint*. Wiley.

Jordan, J. and Orlick, A.L. (2019). Developing people in a time of digital disruption. https://www.imd.org/research-knowledge/articles/Developing-people-in-a-time-of-digital-disruption/.

Lu, G. and Mu, D. (2020). Haier's adaptive strategy wins in the face of Covid-19 challenges. Forrester Blog (15 June).

Moussa, M., Newberry, D., and Urban G. (2021). *The Culture Puzzle*. Berrett-Koehler Publishers.

Neelima (2015). *Haier Is Disrupting Itself – Before Someone Else Does*. CKGCB Knowledge.

Rowles, D. and Brown, T. (2017). *Building Digital Culture*. Kogan Page.

Ruimin, Z. (2007). Raising Haier. *Harvard Business Review* (1 February).

Sengupta, J. (2017). The digital reinvention of an Asian bank. *McKinsey Quarterly* (20 March).

Stackpole, T. (2021). Inside IKEA's digital transformation. *Harvard Business Review* (4 June).

Sundararajan. A. (2014). What Airbnb gets about culture that Uber doesn't. *Harvard Business Review* (27 November). https://hbr.org/2014/11/what-airbnb-gets-about-culture-that-uber-doesnt (accessed 15 November 2021).

Tuff, G. and Goldbach, S. (2018). *Detonate: Why – And How – Corporations Must Blow Up Best Practices (And Bring A Beginner's Mind) To Survive.* Wiley.

Wagner, R. and Harter, J.K. (2006). *12: The Elements of Great*, Gallup Press.

World Economic Forum (2021). *Digital Culture: The Driving Force of Digital Transformation* (June). https://www.weforum.org/reports/digital-culture-the-driving-force-of-digital-transformation (accessed 23 November 2021).

Zappos Culture Book (2022). https://www.zapposinsights.com/culture-book/digital-version (accessed 18 November 2021).

Chapter 4

Civita, M.D. (2020). Why purpose-driven organizations matter in our world today. https://www.forbes.com/sites/forbescoachescouncil/2020/02/18/why-purpose-driven-organizations-matter-in-our-world-today/?sh=55c5a0d8bff8 (accessed 6 December 2021).

Development Dimensions International, Inc. (2018). The Conference Board, Inc. and EYGM Limited, Global Leadership Forecast 2018.

References 291

Domo, Inc., Data never sleeps 9.0. https://www.domo.com/blog/what-data-never-sleeps-9-0-proves-about-the-pandemic/ (accessed 6 December 2021).

Ismail, S. (2014). *Exponential Transformation*. Wiley.

Ismail, S., Palao, F., and Lapierre, M. (2019). *Exponential Transformation: Evolve Your Organization (and Change the World) With a 10-Week ExO Sprint*. Wiley.

LaClair, J.A. and Rao, R.P. (2002). Helping employees embrace change. *McKinsey Quarterly* (1 November).

Ludema, J. and Johnson, A. (2018). Gravity Payment's Dan Price on how he measures success after his $70k experiment. Forbes.com.

McInnis, K.J. (2020). Strategists have forgotten the power of stories. https://foreignpolicy.com/2020/05/19/national-security-policymaking-mythos-logos-strategy/ (accessed 29 October 2021).

Monarth, H. (2010). *Executive Presence: The Art of Commanding Respect Like a CEO*. McGraw-Hill.

Nadella, S. (2020). Coming together to combat Covid-19. https://www.linkedin.com/pulse/coming-together-combat-covid-19-satya-nadella/ (accessed 19 February 2021).

Nieto-Rodriguez, A. and Evrard, D. (2004). *Boosting Business Performance through Programme and Project Management*. PricewaterhouseCoopers.

O'Brien, D., Main, A., Kounkel, S., and Stephan, A.R. (2019). Purpose is everything: how brands that authentically lead with purpose are changing the nature of business today. *Deloitte Insights* (October).

Pink, D. (2011). *Drive: The Surprising Truth About What Motivates Us*. Riverhead Books.

PricewaterhouseCoopers (2016). *Putting Purpose To Work: A Study of Purpose in the Workplace* (June).

Quinn, R.E. and Thakor, A.V. (2018). Creating a purpose-driven organization. *Harvard Business Review* (July–August).

Rozen, M. (2021). How agility, empathy, and purpose steered Mastercard during a pandemic. https://business.adobe.com/blog/the-latest/agility-empathy-purpose-steered-mastercard-during-pandemic (accessed 19 February 2021).

Sinek, S. (2009). *Start with Why: How Great Leaders Inspire Everyone to Take Action*. Penguin.

Uniotomy (2020). How to start to change organizational culture. https://unitonomy.com/how-to-start-to-change-your-organizational-culture/ (accessed 30 October 2021).

Chapter 5

Campbell, A., Gutierrez, M., and Lancelott, M. (2017). *Operating Model Canvas*. Van Haren Publishing.

Chakraborty, S., Charanya, T., de Laubier, R., and Mahesh, A. (2020). *The Evolving State of Digital Transformation*. Boston Consulting Group.

De Jong, M. and van Dijk, M. (2015). *Disrupting Beliefs: A New Approach to Business-Model Innovation*. McKinsey.

Fischer, B. (2021). GE, Toshiba, J&J: reorganizing is not transformation. Forbes (November). https://www.forbes.com/sites/billfischer/2021/11/21/ge-toshiba-jj-reorganizing-is-not-transformati on/?sh=51a089851609 (accessed 3 December 2021).

Fisk, P. (2015). *Gamechangers: Are You Ready to Change the World? Creating Innovative Strategies for Business and Brands*. Wiley.

Ismail, S. (2014). *Exponential Transformation*. Wiley.

Johnson & Johnson Press Release (2021). Johnson & Johnson announces plans to accelerate innovation, serve patients and consumers, and unlock value through intent to separate consumer health business (November 12). https://www.jnj.com/johnson-johnson-announces-plans-to-accelerate-innovation-serve-patients-and-consumers-and-unlock-value-through-intent-to-separate-consumer-health-business (accessed 3 December 2021).

Kering Group. https://www.kering.com/en/finance/ (accessed 4 February 2022).

Lego Ideas. https://ideas.lego.com/.

PricewaterhouseCoopers (2021). Global Consumer Insights Pulse Survey (December). https://www.pwc.com/gx/en/industries/consumer-markets/consumer-insights-survey.html (accessed 5 February 2022).

Rangen, C. (2020). *Building The Transformational Company: A CEO Handbook*. www.strategytools.io/reports (accessed 3 December 2021).

Salesforce (2020). *State of the Connected Customer*. https://www.salesforce.com/resources/research-reports/state-of-the-connected-customer/ (accessed 5 February 2022).

Statista (2021). Global revenue of the Kering Group from 2012 to 2020, by brand (November 2021). https://www.statista.com/statistics/267476/global-revenue-of-the-kering-group-by-brand/ (accessed 5 February 2022).

Westerman, G., Bonnet, D., and McAfee, A. (2014). *Leading Digital. Turning Technology into Business Transformation*. Harvard Business Review Press.

Zhang, Y. (2021). What can luxury brands learn from Gucci's digital strategy? https://hapticmedia.com/blog/what-can-luxury-brands-learn-from-guccis-digital-strategy/ (accessed 5 February 2022).

Chapter 6

Ashkenas, R. and Matta, N. (2021). How to scale a successful pilot project. *Harvard Business Review* (January).

Drucker, P. (2002). The discipline of innovation. *Harvard Business Review* (August).

Highsmith, J.R., Luu, L., and Robinson, D. (2019). *EDGE: Value-Driven Digital Transformation*. Addison-Wesley Professional.

Himowicz, N., The next big thing entrepreneurs and corporate innovators need to consider. https://www.strategyzer.com/blog/the-next-big-thing-entrepreneurs-and-corporate-innovators-need-to-consider?hs_preview=apprcbff-635112179658&utm_content=192806540&utm_medium=social&utm_source=linkedin&hss_channel=lcp-3029520 (accessed 1 February 2022).

Ismail, S. (2014). *Exponential Transformation*. Wiley.

Kaplan, S. (2021). Why "painstorming" is the new brainstorming. *Inc. Magazine* (August). https://www.inc.com/soren-kaplan/why-painstorming-is-new-brainstorming.html (accessed 6 December 2021).

Lankhorst, M. and Matthijssen, P. (2020). *The Adaptive Enterprise: Thriving in an Era of Change*. BiZZdesign.

McKinsey Survey (2021). The new digital edge: Rethinking strategy for the postpandemic era (May). https://www.mckinsey.com/business-functions/mckinsey-digital/our-insights/the-new-digital-edge-rethinking-strategy-for-the-postpandemic-era (accessed 6 December 2021).

Rangen, C., www.Strategytools.io.

Ryan, K.J. (2016). 4 things futurist Alvin Toffler predicted about work back in 1970. *Inc. Magazine* (July). https://www.inc.com/kevin-j-ryan/4-things-futurist-alvin-toffler-predicted-about-work-in-1970.html (accessed 6 December 2021).

Stoop, J., Staffhorset, S., Bekker, R., and Hobma, T. (2016). *The Business Transformation Framework: To Get from Strategy to Execution*. Van Haren Publishing.

Chapter 7

Anthony, S.D., Gilbert, C.G., and Johnson, M.W. (2017). *Dual Transformation: How to Reposition Today's Business While Creating the Future*. Harvard Business Review Press.

Benzell, S., Hersh, J.S., Alstyne, M.W.V., and Lagarda, G. (2021). *How APIs Create Growth by Inverting the Firm*. SSRN eLibrary.

Bezos, J. (1997). Amazon Investor Letter. https://www.sec.gov/Archives/edgar/data/1018724/000119312518121161/d456916dex991.htm (accessed 19 January 2022).

Bucy, M., Schaninger, B., and VanAkin, K. (2021). Losing from day one: why even successful transformations fall short. McKinsey & Company (December).

Carucci, R. (2021). How leaders get in the way of organizational change. *Harvard Business Review* (April).

Drucker Institute (2019). 2019 Drucker Institute company ranking. https://www.drucker.institute/2019-drucker-institute-company-ranking/ (accessed 19 January 2022).

Haas, S., Quinn, B., and Baskin, J. (2019). Inside Strategy Room Podcast – How to move fast: innovation at speed and scale. https://www.mckinsey.com/business-functions/strategy-and-corporate-finance/our-insights/inside-the-strategy-room-podcast (accessed 25 June 2022).

Locke, C. (2019). How to balance business transformation with business as usual. https://www.managementtoday.co.uk/balance-business-transformation-business-usual/innovation/article/1668234 (accessed 19 January 2022).

McKinsey & Company (2019). Decision making in the age of urgency. https://www.mckinsey.com/business-functions/people-and-organizational-performance/our-insights/decision-making-in-the-age-of-urgency (accessed 19 January 2022).

Miller, K. (2020). 5 critical steps in the change management process. *Harvard Business Review* (March).

Musselwhite, C. and Plouffe, T. (2010). Four ways to know whether you are ready for change. *Harvard Business Review* (2 June). https://hbr.org/2010/06/four-ways-to-know-whether-you (accessed 16 January 2022).

Newman, D. (2017). How to capitalize on your digital ecosystem. https://futurumresearch.com/how-to-capitalize-on-your-digital-ecosystem/ (accessed 19 January 2022).

Taneja, Y. (2021). Why did Kodak fail? | Kodak bankruptcy case study. `https://startuptalky.com/kodak-bankruptcy-case-study/ #:~:text=Kodak%20was%20the%20most%20dominant, photography%20and%20videography%2C%20go%20bankrupt%3F` (accessed 19 January 2022).

Van Alstyne, M.W. and Parker, G.G. (2021). Digital transformation changes how companies create value. Harvard Business Review (December).

Weber, L. (2021). How Jeff Bezos has run Amazon, from meetings to managing. `https://www.wsj.com/articles/how-jeff-bezos-has-run-amazon-from-meetings-to-managing-11612314552#:~:text= Most%20meetings%20are%20pointless.&text=Bezos%20is%20 well%2Dknown%20for,a%20meeting%20by%20everyone%20present` (accessed 19 January 2022).

Chapter 8

ARtillery Intelligence (2021). VR Global Revenue Forecast, 2020–2025 (June).

Bitkraft (2021). Reality check: perspectives on extended reality (AR, MR, VR) (October). `https://www.bitkraft.vc/reality-check/` (accessed 4 March 2022).

Bloomberg (2021). Investing in the metaverse (July). `https://www .bloomberg.com/news/videos/2021-07-01/investing-in-the-metaverse-video` (accessed 4 March 2022).

Bornet, P. (2021). How will intelligent automation impact employment? `Forbes.com` (November).

Bornet, P., Barkin, I., and Wirtz, J. (2021). *Intelligent Automation: Welcome to the World of Hyperautomation*. World Scientific Publishing.

Craw, K. (2021). *Atlas of AI*. Yale University Press.

Diamandis, P. and Kotler, S. (2016). *The Six Ds of Exponential Organizations*. Singularity Education Group.

DHL Trend Research (2016). 3D printing and the future of supply chains.

Dilmegani, C. (2022). Bias in AI: what it is, types, examples & 6 ways to fix it in 2022. AIMultiple (February).

Edwards, D. (2022). Global industrial robot density in manufacturing sector doubles over 2021 (February) `www.roboticsandautomationnews.com`.

Gartner (2022). Gartner Top Strategic Technology Trends for 2022. `https:// www.gartner.com/en/information-technology/insights/top-technology-trends` (accessed 25 June 2022).

Google Learning Team (2022). What is artificial intelligence? How does AI work, types and future of it? https://www.mygreatlearning.com/blog/what-is-artificial-intelligence/ (accessed 4 March 2022).

IFR International Federation of Robotics (2021). World Robot Report 2021.

International Data Corporation (IDC) (2022). IDC forecasts companies to increase spend on AI solutions by 19.6% in 2022 (February).

International Data Corporation (IDC) (2022). Worldwide spending on blockchain solutions from 2017 to 2024 (January).

Lardi, K. (2021). Understanding the value of artificial intelligence solutions in your business. Forbes.com (January).

Launchbury, J. (2016). *A DARPA Perspective on Artificial Intelligence.* The Defence Advanced Research Projects Agency (DARPA).

Lee, K.-F. (2021). *AI 2041: Ten Visions for Our Future.* Currency Publishing (Random House).

Luidmila, N. (2021). Social VR Lifestyle Survey 2021 (October).

McCarthy, J. (2004). What is Artificial Intelligence? Stanford University, CA.

Moioli, F. (2022). How to become an AI-driven company today. Forbes.com (March).

Nunes, A. (2021). Automation doesn't just create or destroy jobs – it transforms them. *Harvard Business Review* (November).

Research and Markets, Robotic Process Automation Market Research Report – Global Industry Analysis and Growth Forecast to 2030, November 2021. https://www.researchandmarkets.com/reports/5184615/robotic-process-automation-market-research=report.

Srivastav, S. (2020). Artificial intelligence, machine learning, and deep learning. What's the real difference? https://medium.com/swlh/artificial-intelligence-machine-learning-and-deep-learning-whats-the-real-difference-94fe7e528097 (accessed 4 March 2022).

The European Union Blockchain Observatory & Forum (2020). Convergence of blockchain, AI and IoT (April).

Turing, A.M. (1950). Computing machinery and intelligence. *Mind* 59: 433–460.

Vigros, A. et al. (2021). XR and its potential in Europe. Ecorys (April).

Acknowledgments

This book has been developing in my mind for several years. As I advised companies across regions and industries on digital business transformation, the ideas and insights grew and eventually overflowed to a point that I needed to write it down. As I poured my heart and soul into the contents, I realized that there were key people around me who contributed, supported, and motivated me to complete this challenging process.

First and foremost, my husband and daughter (and dog), who have been my cheerleaders, comforters, and motivators, keeping me going every time I came close to giving up or slowing down. You make it all worthwhile. And thank you to my family and friends, who always believed that I could achieve the big dreams in my heart.

I am also eternally grateful to the people that I have engaged with throughout my professional journey, including clients, partners, collaborators, and technologists. I am grateful to have shared this two-decade journey with you.

Finally, I would like to convey my deepest gratitude to the experts and leaders who contributed their time and insights for the book interviews. Despite achieving greatness in your own respective fields, you demonstrated generosity in sharing your expertise, experiences, and insights with full openness.

About the Author

Kamales Lardi is a bold and strategic thinker in digital and business transformation. She combines over 22 years of deep cross-industry experience with the latest digital and technology solutions. Kamales is listed in the "Top 10 Global Influencers & Thought Leaders in Digital Transformation" (Thinkers360) and "Top 50 Women in Tech Influencers 2021" (*The Awards* Magazine). She often says that "technology is not a silver bullet solution, a clear value proposition should drive any transformation effort." This approach resonates well with business leaders and has helped her stand out in the global digital space. Kamales has advised many multinational companies across various industries in Europe, Asia, and Africa, winning the company she founded and managed for over a decade the Business Worldwide Magazine 2020 Global Corporate Excellence Award for "Digital Business Transformation Firm of the Year."

Kamales believes in the transformative impact of emerging technologies. She has developed deep knowledge and practical experience in a range of emerging technology solutions, such as blockchain, AI, virtual and augmented reality, 3D-printing, IoT and sensor technologies, and robotics process automation, among others.

Kamales is a Teaching Fellow at Durham University Business School, and is the first Chair of the FORBES Business Council Women Executives. She is a dynamic and influential speaker and presents regularly at corporate and industry conferences. In 2022, Kamales was recognized in International 40 Over 40—The World's Most Inspiring Women by CapGemini Invent and Female One Zero.

In addition, Kamales is a strong advocate for diversity in the tech scape. She believes that diversity of knowledge, culture, gender, sexual orientation, and experience plays a critical role in developing technology solutions that have a transformative impact in business and society. Kamales is Malaysian, and has lived and worked in Switzerland since 2005.

Index

Page numbers followed by *f* and *t* refer to figures and tables, respectively.

301

Sustainable digital business transformation, 22, 97, 165–167. *See also* Digital Business Transformation Strategy framework
Sustainable digital transformation, 123–127, 125*f*

T
Talent, matching initiatives and, 216
Target Operating Model (TOM), 197, 197*f*, 198, 201–203, 202*f*
Task Rabbit, 45
Teams:
changing structures/approaches of, 23
as critical success factor, 28
for digital business transformation, 221–226
digital skills of, 141–142
implementation, 225–226, 232–233
innovation, 180
Technology(-ies), 1–4
adoption life cycle for, 39–40, 40*f*
in change management, 95
convergence of humans and, 246–247, 246*f*
as critical success factor, 27
in Digital Maturity & Readiness Assessment, 155*f*, 156
disruptive, *see* Disruptive technologies

emerging, *see* Emerging technologies
evolution of, 12
investments in, 21
leveraging, 19–20
SMAC, 19
workforce impact of, 269
Technology experts, 224
Technology trends, 11–18
emerging technologies and breakthrough solutions, 12–13
evolving consumer behavior, 13–16
rise of low-touch economy, 18
shifting competitive landscape, 16–17
TED Talks, 108
Thinking big, 226–229
Think like an agile start-up, 231–236
Thomas-Hunt, Melissa, 52
3D printing, 188, 266–268
Thunberg, Greta, 47–48
TikTok, 13–14
Toffler, Alvin, 185, 186
Top-Down Health Check, 171, 176, 176*f*, 178–179
Toshiba, 123–124, 126
Transformation, digital transformation vs., 127–131
Transformational changes, 242
Transformational maturity level, 157*f*, 159
Transparency, 52
Trend Scan, 177, 180–184, 181*f*–183*f*, 199